N. Magnenat-Thalmann
D. Thalmann (eds.)

Computer Animation
and Simulation 2001

Proceedings of the Eurographics Workshop
in Manchester, UK,
September 2–3, 2001

Eurographics

SpringerWienNewYork

Prof. Dr. Nadia Magnenat-Thalmann
MIRA Laboratory
University of Geneva
Geneva, Switzerland

Dr. Daniel Thalmann
Computer Graphics Laboratory
Swiss Federal Institute of Technology
Lausanne, Switzerland

© 2001 Springer-Verlag/Wien
Printed in Austria

Typesetting: Camera-ready by authors
Printing: Novographic, A-1238 Wien
Binding: Papyrus, A-1100 Wien

Printed on acid-free and chlorine-free bleached paper

SPIN: 10847739

With 79 partly coloured Figures

ISSN 0946-2767
ISBN 3-211-83711-6 Springer-Verlag Wien New York

Preface

This volume contains the research papers presented at the 12th Eurographics Workshop on Computer Animation and Simulation, Manchester, UK, September 2-3, 2001.

The workshop is an international forum for research in computer-animation and simulation. This year, we choose to give a special focus on the modelling and animation of complex phenomena. This includes the modelling of virtual creatures - from their body-parts to the control of their behavior, and the animation of natural phenomena such as water, smoke, fire and vegetation.

The call for papers required submission of the full papers for review, and each paper was reviewed by at least 2 members of the international program committee and additional reviewers. Based on the reviews, 16 papers were accepted. We added to the final program an invited talk by Jos Stam.

We wish to thank all reviewers for their time and effort in working within the rigid constraints of the tight schedule, thereby making it possible to publish this volume in time for the workshop. We also thank the authors for their contributions to the workshop, without whom this unique forum for animation and simulation work would not exist.

We are grateful to the Eurographics Association and especially to Werner Purgathofer from the Technical University of Vienna, for his support in publishing the workshop as a volume of the Springer-Verlag Eurographics Series. We also thank the Eurographics '2001 organisers, especially Roger Hubbold, and Heinrich Müller from the EG board. We are also very grateful to Zerrin Celebi for the organization of the review process.

Marie-Paule Cani
Nadia Magnenat-Thalmann
Daniel Thalmann

Program Committee

Marie-Paule Cani (iMAGIS INP Grenoble, France)
Nadia Magnenat-Thalmann (University of Geneva, Switzerland)
Daniel Thalmann (EPFL, Lausanne, Switzerland)

Bruno Arnaldi (IRISA, Rennes, France)
Norm Badler (University of Pennsylvania, USA)
Ronan Boulic (EPFL, Lausanne, Switzerland)
Michael Cohen (Microsoft, Seattle, USA)
Mathieu Desbrun (University of Southern California, USA)
Francois Faure (iMAGIS, University of Grenoble I, France)
Michael Gleicher (University of Wisconsin, USA)
Marcelo Kallmann (EPFL, Lausanne, Switzerland)
Ming Lin (University of North Carolina, USA)
Laurent Moccozet (University of Geneva, Switzerland)
Hong Qin (State University of New York, USA)
Hansrudi Noser (University of Zurich, Switzerland)
Werner Purgathofer (Technical University of Wien, Austria)
Frank van Reeth (Limburgs University Center, Belgium)
Pascal Volino (University of Geneva, Switzerland)

Reviewers

Eric G. Aaron (University of Pennsylvania, USA)
Jan M. Allbeck (University of Pennsylvania, USA)
Koji Ashida (University of Pennsylvania, USA)
Kevin T. McDonnell (State University of New York, USA)
Olaf Etzmuss (University of Tuebingen, Germany)
Chris Faisstnauer (Technical University of Wien, Austria)
Jing Hua (State University of New York, USA)
Heinrich Hey (Technical University of Wien, Austria)
Seung-Joo Lee (University of Pennsylvania, USA)
Jean-Sebastien Monzani (EPFL, Lausanne, Switzerland)
Yannick Remion (University of Reims, France)
Etienne de Sevin (EPFL, Lausanne, Switzerland)
Branislav Ulicny (EPFL, Lausanne, Switzerland)
Alexander Wilkie (Technical University of Wien, Austria)
Michael Wimmer (Technical University of Wien, Austria)
Jian Jun Zhang (Bournemouth University, UK)
Liwei Zhao (University of Pennsylvania, USA)

Contents

X

5. Hair Animation

6 . High Level Motion Planning

1

Motion Capture and Control

Markerless Motion Capture of Complex Full-Body Movement for Character Animation

Andrew J. Davison, Jonathan Deutscher and Ian D. Reid

Robotics Research Group
Department of Engineering Science
University of Oxford
Oxford OX1 3PJ, UK
[ajd,jdeutsch,ian]@robots.ox.ac.uk

Abstract. Vision-based full-body tracking aims to reproduce the performance of current commercial marker-based motion capture methods in a system which can be run using conventional cameras and without the use of special apparel or other equipment, improving usability in existing application domains and opening up new possibilities since the methods can be applied to image sequences acquired from any source. We present results from a system able to perform robust visual tracking with an articulated body model, using data from multiple cameras. Our approach to searching through the high-dimensional model configuration space is an algorithm called *annealed particle filtering* which finds the best fit to image data via multiple-layer propagation of a stochastic particle set. This algorithm efficiently searches the configuration space without the need for restrictive dynamical models, permitting tracking of agile, varied movement. The data acquired can readily be applied to the animation of CG characters. Movie files illustrating the results in this paper may be obtained from **http://www.robots.ox.ac.uk/~ajd/HMC/**

1 Introduction

Motion capture aids animators in the time-consuming task of making computer graphics characters move in realistic ways by enabling movement data to be recorded straightforwardly from observation of an actor performing the desired motions. Commercial human motion capture technology [16] has now been used for CG character animation for a number of years. In typical current systems, a number of retro-reflective markers are attached in known positions to the actor's body and viewed by infra-red cameras emitting light and filtered to remove background signals. The easily-recovered image positions of the markers are transformed into 3D trajectories via triangulation of the measurements from multiple cameras, and a parameterised representation of the actor's movements can be calculated.

It is a sign of the growing synergy between graphics and computer vision (seen recently in areas such as augmented reality [15]) that visual processing can in fact be used to recover motion data *directly from images*, without markers, and many analogues can be seen in the processes used for tracking and those used later on to reanimate the data in graphical output. The use of markers is intrusive and restricting, necessitates the use of expensive specialised capture hardware, and requires footage to be taken specially. The goal of markerless motion capture is to reproduce the performance of marker-based methods in a system which could be run using conventional cameras and without the use of special apparel or other equipment.

Such a system would of course be able to replace current marker-based systems, improving usability in studio scenarios, but also potentially be used in a variety of new domains such as sports broadcasting. However, full-body tracking from standard images is a challenging problem, and research has so far failed to produce a full-body tracker general enough to handle real-world applications. In particular, no markerless system presented to date has convincingly achieved the following combination of capabilities of current marker-based systems which would make it a viable alternative in animation applications: full 3D motion recovery; robust tracking of rapid, arbitrary movement; high accuracy; easy application to new scenarios.

A number of effective systems able to recover 2D motion from a single camera have been presented [6, 10]. While these might be useful in simple applications, tracking "side-on" planar movements, they do not provide output in the form of 3D model configurations that are needed in general for character animation.

Bregler and Malik [2] produced some of the best-known results to date in 2D and 3D body tracking. Their approach was based on frame-to-frame region-based matching using a gradient-descent search and was demonstrated on several short multi-camera image sequences. However, this simple search scheme is not capable of tracking agile motions with cluttered backgrounds, and their method of locating body parts by frame-to-frame matching of image regions will cause drift over long sequences. Howe *et al.* [8] present a system for single-camera tracking which combines a 2D tracker with learned models of 3D configuration to produce 3D pose output for simple sequences.

Gavrila and Davis [5] use an explicit hierarchical search, in which parts of the body's kinematic chain are located sequentially (e.g. torso, followed by upper arm, lower arm and then hand), a process which greatly reduces search complexity. Without the assistance of artificial labelling cues (such as colour), however, it is very hard to localise specific body parts independently in realistic scenarios. This is due to the fact that limited measurements of a specific body part itself may not be sufficient to recover its own position: information on the location of parts further down the kinematic hierarchy also give vital information (for instance the orientation of the torso may not be apparent until arms are observed).

In work with many similarities to that in this paper, Sidenbladh *et al.* [14] have taken a mathematically rigorous approach to full-body tracking based on Condensation (see Section 2.1), using learned dynamical models and a generative model of image formation. They tracked short sequences of 3D motion from a single camera, though the very strong dynamical models used restrict the applicability of the system to general motion tracking and the system runs slowly due to the large number of particles required.

Building on previous work in [4], in this paper we present a method for full body tracking using multiple cameras. Our approach is characterised by the following: 1. articulated body model, 2. weak dynamical modelling, 3. edge and background subtraction image measurements, and 4. a particle-based stochastic search algorithm. The latter uses a continuation principle, based on annealing, to introduce the influence of narrow peaks in the fitness function gradually. The algorithm, termed *annealed particle filtering*, is shown to be capable of recovering full articulated body motion efficiently, and demonstrated tracking extended walking, turning and running sequences.

We will introduce and review visual tracking in general in Section 2, then move on to a discussion of the specifics of full-body tracking in Section 3. The annealed particle filtering approach which this problem has led us to take is described in Section 4. Section 5 presents results from tracking agile walking, running and handstand movments.

2 Visual Tracking

Full-body motion capture is an example of *model-based tracking*, in that it is the process of sequentially estimating the parameters of a simplified model of a human body over time from visual data. The parameters X needed to specify a particular state of the model are called its degrees of freedom. As well as models representing the *shape* and *motion* of the target, a model of the *measurement* process, through which information is gained from images in the form of measurement parameters Z, is required.

In early model-based tracking using vision (e.g. [11]), the targets were simple objects which could closely be modelled with mathematically convenient geometrical shapes, and clear edges or other image features were available as reliable measurements. In cases like these, localising the object at each time step can proceed as a gradient-descent search in which a measure of fit of a hypothesized model configuration is repeatedly evaluated based on how well it predicts the measurements obtained with the model degrees of freedom deterministically adjusted to find the global best fit. Bregler and Malik [2] used a similar method in their work on full-body tracking.

An unconstrained search of this type, generally initialised at each new time step at the model configuration found in the previous frame, can get into trouble with local maxima in the search space, and will not be able to track rapid movement. It is profitable to constrain the search area using information which is available about the possible motion of the object: given knowledge about where the object was at a sequence of earlier time steps, it is possible to make a prediction, with associated uncertainty, about where it will be at the current time, and limit search to this part of configuration space.

When combining motion and measurement information in this way however, we can do better than simply using motion information to initialise a search by putting both types of information into an absolute, Bayesian probabilistic framework. The Extended Kalman Filter (EKF) has been widely used in visual tracking [7] to achieve this. The "goodness of fit" function associated with measurements must now take the form of a likelihood $p(Z|X)$ which describes the probability of measurements Z given a state X, and the motion model has the form $p(X_k|X_{k-1})$. Tracking now proceeds as a sequential propagation of a probability density function in configuration space: the estimate of model configuration at any time step is a weighted combination of both information from the most recent set of measurements and, via motion continuity, that from previous measurements.

In more difficult tracking problems, where the models were now for example deformable 2D templates tracking complicated objects with agile motion, EKF-based tracking was enhanced with the use of learned motion models [13]: analysis of a training data set enabled probabilistic models of motion to be built, giving much better tracking of future motions of the same type. Baumberg and Hogg applied methods of this kind to the tracking of human figures from a single camera [1], obtaining good estimates of global movement but not the details of articulation needed for motion capture.

2.1 Particle Filters

The EKF provides a probabilistic framework for tracking, but supports only the case where observation and motion probability density functions can be approximated as multi-variate Gaussians. While Gaussian uncertainty is sufficient for modelling many motion and measurement noise sources, the EKF has been shown to fail catastrophically in cases where the true probability function has a very different shape. Attempts to track objects moving against a very cluttered background, where measurement densities include the chance of detecting erroneous image features, led to the first application of particle filtering in visual tracking [9] in the form of the Condensation algorithm.

In particle filtering, the posterior density $p(\mathbf{X}|\mathbf{Z}_k)$ representing current knowledge about the model state after incorporation of all measurements is represented by a finite set of *weighted particles*, or samples, $\{(\mathbf{s}_k^{(0)}, \pi_k^{(0)}) \ldots (\mathbf{s}_k^{(N)}, \pi_k^{(N)})\}$ where the weights $\pi_k^{(n)} \propto p(\mathbf{Z}_k|\mathbf{X} = \mathbf{s}_k^{(n)})$ are normalised so that $\sum_N \pi_k^{(n)} = 1$. The state $\mathcal{X}_k$ at each time step t_k can be estimated by the sample mean:

$$\mathcal{X}_k = \mathcal{E}_k[\mathbf{X}] = \sum_{n=1}^{N} \pi_k^{(n)} \mathbf{s}_k^{(n)} \tag{1}$$

or the mode

$$\mathcal{X}_k = \mathcal{M}_k[\mathbf{X}] = \mathbf{s}_k^{(j)}, \pi_k^{(j)} = \max(\pi_k^{(n)}) \tag{2}$$

of the posterior density $p(\mathbf{X}|\mathbf{Z}_k)$. Variance and other high-order moments of the particle set can also easily be calculated.

Essentially, a smooth probability density function is approximated by a finite collection of weighted sample points, and it can be shown that as the number of points tends to infinity the behaviour of the particle set is indistinguishable from that of the smooth function. Tracking with a particle filter works by: 1. Resampling, in which a weighted particle set is transformed into a set of evenly weighted particles distributed with concentration dependent on probability density; 2. Stochastic movement and dispersion of the particle set in accordance with a motion model to represent the growth of uncertainty during movement of the tracked object; 3. Measurement, in which the likelihood function is evaluated at each particle site, producing a new weight for each particle proportional to how well it fits image data. The weighted particle set produced represents the new probability density after movement and measurement.

Particle filtering works well for tracking in clutter because it can represent arbitrary functional shapes and propagate multiple hypotheses. Less likely model configurations will not be thrown away immediately but given a chance to prove themselves later on, resulting in more robust tracking.

The complicated nature of the observation process during human motion capture causes the posterior density to be non-Gaussian and multi-modal as shown experientally by Deutscher *et al.* [3], and Condensation has been implemented successfully for short human motion capture sequences by Sidenbladh *et al.* [14]. However, serious problems arise with Condensation in the high-dimensional configuration spaces occurring in human motion capture and other domains: essentially, the number of particles needed to populate a high-dimensional space is far too high to be manageable. We will explain the specifics of the full-body tracking problem in the following section, then present our approach to efficient particle filtering in Section 4.

3 Models for Full-Body Tracking

3.1 Kinematics and Dynamics

In common with the majority of full-body tracking approaches, we have used an articulated model in which the body is approximated as a collection of rigid segments joined by rotating joints. Degrees of freedom (DOF) in the model are close approximations to the the way the human skeleton moves. In joints (such as the shoulder) which have

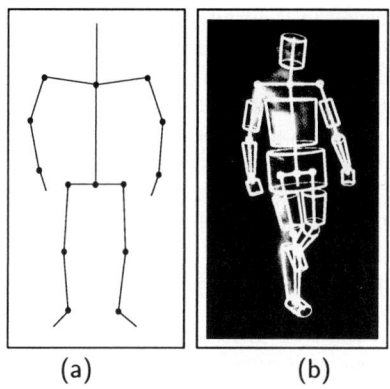

(a)   (b)

Fig. 1. (a) Typical kinematic model with 33 degrees of freedom based on a kinematic chain consisting of 18 segments. Six degrees of freedom are given to base translation and rotation. The shoulder and hip joints are treated as sockets with 3 degrees of freedom, the clavicle joints are given 2 degrees of freedom and the neck, elbows, wrists, hips, knees and ankles are modelled as hinges requiring only one. This results in a configuration vector $\mathbf{X} = \{x_1 \ldots x_{33}\}$. The model is fleshed out by conical sections (b).

more than one DOF, rotations are parameterised with sequential rotations about perpendicular axes (simlilar to Euler Angles). A reasonable articulated model of the human body usually has at least 25 DOF; we have most commonly used a model with 33 DOF (see Figure 1). Models for commercial character animation usually have over 40 DOF.

In our system, kinematic models are specified in a format commonly used in CG packages, meaning that they are easily reconfigurable and the data acquired readily applied to character animation. In addition to defining degrees of freedom, we specify range limits for each joint, hard constraints beyond which movement is not allowed. Depending on the application, decisions are made about exactly how closely to model the skeleton: commonly, it will be more important to recover gross body motion robustly than to capture in detail the positions of hands and feet for instance. In general, stable tracking becomes more difficult as the number of degrees of freedom in the model increases, since a model with high dimensionality is "looser" and more easily distracted by ambiguous image data. There is a strong argument in fact for using *different* models for tracking and animation, since finely-detailed movements (of the hands and feet for example) can potentially be added to an animation at a later stage. In the long-term, it will be desirable to refine a tracking model which can be used in many different situations: progress towards this can be seen in the slightly more advanced model used to track the handstand sequence of Section 5.

While we have taken care with our *kinematic* model to represent possible body movements realistically, a much looser approach has been taken to *dynamic* modelling of the way that the position of the body at one time step affects the position at the next: we have either dispensed with a motion model altogether, initialising the search for each time step from the model configuration found previously, or used a very simple damped velocity model for the motion at each joint (although our method does not preclude the use of an arbitrarily complex motion model).

Specifically, we have chosen not to used trained dynamical models [13, 14]. While these models aid robust tracking greatly, they restrict the motions which can be tracked to be similar to those observed in the training set. In character animation, the value of motion capture is to be able to supply interesting and unusual movements automatically, and these movements will often not be in a training set. In addition, a strong dynamical model is time-consuming to train, and a requirement of a workable motion capture system is the ability to apply it quickly in new situations. Depending on the application, there may be a desire to change the details of the model — for instance the number of degrees of freedom, or perhaps to use only a partial body model. It would be impractical to provide pre-trained models for each of these situations.

3.2 Appearance Modelling and Image Measurement

Orthogonal to the specification of kinematic and dynamic models is the choice of method used to evaluate how well hypothesized model configurations agree with image data: the role of markers in current commercial motion capture systems must be replaced by repeatable image-based measurement. In a particle filter framework, each particle representing a hypothesized model configuration must be assigned a *weight* (technically a likelihood) representing its fit to current image data.

Unlike some recent authors [14], we use a tracking model which does not aim to be *generative* in the sense that can be used to render realistic images of a person. Such a model, while desirable from the Bayesian point of view, requires a form of texture mapping, and potentially complicated effects such as lighting conditions to be taken into account, making it highly specific to a particular person, set of clothing and conditions. Our image measurement strategy was chosen considering the following criteria:

- *Generality.* The image features used should be invariant under a wide range of conditions so that the same tracking framework will function well in a broad variety of situations.
- *Simplicity.* In an effort to make the tracker as efficient as possible the features used must be easy to extract.

Two image types of image feature were chosen to construct a weighting function: 1. *edges* and 2. *foreground segmentation*. From a particular hypothesized model configuration, the locations in images at which these features are expected to appear can be predicted: i.e. edges at the boundaries of body parts, non-background regions at any positions covered by body parts. A test can then be made against the actual edges and foreground regions found in the images from bottom-up image processing to evaluate this configuration and assign it a weight. The process is described in detail in Figure 2.

Sum-of-squared difference (SSD) measures $\Sigma^e(\mathbf{X}, \mathbf{Z})$ and $\Sigma^r(\mathbf{X}, \mathbf{Z})$ are computed for the edge and foreground measurements respectively: these functions represent the degree of fit between the hypothesized model configuration and edge and foreground measurements with single numbers (in both cases the 0 corresponds to a perfect fit):

$$\Sigma^e(\mathbf{X}, \mathbf{Z}) = \frac{1}{N^e} \sum_{i=1}^{N^e} (1 - p_i^e(\mathbf{X}, \mathbf{Z}))^2 \quad ; \quad \Sigma^r(\mathbf{X}, \mathbf{Z}) = \frac{1}{N^r} \sum_{i=1}^{N^r} (1 - p_i^r(\mathbf{X}, \mathbf{Z}))^2 . \quad (3)$$

To combine the edge and region measurements the two SSD's are added together and the result exponentiated to give:

$$w(\mathbf{X}, \mathbf{Z}) = \exp - \left(\Sigma^e(\mathbf{X}, \mathbf{Z}) + \Sigma^r(\mathbf{X}, \mathbf{Z}) \right) . \quad (4)$$

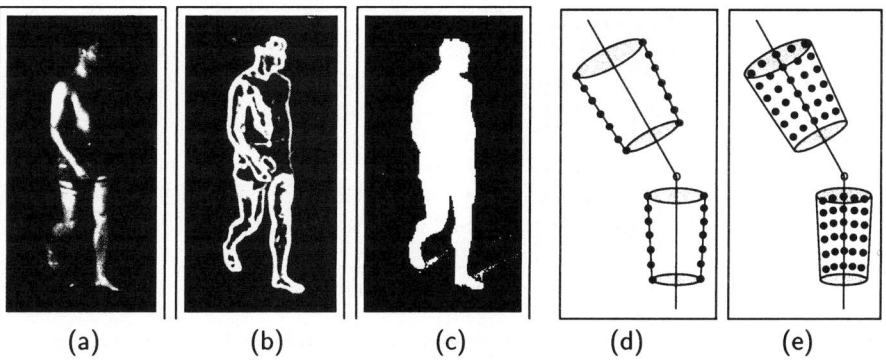

(a)   (b)   (c)   (d)   (e)

Fig. 2. Image measurement. Starting with input image (a), **two** types of bottom-up image processing are applied: (b) an edge detection mask is used to find edges, which are thresholded and smoothed using a Gaussian mask to produce a pixel map in which the value of each pixel ranges from 0 to 1 according to its proximity to an edge; (c) the foreground is segmented using thresholded background subtraction (a reference image with no target present is subtracted pixel-by-pixel from the current image) to produce a pixel map in which the value 1 correponds to foreground regions and 0 to background. These two measured pixel maps are then sampled at sites determined by each hypothesized model configuration: (d), for the edge pixel map, at sites lying along the occluding contours of the model's cone segments, providing N^e measurements with values p_i^e, and (e), for the foreground segmentation map, at sites evenly spread across the image regions spanned by the cones, providing N^r measurements with values p_i^r.

The function is trivially extended to simultaneous measurements from multiple cameras: the SSD's from each camera are simply added together:

$$w(\mathbf{X}, \mathbf{Z}) = \exp - \left(\sum_{i=1}^{C} \left(\Sigma_i^e(\mathbf{X}, \mathbf{Z}) + \Sigma_i^r(\mathbf{X}, \mathbf{Z}) \right) \right) \tag{5}$$

where C is the number of cameras and $\sum_i^*(\mathbf{X})$ is from camera i. An example of the output of this weighting function, demonstrating its ability to differentiate between hypothesized configurations around a good match, can be seen in Figure 3.

Both of these measurement types can be expected to work in general imaging conditions, though clearly their performance depends on the characteristics of the particular images: neither would perform well if the target person was of an intensity profile similar to the background and therefore poorly distinguished. Foreground segmentation of the type used here of course relies on the cameras being stationary and there being little background motion. Edge measurements may fail if the person is wearing loose clothing which moves significantly relative the the rigid structure of the skeleton.

4 A Particle Filter for High-Dimensional Spaces

Particle filters such as Condensation permit robust tracking by representing arbitrary probability density functions and propagating multiple hypotheses, but a price is paid for these attributes in computational cost. The most expensive operation in the standard Condensation algorithm is an evaluation of the likelihood function $p(\mathbf{Z_k}|\mathbf{X} = \mathbf{s}_k^{(n)})$ and this has to be done once at every time step for every particle. To maintain a fair

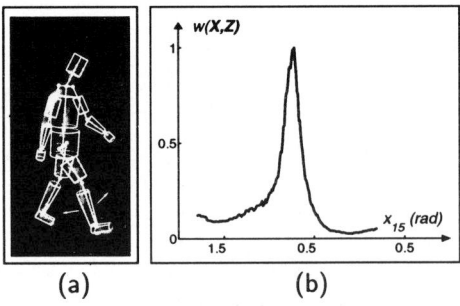

(a)   (b)

Fig. 3. Example output of the weighting function obtained by varying only component x_{15} of **X** (the right knee angle) using the image and model configuration seen in (a). The function is highly peaked around the correct angle of -0.7 radians (b).

---

representation of $p(\mathbf{X}|\mathbf{Z_k})$ a certain number of particles are required, and this number grows with the size of the model's configuration space. In fact it has been shown by MacCormick and Blake [12] that

$$N \geq \frac{\mathcal{D}_{min}}{\alpha^d} \,, \tag{6}$$

where N is the number of particles required and d is the number of dimensions. The survival diagnostic $\mathcal{D}_{min}$ and the particle survival rate α are both constants with $\alpha << 1$. When d is large, as in full-body tracking, normal particle filtering becomes infeasible.

Given this critical factor, combined with the fact the we have already moved away from a purely Bayesian framework in our choice of simple and generic measurement processes, it was decided to reduce the problem from propagating the conditional density $p(\mathbf{X}|\mathbf{Z_k})$ using $p(\mathbf{Z}|\mathbf{X})$ to finding the configuration $\mathcal{X}_k$ which returns the maximum value from a simple and efficient weighting function $w(\mathbf{Z_k}, \mathbf{X})$ at each time t_k, given $\mathcal{X}_{k-1}$. By doing this gains will be made on two fronts. It should be possible to make do with fewer likelihood (or weighting function) evaluations because the function $p(\mathbf{X}|\mathbf{Z_k})$ no longer has to be fully represented, and an evaluation of a simple weighting function $w(\mathbf{Z_k}, \mathbf{X})$ should require minimal computational effort when compared to an evaluation of the observation model $p(\mathbf{Z_k}|\mathbf{X})$.

We continue to use a particle-based stochastic framework because of its ability to handle multi-modal likelihoods during the search process, or in the case of a weighting function, one with many local maxima. The question is: *What is an efficient way to perform a particle based stochastic search for the global maximum of a weighting function with many local maxima?* We use a solution derived from simulated annealing.

4.1 Annealed Particle Filtering

Simulated annealing is a well known procedure in optimisation for finding the global maximum of a function which has multiple local peaks. Taking its name from the sequential coarse-to-fine adjustment of temperature needed to remove imperfections from solid structures in physics, it is the process of searching for functional maxima by first searching coarsely over a wide area, aiming to locate the approximate position in model space of the global maximum and avoid getting trapped by local maxima, and then perturbing the results achieved by smaller and smaller amounts until the global maximum can be settled on with accuracy. The amount of perturbation applied at each step, or *layer*, is the analogue of temperature in physics.

The annealed particle filter, explained in detail in [4], has the following key features which differentiate it from Condensation:

1. A layered search, in which a particle set is resampled, dispersed and weighted depending on measurements multiple times for each tracking time-step. The amount of dispersal, implemented as stochastic movement of the particle set, decreases layer-by-layer.
2. The output of the search is no longer a particle set which meaningfully represents a probability distribution, but a highly clustered group indicating the global maximum of the search.
3. The use of noise functions in the dispersion step which no longer represent purely the uncertainty associated with motion: since only a single peak of the distribution is being maintained, this additive noise must also take into account the possibility that the current estimate is substantially wrong if it is to be possible to recover from temporary tracking failures.

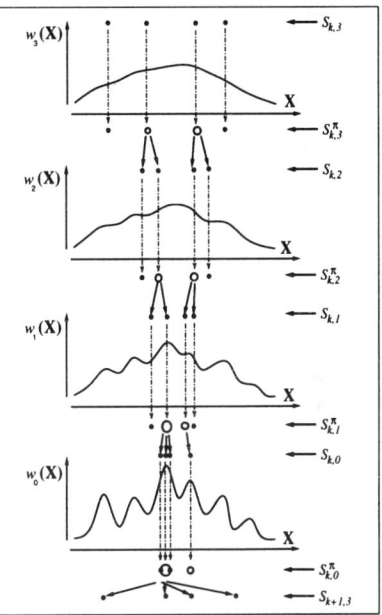

1. For every time step t_k an annealing run is started at layer M, with $m = M$.
2. Each layer of an annealing run is initialised by a set of unweighted particles $S_{k,m}$.
3. Each of these particles is then assigned a weight $\pi_{k,m}^{(i)} \propto w_m(\mathbf{Z}_k, \mathbf{s}_{k,m}^{(i)})$ which are normalised so that $\sum_N \pi_{k,m}^{(i)} = 1$. The set of weighted particles $S_{k,m}^{\pi}$ has now been formed.
4. N particles are drawn randomly from $S_{k,m}^{\pi}$ with replacement and with a probability equal to their weighting $\pi_{k,m}^{(i)}$. As the nth particle $\mathbf{s}_{k,m}^{(n)}$ is chosen it is used to produce the particle $\mathbf{s}_{k,m-1}^{(n)}$ using $\mathbf{s}_{k,m-1}^{(n)} = \mathbf{s}_{k,m}^{(n)} + \mathbf{B}_m$ where $\mathbf{B}_m$ is a multi-variate gaussian random variable with variance $\mathbf{P}_m$ and mean $\mathbf{0}$.
5. The set $S_{k,m-1}$ has now been produced which can be used to initialise layer $m - 1$. The process is repeated until we arrive at the set $S_{k,0}^{\pi}$.
6. $S_{k,0}^{\pi}$ is used to estimate the optimal model configuration $\mathcal{X}_k$ using $\mathcal{X}_k = \sum_{i=1}^{N} \mathbf{s}_{k,0}^{(i)} \pi_{k,0}^{(i)}$.
7. The set $S_{k+1,M}$ is then produced from $S_{k,0}^{\pi}$ using $\mathbf{s}_{k+1,M}^{(n)} = \mathbf{s}_{k,0}^{(n)} + \mathbf{B}_0$. This set is then used to initialise layer M of the next annealing run at t_{k+1}.

Fig. 4. Annealed particle filter algorithm and graphical depiction. With a multi-layered search the sparse particle set is able gradually to migrate towards the global maximum without being distracted by local maxima. The final set $S_{k,0}^{\pi}$ provides a good indication of the weighting function's global maximum.

The annealed particle filter algorithm is given in Figure 4, along with an illustration of its action in a one-dimensional diagram which can be thought of as a "slice" through multi-dimensional configuration space. The particle set, initially widely and evenly spread, becomes drawn first globally towards the global function maximum, and then explores that area of configuration space in increasing detail, able to jump out of

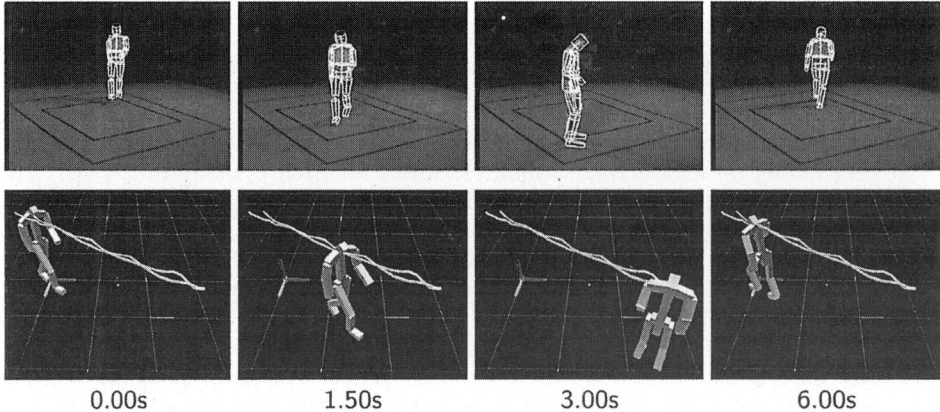

| 0.00s | 1.50s | 3.00s | 6.00s |

Fig. 5. Walking and turning sequence: the subject walks in a straight line, turns, and walks back. In the upper row, the tracked model template is shown superimposed on the raw images from one of the three cameras used. The lower row shows synchronised animation of a character seen from a viewpoint different to that of any of the input cameras; the waving line seen is the trajectory of the character's root segment, defined at the neck.

local maxima. The parameters of the process (in particular the number of layers M, the number of particles N and the annealing rate, which determines the rate of convergence) must be adjusted such that accurate tracking can be performed with a minimum amount of computational cost; in typical operation, 10–30 layers were used with 200–500 particles. The annealing rate is closely related to the particle survival rate α of MacCormick and Blake [12], affecting the number of particles which are usefully propagated from one layer to the next.

5   Results

We present results from three image captures of a subject wearing normal clothing moving freely within an workspace area of around 5×3 metres. Images were taken from three cameras spaced horizontally at regular intervals around this area, and capture was at 60Hz. Calibration to determine the positions of cameras and their internal parameters to a high accuracy was obtained via a commercial marker-based system.

Image processing was carried out offline using both an SGI Octane workstation and a 1GHz Pentium PC (the two having similar performance), and required around 30 seconds for each frame of video (a rate corresponding to 30 minutes per second of video footage). Although this processing is still a large factor away from the long-term target of real-time, it compares very favourably with other systems in the literature. The sequences tracked in this paper are only a few seconds long, but this shortness is due more to difficulties with managing the very large amounts of image data involved (10 seconds of uncompressed footage from 3 cameras fills a CD-R disc), and the processing time required, than to limitations of the tracker. See the web site given in the abstract of this paper for movie files of these results.

In the first image sequence (Figure 5), the subject walks in a straight line, turns through 180°, and walks back in a total movement of just over 6 seconds. The most challenging part of this sequence from a tracking point of view is the sharp turn, when the subject's arms and legs are close together and likely to be confused, and some tracking inaccuracies are observed here. The second sequence (Figure 6) shows the subject running and dodging in a triangular pattern over nearly 3 seconds. Although tracking rapid movement of this type is generally more difficult due to the larger frame-to-frame displacements involved, the subject's limbs are generally away from his body in this example and could be localised accurately. The third sequence (Figure 7) emphasizes the lack of movement constraints imposed in our tracking framework by tracking a handstand motion. The character model used in this last sequence was augmented with extra degrees of freedom in the back to capture the bending involved.

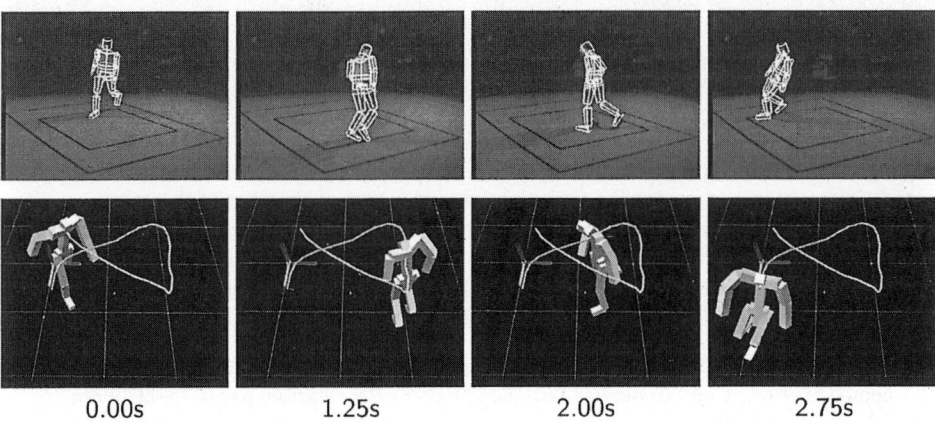

| 0.00s | 1.25s | 2.00s | 2.75s |

Fig. 6. Running and dodging sequence: the subject runs in a roughly triangular pattern, changing direction abruptly.

6 Conclusions

We have presented convincing results from a system able to perform robust visual motion capture in 3D without artificial markers, and shown that the data obtained can be used to animate a CG character. Annealed particle filtering is able to cut efficiently through the high-dimensional configuration space of an articulated model to recover varied and agile motions without the need for restrictive dynamical models.

Acknowledgements: This work was supported by Oxford Metrics and EPSRC grant GR/M15262.

References

1. A. Baumberg and D. Hogg. Generating spatiotemporal models from examples. In *Proc. British Machine Vision Conf.*, volume 2, pages 413–422, 1995.
2. C. Bregler and J. Malik. Tracking people with twists and exponential maps. In *Proc. CVPR*, 1998.
3. J. Deutscher, A. Blake, B. North, and B. Bascle. Tracking through singularities and discontinuities by random sampling. In *Proc. 7th Int. Conf. on Computer Vision*, volume 2, pages 1144–1149, 1999.

14

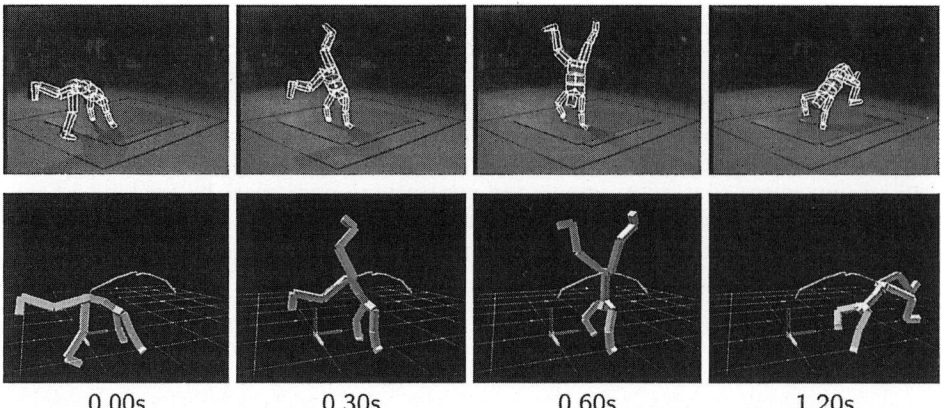

| 0.00s | 0.30s | 0.60s | 1.20s |

Fig. 7. Handstand sequence: the subject executes a poorly-balanced handstand, toppling rapidly over. In this sequence the trajectory shown is that of the base of the spine.

4. J. Deutscher, A. Blake, and I Reid. Articulated body motion capture by annealed particle filtering. In *Proc. Conf. Computer Vision and Pattern Recognition*, volume 2, pages 1144–1149, 2000.

5. D. Gavrila and L.S. Davis. 3d model-based tracking of humans in action: a multi-view approach. *Proc. Conf. Computer Vision and Pattern Recognition*, pages 73–80, 1996.

6. I. Haritaoglu, D. Harwood, and L. Davis. w^4s: A real-time system for detecting and tracking people in 2.5D. In *Proc. 5th European Conf. Computer Vision*, volume 1, pages 877–892, Freiburg, Germany, June 1998. Springer Verlag.

7. C. G. Harris. Tracking with rigid models. In A. Blake and A. Yuille, editors, *Active Vision*. MIT Press, Cambridge, MA, 1992.

8. Nicholas R. Howe, Michael E. Leventon, and William T. Freeman. Bayesian reconstruction of 3D human motion from single-camera video. In *Advances in Neural Information Processing Systems 12*, pages 820–826. MIT Press, 2000.

9. M.A. Isard and A. Blake. Visual tracking by stochastic propagation of conditional density. In *Proc. 4th European Conf. Computer Vision*, pages 343–356, Cambridge, England, Apr 1996.

10. S.X. Ju, M.J. Black, and Y. Yacoob. Cardboard people: A parameterized model of articulated motion. In *2nd Int. Conf. on Automatic Face and Gesture Recognition, Killington, Vermont*, pages 38–44, 1996.

11. D.G. Lowe. Robust model-based motion tracking through the integration of search and estimation. *Int. J. Computer Vision*, 8(2):113–122, 1992.

12. J. MacCormick and A. Blake. Partitioned sampling, articulated objects and interface-quality hand tracking. In *Accepted to ECCV 2000*, 2000.

13. D. Reynard, A.P. Wildenberg, A. Blake, and J. Marchant. Learning dynamics of complex motions from image sequences. In *Proc. 4th European Conf. Computer Vision*, pages 357–368, Cambridge, England, Apr 1996.

14. H. Sidenbladh, M. J. Black, and D. J. Fleet. Stochastic tracking of 3D human figures using 2d image motion. In *Proceedings of the 6th European Conference on Computer Vision, Dublin*, 2000.

15. R. A. Smith, A. W. Fitzgibbon, and A. Zisserman. Improving augmented reality using image and scene constraints. In *Proc. 10th British Machine Vision Conference, Nottingham*, pages 295–304. BMVA Press, 1999.

16. Vicon web based literature. URL http://www.metrics.co.uk, 2001.

Implementation of a 3D Virtual Drummer

Martijn Kragtwijk, Anton Nijholt, Job Zwiers

Department of Computer Science
University of Twente
PO Box 217, 7500 AE Enschede, the Netherlands
Phone: 00-31-53-4893686
Fax: 00-31-53-4893503
email: {kragtwij,anijholt,zwiers}@cs.utwente.nl

Abstract.
We describe a part of a system which generates a 3D animated drummer based
on the contents of a sound wave. The focus of this paper will be on the automatic
generation of 3D animations, based on an abstract representation of the music
(a MIDI file). The system is implemented in Java and uses the Java3D API for
visualisation.

1 Introduction

In this paper we describe preliminary results of our research on virtual musicians. The
objective of this project is to generate animated virtual musicians, that play along with
a given piece of music. The input of this system consists of a sound wave, originating
from e.g. a CD or a real-time recording.

There are many possible uses for an application like this, ranging from the automatic
generation of music videos to interactive music performance systems where musicians
play together in a virtual environment. In the last case, the real musicians could be
located on different sites, and their virtual counterparts could be viewed in a virtual
theatre by a worldwide audience. Additionally, our department is currently working on
instructional agents that can teach music, for which the work we describe in this paper
will be a good foundation.

For our first virtual musicians application, we have restricted ourselves to an animated drummer. However, the system is flexible enough to allow an easy extension to
other instruments.

As figure 1 shows, the total task can be separated into two independent subtasks:

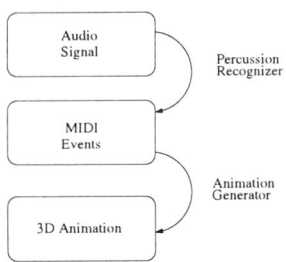

Fig. 1. An overview of the entire system

- Percussion recognition: the translation from a 'low level' description of the music (the sound wave) to a abstract, 'high level' description of all percussion sounds that are present in the signal. The recognised notes are stored as MIDI events. This part of the system is subject of our still ongoing research, and will therefore not be further explained here. For an introduction on how we plan to solve this problem, please refer to [6].

- Animation generation: the creation of the the movements of a 3D avatar playing on a drum kit. For the remainder of this article, we will focus on this part of the systen. In section 2, the transformation from MIDI to animation is described using a number of relatively simple algorithms, to maintain a clear view on the system as a whole. In section 3, some more advanced techniques are described, that result in more 'natural' motion.

In this section, we describe how our system generates animations automatically. The various algorithms discussed here are kept rather simple on purpose, to maintain a clear view on the system as a whole. In section 3, more advanced techniques (that give better results) will be explained.

2 Basic Algorithms

2.1 Overview of the system

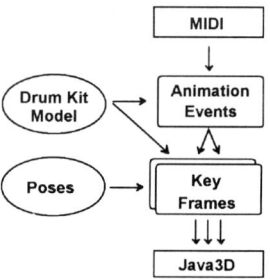

Fig. 2. Animation generation

A general overview of the animation generation is shown in figure 2. An abstract description of the animation (in this case, a list of time-stamped MIDI events) is transformed into a 'concrete' animation. This lower-level description of the animation is defined in terms of 'key frames' [2] that can directly be used by the graphical subsystem to animate objects in the scene.

Our implementation uses the Java3D engine for visualisation purposes [4]; the geometry of the 3D objects we have used has been created using Virtual Reality Modeling Language (VRML, [10]).

2.2 'Pre-calculated' versus 'real-time' animation

In our current off-line implementation, the piece of music to be played is completely known in advance as a list of MIDI events. Therefore, the entire animation can be computed before it is started. In a real-time situation, where the system has to respond to incoming MIDI events, this would not possible. In that case, a short animation should be constructed and started immediately for each note that occurs in the input.

A great advantage of pre-calculating the entire animation is that the transitions between strokes will be much smoother: for each note we already know which drum will be struck next, and the arm can already start moving towards that drum.

2.3 Polyphony Issues

Monophonic instruments (such as the trumpet or the flute) are relatively easy to animate, because each possible sound corresponds to exactly one 'pose' of all fingers, valves, etc., and only one pose can be active at each moment in time. Highly polyphonic instruments (such as the piano) are much more difficult, because there are many different ways ('fingerings') to play the same piece of music, and a search method is needed to find a good solution [5]. The drum kit could be viewed in between these two extreme examples: up to four sounds can be started simultaneously.

2.4 Drum Kit Model

In this section we will describe the parameters that are used to model different drum kits.

Event Types. The General MIDI standard [8] defines 47 different percussive sounds. The standard includes different versions of the same sound, for example "Crash cymbal 1" and "Crash cymbal 2". Our application should treat both events in the same way.

Additionally, there are six different tom-tom sounds, while a 'real' drum kit usually only has 2 or 3 tom-toms. It may be clear that we have to define a smaller set of 'animation event types' in the drum kit model. The MIDI events from the input file can then be mapped onto animation events, that have a type code.

Our current implementation distinguishes between the following animation event types: BASS, SNARE, RIM, HIGHTOM, MIDTOM, FLOORTOM, CRASH, RIDE, RIDEBELL, SPLASH, CHINA, HIHATOPEN, HIHATCLOSED, HIHATPEDAL, COWBELL.

The animation event types do not neccesarily have to have a one-on-one correspondence with the objects in the 3D scene, because 2 or more event types can belong to the same drum/cymbal, with a different 'hit point'.

Other Parameters. Other parameters that are defined in the drum kit model:

- For each event type, a preferred hand: -1 ("left") or 1 ("right").
- For each event type, a parameter $minTimeGap$ that determines how fast that particular event type can be played with one hand. This parameter will be explained in more detail in section 2.6.

2.5 MIDI Parsing

First, the list of MIDI events is transformed into a list of 'animation events' according to the mapping defined in the drum kit model (see section 2.4). Besides having a type code, an animation event has an associated velocity vel_{event} in the range [0..1].

Secondly, the list of animation events is parsed to remove double events [1] and distribute the events over the different animated objects. Objects in the scene respond to a

---

[1] some MIDI files that were used contained 'double events', that is: multiple events on the same channel, with the same time stamp, the same note number and the same velocity. These extra events do not contain new information, nor do they increase the velocity, therefore we can discard them.

subset of animation event types.

Three new event lists are created (one for the hands, one for the left leg and one for the right leg) and the animation events from the original list are distributed between them. The event list that is used for the hands will later be subdivided for the left and right hand; this is discussed in section 2.6.

2.6 Event Distribution

Animation events that can be played by both hands (i.e. all events except BASS and HIHATPEDAL) need to be distributed between the left and right hand in a natural looking way.

The first hand assignment algorithm that we have tested was designed to be as simple as possible. It is based on the following principles:

1. No more than two events, that are played with the hands, can have the same time stamp.
2. For each event type, there is a preferred (default) hand that should be used if possible.
3. When playing fast rolls, both hands should be used.

In our system, these principles were implemented in the following way:

- When more than two events (that should be played with the hands) are found to have the same time stamp, all but two are deleted.
- A parameter $defaultHand_{eventType}$ is specified for all event types. In our implementation, the SNARE and RIM events have the default hand set to 'left', while 'right' is the default hand for all other events.
- A parameter $minTimeGap$ is defined, that determines how fast an event can be played with *one* hand. This parameter can have a different value for different event types, because the tendency to alternate hands varies from one drum type to another. For example, the hi-hat is usually played with the right hand; only in very demanding situations (fast rolls) both hands will be used. On the other hand, hand alternation on the high tom is much more common.

These principles are implemented in algorithm 2.1. It consists of two phases:

1. default hand assignment
2. hand alternation

Algorithm 2.1 A simple algorithm for event distribution

```
iterate over all events e:
    hand(e) := preferredHand(type(e))
iterate over all triplets of subsequent events (e1,e2,e3):
if    hand(e1)=hand(e2)=hand(e3)
    AND
            Time(e2) - Time(e1) <= minTimeGap(type(e1))
        OR
            Time(e3) - Time(e2) <= minTimeGap(type(e3))
    then
    hand(e2) := otherHand(hand(e2))
```

2.7   Pose Creation

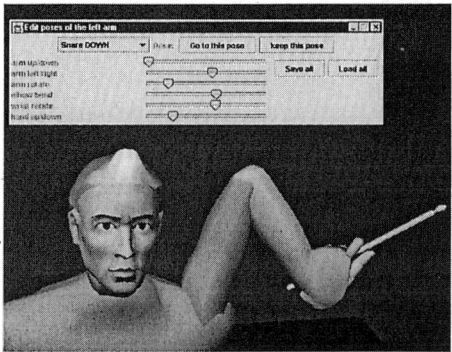

Fig. 3. The graphical poser interface, applied to the left arm

A graphical user-interface (GUI) is provided to create 'poses' manually. Figure 3 shows a screenshot of the GUI applied to the left arm. A pose consists of a set of angles or translation values: one for each degree of freedom. With the horizontal sliders, the user can change these values.

Fig. 4. 'MID TOM UP'

Fig. 5. 'MID TOM DOWN'

For each limb, two poses should be specified for each animation event type that it supports: the 'DOWN' pose (the exact situation on contact) and the 'UP' pose (the situation just before and just after the hitting moment). Examples of 'UP' and 'DOWN' poses are shown in figures 4 and 5.

Once a good position is achieved, it can be stored in the pre-defined list of poses. The entire list can be saved to disk, to preserve the information for a next session.

Motivation. We have chosen for manually setting the poses through a GUI interface, instead of using motion capture [11] or inverse kinematics for the following reasons:

Costs: Motion capture equipment is expensive, and requires a complete setup with a real drum kit that matches the 3D kit. If one would want to change something in the 3D drum kit (for example, moving a tom-tom) the whole capturing would have to be done all over again.

Simplicity: there are only a small number of poses, and they have to be set only once for a new drum kit configuration.

Flexibility: besides for the setting of poses for the arms and legs, the interface can also be used for the hi-hat stand and pedal, the cymbal stands, the parts of the bass pedal, and giving the snare, bass drum and tom-toms their position and orientation in the 3D scene.

2.8 Key Frame Generation

In this section, the transformation from lists of 'abstract' animation events to time lines (containing 'concrete' key frames) is discussed. Since a different approach is used for the avatar and the drum kit, they are discussed separately.

Avatar Animation. The poses that were created with the GUI interface (see section 2.7) are used to create key frames for the animation of the limbs. For each joint, the list of animation events that should be played by the corresponding limb is parsed in the correct temporal order.

For each abstract animation event e, three key frames (a 'stroke') are added to the animation time line: $[e_{before}, e_{contact}, e_{after}]$. In the simplest version of the algorithm, these are equal to th UP, DOWN and UP poses for the corresponding event type. A constant $delta$ determines the time between the key frames within a stroke (100ms is a useful value). See figure 6 for a graphical representation of a stroke that will be used throughout this chapter.

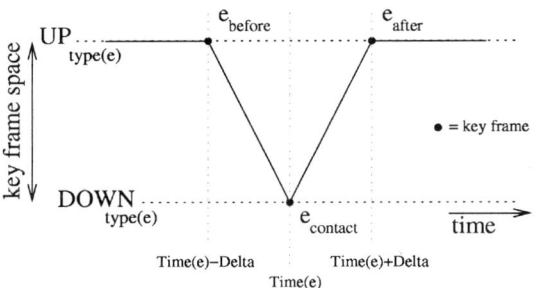

Fig. 6. A basic stroke, consisting of key frames 'before', 'contact' and 'after'

If the time gap between subsequent animation events $e1$ and $e2$ is less then $delta$, their key frames will overlap, and special care has to be taken. We distinguish between two cases:

- If $e1$ and $e2$ are of the same event type (e.g. both are 'SNARE' events), the last key frame of $e1$ and the first key frame of $e2$ are replaced by an interpolated key frame $eNew$: the less time between $e1$ and $e2$, the closer the new key frame will be to the 'DOWN' key frame, as can be seen from figure 7.

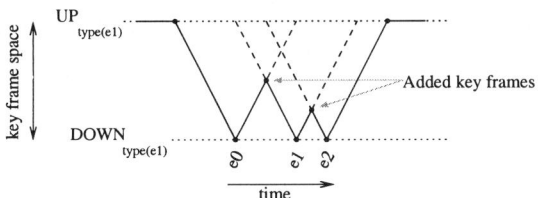

Fig. 7. New key frames in the case of overlapping events of the same event type

- If $e1$ and $e2$ are of different event types (e.g. a 'SNARE' and a 'HIGHTOM' event), more time is needed to bring the arm from the 'after' key frame of $e1$ to the 'before' key frame of $e2$. To accomplish this, the time difference between $e1_{contact}$ and $e1_{after}$, and between $e2_{before}$ and $e2_{after}$ is shortened. A parameter a $(0 < a < 1)$ determines the fraction of the time between the events that is used for moving the arm from $e1_{after}$ to $e2_{before}$.

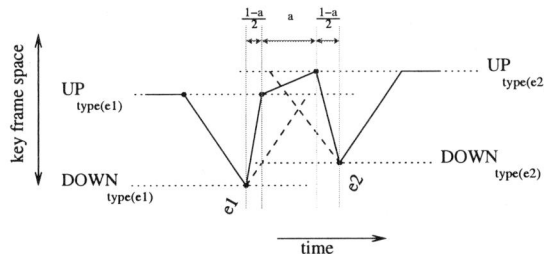

Fig. 8. New key frames in the case of overlapping events of different event types

Drum Kit Animation. The original event list, containing all animation events (i.e. for all limbs) is used to animate the 3D drum kit.

Pedals: The bass pedal and the hi-hat are animated through the same kind of strokes as are used for the avatar. Because the pedals and the feet have their 'UP' and 'DOWN' key frames at exactly at the same moments in time, the illusion is created that the feet really 'move' the pedals.

Cymbals: For the vibration animation of a cymbals, a number of key frames are added to its time line starting at the 'contact' time stamp of a cymbal event. These key frames are computed by rotating the cymbal object around its local X and / or Z axis. The angles are sampled from an exponentionaly decaying sinusoid:

$$angle(t) = \eta^t \alpha_{max} \sin(\beta t)$$

In the above equation,

- α_{max} represents the maximum angle
- η is the damping factor of the vibration $(0 < \eta < 1)$: low values for η result in a fast decay.

- β determines the speed of the vibration: a higher value for β corresponds to a shorter swing period.

Overlapping vibrations are much easier to deal with than overlapping strokes. When the first time stamp of a new vibration falls within the time range of an previous one, the remaining key frames are deleted[2].

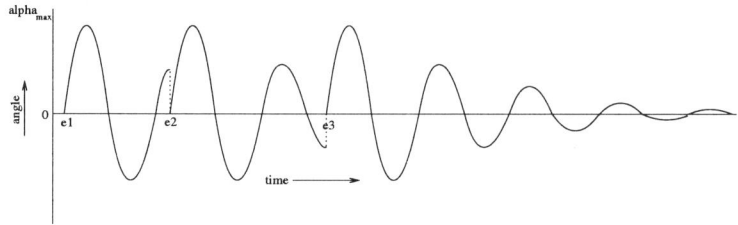

Fig. 9. overlapping vibrations for events [e1,e2,e3]

3 Advanced algorithms

In this section, some advanced techniques will be discussed that extend the system as described in section 2. These techniques are designed to make the motion of the virtual drummer appear to be more 'natural' and 'realistic'. One should keep in mind, however, that although some general rules can be followed, human drummers can play the same piece of music in many different ways. Every drummer will have his/her own playing style, with differences in terms of

- the parts of the drum kit: how many and what type of cymbals, toms etc. are used?
  Is there one bass drum with a single pedal, one bass drum with a double pedal, or two bass drums with two seperate pedals?
- the setup of the drum kit: 'normal' (with the hi-hat on the left side and the lowest tom on the right side, this setup is used by right-handed players) or 'mirrored' (for left-handed drummers)? Where are the cymbals placed?
- The hand patterns used on a certain 'roll': LLRR, LRLR, LRRL, etc.
- 'grip', the way of holding the drum sticks: either 'matched' [3] or 'traditional' [4]?
- the way of striking the drums: are the palms of the hands kept vertical or more horizontal?

Almost all of these parameters can easily be saved in a drummer 'profile', which also incorporates the parameters from the drum kit model, and the 'UP'/'DOWN' poses for all event types.

---

[2]Note that this will sometimes cause a sudden discontinuity in the angle, when a new vibration overrides an existing one at a moment that the angle was not 0. In practice, however, this effect is hardly noticed; probably because the viewer's eye already expects a sharp change in the motion of the cymbal, once it gets hit by the stick.

[3]in matched grip, both hands hold their stick between thumb and index finger

[4]the traditional grip is often used by jazz drummers. The right hand grip (for right-handed players) is the same as with matched grip, while the left hand holds the stick between thumb and index finger and also between ring and middle finger

3.1   Event Distribution

The hand assignment algorithm described in section 2.6 is easy to model and gives satisfactory results in most situations. However, a number of problems arise:

- when two simultaneous events have the same default hand (for example, MID-TOM and LOWTOM), the original algorithm would remove one of the events from the list, even when the other hand could have played that event.
- in some cases, the arms are crossed when this is not necessary: consider for example a fast sequence HIHATOPEN-RIDE-HIHATOPEN. Both RIDE and HI-HATOPEN have 'right' as default hand, and the hand alternation algorithm will assign the RIDE event to the left hand. Most drummers, however, would in this case prefer to play the HIHATOPEN with the left hand and the RIDE with the right hand.

Our second algorithm, that solves these shortcomings, uses default hand assignments for all possible *pairs* of events. For example, we can define that whenever RIDE and HIHATOPEN are played together, the RIDE is played with the right hand and the HIHAT with the left. We should keep some flexibility, as these constraints do not have to be equally strong for all pairs: for example, SNARE+CRASH can be played as left-right just as easy as right-left.

The drum kit model is extended with a function $pair(eventType, eventType)$, that returns a floating-point value in the range [-1..1]. The semantics of this value are as follows:

$$-1 \equiv \text{strictly left-right}$$
$$0 \equiv \text{don't care}$$
$$1 \equiv \text{strictly right-left}$$

The improved hand assignment algorithm uses just the $pair(a, b)$ function for simultaneous events. For events $[e1, e2]$ with a time gap Δt greater that zero, the default hand values are taken into account as well.

For a pair [e1,e2] the hand assignment values $(hand(e1), hand(e2))$ are calculated in the following way:

$$\Delta t = Time(e2) - Time(e1)$$
$$hand(e1) = \rho^{\Delta t} pair(e1, e2) + (1 - \rho^{\Delta t})$$
$$\times defaultHand(e1)$$
$$hand(e2) = \rho^{\Delta t}(-pair(e1, e2)) + (1 - \rho^{\Delta t})$$
$$\times defaultHand(e2)$$

The decreasing exponential function $\rho^{\Delta t}$ $(0 < \rho < 1)$ ensures that the default hand values are taken more into account when there is more time between e1 and e2, at the same time lowering the influence of the pair-wise hand preference.

For each event with index I in the event list, a hand assignment value is calculated twice: in the pair [event(I-1),event(I)] and in the pair [event(I),event(I+1)]. Afterwards, these two values are averaged to yield the final hand assignment value for event(I).

Shortest path methods. A third possible solution to the hand assignment problem might be found in shortest-path methods, as used in [5, 7]. These methods consist of the following steps:

1. generate all possible solutions
2. assign a distance value to each solution (e.g. based on distances between drums, penalties for using a certain hand for a certain event type, etcetera)
3. take the solution with the lowest distance value.

Problems with this approach lie in the design of a good distance function, and in the large number of possible solutions[5]. We have not (yet) implemented a shortest-path algorithm in our system.

3.2 Key Frame Generation

Drum Elasticity. In a real drum kit, one can observe that some drums or cymbals are more 'elastic' than others, i.e. the drum stick 'bounces' more on one object than on another. Besides the object itself, the elasticity is also dependent on the way of playing: the stick will bounce back more on the hi-hat when it is played 'closed' than when it is played 'open'.

To simulate this phenomenon, we extend the drum kit model with an elasticity parameter $el_{eventType}$ in the range $[0..1]$ for each animation event type. The value of $el_{eventType}$ determines how far the drum stick should bounce back to its initial position after contact. In this definition, 0 means "no elasticity" while 1 corresponds to "maximum elasticity".

Note Velocities. In the basic algorithm (see section 2.5), we did not take the velocities vel_{event} of the animation events into account. Using different animations for different velocities results in a more 'natural' animation: the 'UP' position should be closer to the drum surface for softer notes, and further away in the case of loud notes.

The note velocities and the elasticity values are used to calculate the key frames (for each joint) for an event e, by interpolating between the 'UP' and the 'DOWN' poses for the corresponding event type:

$$e_{before} = DOWN_{eventType} + vel_{event} \times diff$$
$$e_{contact} = DOWN_{eventType}$$
$$e_{after} = DOWN_{eventType} + vel_{event} \times el_{eventType} \times diff$$
$$diff = UP_{eventType} - DOWN_{eventType}$$

For the drum kit animation, the note velocities can easily be used to scale the amplitudes of the cymbal vibrations.

Extra avatar animation. In this section, a number of extensions are discussed that animate parts of the avatar that were not animated at all in the basic system. This helps a great deal to make the avatar look 'alive'.

---

[5]This is of exponential complexity, as n events can be distributed over the 2 hands in 2^n ways

The head: The head of the avatar is animated, to create the effect that the avatar 'follows' his hands with his eyes. First, we create poses for the head: one for each event type that is supported by the hands. These poses rotate the head so that the eyes are pointed at the associated drum / cymbal. If we then use all events that are played by e.g. the right hand to create a key frame time line, the head appears to 'follow' this hand.

The neck: The neck joint is used to make the avatar nod with his head on the beat: 'UP' and 'DOWN' poses are defined for the neck joint, and for each 'beat' note a stroke is created. We have used the SNARE event on the left hand as an approximisation of beat notes.

Finding the 'real' beat in a MIDI file is far from trivial, and many other researchers have addressed this problem [1, 3]. Our system could very well be integrated with an intelligent beat detector to create even better looking behaviour.

Key Frame Interpolation. After the basic key frames are set, the motion is fine-tuned by inserting extra key frames according to interpolation 'scripts'. Different interpolation scripts can be used between specific pairs of key frame types (e.g. between 'before' and 'contact'). Of course, scripts can also vary between different joints.

Figure 10 shows example scripts shown in create rather convincing results, because the stick moves slightly 'behind' the hand, and the hand moves 'behind' the elbow, resulting in a whip-like motion. These interpolation scripts are derived by observing the motion of a human drummer.

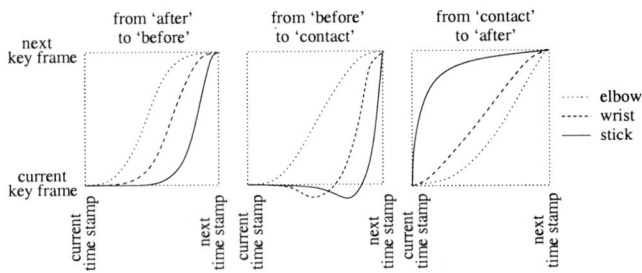

Fig. 10. example interpolation scripts for the elbow and the wrist and stick joints

3.3 Implementation Notes

The Java3D API is used for the implementation, because it is platform-independent and supports a wide range of geometry file formats. Moreover, our virtual theatre [9] is currently being ported from VRML to Java3D.

The SMF format (Standard MIDI File) is used as intermediate file format between the percussion recogniser and the animation generator. A great advantage of using the SMF is that it allows us to use MIDI files (which are widely available on the WWW) to test the animation generator independent from the percussion recognizer.

For the synchronisation of the animation and the sound, a seperate thread is used, which looks up the current audio position and adjusts the start time of the animation accordingly.

4   Conclusions

We have presented some algorithms that allow for the automatic generation of 3D animated musicians, based on an abstract representation of the musical part that has to be played. Using this, we have implemented a virtual drummer, but the system could easily be applied to other kinds of instruments.

The algorithms that create the realistic animation of the limbs and sticks *before* the contact moments, as well as the improved hand assignment algorithm (which makes use of the time intervals between subsequent events) can only be used for pre-calculated animations.

Instead of motion capture or inverse kinematics, a simple GUI-based pose editor is used. This proved to be very useful, because there are only a small number of poses, and they have to be set only once for a new drum kit configuration.

The animation results can be viewed at our web site: http://wwwhome.cs.utwente.nl-Γ kragtwij/science/

References

1. P. Desain and H. Honing. Can music cognition benefit from computer music research? from foot tapper systems to beat induction models. In *Proceedings of the ICMPC*, pages 397–398, Liege: ESCOM, 1994.
2. J. D. Foley, A. van Dam, S. K. Feiner, and J. F. Hughes. *Computer Graphics: Principles and Practice*. Addison-Wesley Publishing Company, second. edition, 1990.
3. M. Goto and Y. Muraoka. Music understanding at the beat level: Real-time beat tracking for audio signals. In *Working Notes of the IJCAI-95 Workshop on Computational Auditory Scene Analysis*, pages 68–75, Montreal, Aug. 1995.
4. The Java3D API. http://java.sun.com/products/java-media/3D/.
5. J. Kim. Computer animation of pianist's hand. In *Eurographics '99 Short Papers and Demos*, pages 117–120, Milan, 1999.
6. M. Kragtwijk, A. Nijholt, and J. Zwiers. An animated virtual drummer. In *Proceedings of the ICAV3D International Conference on Augmented, Virtual Environments and Three-Dimensional Imaging*, pages 319–322, Mykonos, Greece, 2001.
7. T. Lokki, J. Hiipakka, R. Hänninen, T. Ilmonen, L. Savioja, and T. Takala. Real-time audio-visual rendering and contemporary audiovisual art. *Organised Sound*, 3(3):219–233, 1998.
8. The general midi specification. http://www.midi.org/about-midi/gm/gm1sound.htm.
9. A. Nijholt and J. Hulstijn. Multimodal interactions with agents in virtual worlds. In N. Kasabov, editor, *Future Directions for Intelligent Systems and Information Science*, Studies in Fuzziness and Soft Computing, chapter 8, pages 148–173. Physica-Verlag, 2000.
10. Web3d consortium. http://www.vrml.org/.
11. V. B. Zordan and J. K. Hodgins. Tracking and modifying upper-body human motion data with dynamic simulation. In *Computer Animation and Simulation '99*. Springer-Verlag Wien, 1999.

2

Deformations for Animation

Animating with the "Multidimensional deformation tool"

Dominique Bechmann, Mehdi Elkouhen

Université Louis Pasteur - LSIIT
Pôle API - Boulevard Sébastien Brant
67400 Strasbourg France
[bechmann, elkouhen]@dpt-info.u-strasbg.fr

Abstract.
This paper describes our "Multidimensional deformation tool" defined to be used in geometrical modeling and animation. It is a space-time deformation tool defined as a combination of three free-form deformation tools. The first one is Chang and Rockwood's axial tool and the two others are its extensions to a tool defined by a Bezier patch and a tool defined by a Bezier trivariate volume.
The presentation of our "Multidimensional deformation tool" will start by a description of each of the elementary tools to finish with a description of the rules that unite the deformations defined by a set of tools in a unique deformation.

Introduction

Sederberg and Parry's [16] free-form deformation tools have been on one hand extended in their shape [7] and topology [14, 1] to cope with complex shapes and on the other hand specialized to ease control during deformations [12, 6, 10, 15]. They have also been adapted to key frame animation systems [8].

In order to define a uniform framework of deformations which generates arbitrary shaped deformations and animations, we extended three free-form deformation tools, and set rules to define the way they collaborate (*cf.* section 4). The first tool is Chang and Rockwood's axial tool (*cf.* section 1); the two others are its extensions to a tool defined by a Bezier rectangular mesh (*cf.* section 2) and a tool defined by a Bezier lattice (*cf.* section 3).

Remarks

To describe our elementary tools we will use the same vocabulary than the one used for Bezier curves, surfaces and volumes. For example, an axial tool that has $n + 1$ points of control is said to be of degree n.

We will note $Tool(M)$ the result of the deformation by a tool $Tool$ applied to the point M.

1 Generalized De Casteljau tool

An interpretation of De Casteljau's algorithm is that it deforms the segment $[0, 1]$ in a Bezier curve. This observation lead Chang and Rockwood [6] to generalize the former interpolation scheme into a deformation algorithm. They modified it in order to take in input points of $\mathbb{R}^3$ and for the sake of the generalization enriched the control polygon (which defines the Bezier curve) by associating to each segment of control two handles (or vectors) S and T. In fact, the handles define the way the deformed points are placed around the Bezier curve.

We will explain how a designer creates and manipulates (*cf.* section 1.1) an axial tool, give the area of influence (*cf.* section 1.2) and finally describe the algorithm of deformation (*cf.* section 1.3). Except for the mathematical formalism of this tool, we will try to be as less redundant as possible.

1.1 Tool creation

In our modeler known as STIGMA [5], a designer can create a tool in two manners. The first way consists of specifying a linear control polygon and two directions A and B: the tool is linear and all the handles S (resp. T) share the same direction A (resp. B). The user can also choose to create a tool by simply creating a Bezier curve; the handles are computed automatically.

When using this tool, one manipulates the position of the control points, the orientation of the handles and their lengths. By giving examples, we will explain how the modification of each parameter is linked to the shape of the deformation. And as the placement of handles is linked to the control, we will explain by the way how they are computed when a tool is created.

By controlling the position of the control points, one controls the shape of the Bezier curve associated to the tool and so the bending the deformed object undergoes. In plate 1(a), a cube is bent.

In plate 1(b), handles were turned around the control polygon: the cube is twisted. To limit unwanted twisting, orientation of handles is initially computed by an algorithm based on the rotation minimizing frame [11]. In this way, bad orientation of handles which lead to unintuitive deformations (plate 1(e)) are eliminated (plate 1(f)).

The algorithm is iterative. It first sets the handles S_0 and T_0 as the binormal and the main normal of the Bezier curve at its origin. Afterwards the algorithm computes the handle S_{i+1} (resp T_{i+1}) by rotation of the handle S_i (resp T_i); it is the rotation that turns the vector $P_i P_{i+1}$ into the vector $P_{i+1} P_{i+2}$.

In plate 1(c), a handle is pulled : the cube is tapered. To limit unwanted tapering, lengths of handles are initially set to 1.

As these three parameters are not linked, one tool can twist, bend and taper simultaneously (plate 1(d)).

1.2 Influence area

After having created a tool, the designer places the object to deform in the area of influence of the tool. Because of the convex hull property of Bezier curves, our implementation of this tool deforms a point only if its abscissa is between 0 and 1. In this way, objects warp on the Bezier curve defined between 0 and 1.

As precised by Blanc [3], every tool has its own local frame $< \Omega, X, Y, Z >$ which enables designers to place correctly the tool regarding the object to deform. In this way, to apply a deformation on a point P one must compute the coordinates of this point in the frame of the tool, apply the deformation and compute the coordinates of the deformed point in the frame of the object. The frame associated to this tool is $< P_0, P_n P_0, S_0, T_0 >$.

1.3 Deformation algorithm

As the deformation algorithm is a generalization of the De Casteljau algorithm, it is important to have in mind the original algorithm. For a curve defined by the control polygon $\{P_i\}_{0 \le i \le n}$, the iterations to compute the point with parameter value u on the Bezier curve which is given by the point $P_0^n(u)$ are now described.

$$
\begin{cases}
P_i^0(u) = P_i & 0 \le i \le n \\
P_i^j(u) = (1-u)P_{i-1}^{j-1}(u) + uP_i^{j-1}(u) & \begin{cases} 1 \le j \le n \\ 0 \le i \le n-j \end{cases}
\end{cases}
$$

In this algorithm, each intermediate point $P_i^j(u)$ is computed as the point of coordinates u in the 1D frame $< P_{i-1}^{j-1}(u), P_i^{j-1}(u)P_{i-1}^{j-1}(u) >$. Chang and Rockwood generalized this to compute the point $P_i^j(M)$: it is the point of coordinates (x,y,z) in the 3D frame $< P_{i-1}^{j-1}(M), P_i^{j-1}(M)P_{i-1}^{j-1}(M), S_i, T_i >$. But as it is cumbersome and not necessary to define handles for each iteration i, the handles are set to the null vector except for the first iteration.

In this way, they obtained this formal description of the deformation of the point M of coordinates (x,y,z) by a tool of degree n : the deformed point is $P_0^n(M)$.

$$
\begin{cases}
P_i^0(M) = P_i & 0 \le i \le n \\
P_i^1(M) = \Theta[P_{i-1}^0(M), P_i^0(M), S_i, T_i] & 0 \le i \le n-1 \\
P_i^j(M) = \Theta[P_{i-1}^{j-1}(M), P_i^{j-1}(M), \vec{0}, \vec{0}] & \begin{cases} 1 \le j \le n \\ 0 \le i \le n-j \end{cases}
\end{cases}
$$

With Θ defined as following :

$$
\Theta[O, X, j, k] \begin{pmatrix} x \\ y \\ z \end{pmatrix} = O + xOX + yj + zk
$$

In plates 1(g), 1(h) and 1(i) the iterations of the deformation of a cube are illustrated. The cube is first duplicated in each frame. Then the duplicated cubes are successively interpolated two by two; the final cube is the deformed cube.

The explicit formulation of the deformation of a point M of coordinates x, y and z is given by the two equivalent formulas :

$$
Axial(M) = \Sigma_{i=0}^{n-1} B_i^{n-1}(x)(P_i + xP_iP_{i+1} + yS_i + zT_i)
$$
$$
Axial(M) = \Sigma_{i=0}^{n} B_i^n(x)P_i + y\Sigma_{i=0}^{n-1} B_i^{n-1}(y)S_i + z\Sigma_{i=0}^{n-1} B_i^{n-1}(z)T_i
$$

The first equation means that the deformation is an interpolation of affine transformations of space, and the second one is a handy rewrite of the first one. It can be used to define geometric continuity [6] of deformation between two axial tools, and also to extend the shape of this axial tool in the same way the FFD was extended into the EFFD tool.

In order to take into account the t component of a 4D point during deformation, we simply add it to the result of the deformation by the previous algorithm.

$$
Axial4D(x,y,z,t) = Axial(x,y,z) + (0,0,0,t)
$$

This algorithm of deformation was constructed as an interpolation of affine transformations of space. We will present in next section our surfacic tool which is defined as an interpolation of axial tools, and so generates a broader class of deformations.

2 Generalized Bezier surfacic tool

This tool is defined by an enriched Bezier surface; handles are still associated to the control points. The point on using handles is to define a way to place deformed points in height regarding the mesh, so we associate only one handle to a control point. We will precise how in (*cf.* section 2.2).

The way to create and use this tool will be described in (*cf.* section 2.1), and the algorithm of deformation in (*cf.* section 2.2).

2.1 Tool creation

Designers can create a tool in two ways. In the first method, one specifies a regular rectangular mesh and a direction A : the tool is defined by a regular rectangular Bezier patch and all it handles share the same direction A. In the second method, one creates the rectangular mesh in a free way; the handles are computed automatically.

By giving two examples of deformed grids, we will show how intuitive this tool is.

In plate 1(k), we modified the position of the control points by creating a bump on the mesh : the grid is bumped.

In plate 1(j), we selected control points along an "S" and pulled the handles of the corresponding control points: an S appears on the grid.

As for the previous tool, we had to define a method to place the handles on a tool when it is created using the interactive way. We compute the handle T_{ij} as the normalized vector product of the two vectors $P_{i+1j}P_{ij}$ and $P_{ij+1}P_{ij}$. In this way, the handles are all oriented in the same way regarding the surface and share the same norm : self-intersections and tapering are avoided.

2.2 Deformation algorithm

As a Bezier patch is evaluated for parameter values (u,v) with $u \in [0,1]$ and $v \in [0,1]$, then our two dimensional tool only deforms points $P(x,y,z)$ if there coordinates x and y are between 0 and 1. The local frame associated to a tool of degree $m*n$ is $< P_{00}, P_{m0}P_{00}, P_{0n}P_{00}, T_{00} >$

In this section we will present the algorithm of deformation of a point M by a tool *Surf* defined by a rectangular mesh P_{ij} of degree $m*n$ and a set of handles T_{ij}; the handle $\{T_{ij}\}_{0 \leq i < m, 0 \leq j < n}$ is associated to the control point P_{ij}.

We define for almost each row of the mesh an axial tool $\{Axial_j\}_{0 \leq j < n}$ defined by the control polygon $\{P_{ij}\}_{0 \leq i \leq m}$. Except for the last control point, we associate to each control point a handle of type S equal to the vector $P_{ij+1}P_{ij}$ and a handle of type T which is the vector T_{ij}.

Each tool $Axial_j$ is applied on M, the result is memorized in the point I_j. Finally the I_j's are interpolated with respect with y. We obtain this formula to compute a deformation :

$$Surf(M) = \sum_{j=0}^{n-1} Axial_j(M)B_j^{n-1}(y)$$

In this section, we will give two extensions of this surfacic tool into a volumic tool. We will show their difference and explain why we chose a solution similar to the FFD.

3 Generalized Bezier volumic tool

This tool is defined by a lattice of control points P_{ijk}; handles dissapear in this tool (plate 1(1)).

3.1 Tool creation

The designer creates a Generalized Bezier volumic tool using the classic operations : extrusion of a mesh,... The only restriction is that the topology of the tool must be of a parallelepiped.

3.2 Deformation algorithm

A point is in the area of influence of this tool if its coordinates x, y and z are between 0 and 1. The frame associated to a tool of degree $m*n*p$ is $< P_{000}, P_{m00}P_{000}, P_{0n0}P_{000}, P_{00p}P_{000} >$.

The first algorithm we propose to associate to this tool is the one that evaluates Bezier trivariate volumes and consequently the one used by FFD's. To deform a point M by a tool Vol of degree $m*n*p$ is obtained by the following computation :

$$Vol(M) = \sum_{i=0}^{m} \sum_{j=0}^{n} \sum_{k=0}^{p} P_{ijk}B_i^m(x)B_j^n(y)B_k^p(z)$$

A similar approach to the one presented in (cf. section 2.2) can be followed to define another algorithm of deformation. It requires to define a set of Generalized Bezier surfacic tools as sections of this tool, and define the deformation induced by this tool as an interpolation of the deformations induced by each surfacic tool.

We define p Generalized surfacic tools $Surf_l$ from sections of the lattice P_{ijk} of degree $m*n*p$. The tool $Surf_l$ is defined by the grid of points $\{P_{ijl}\}_{0\leq i\leq m,0\leq j\leq n}$; the handle $P_{ijk+1}P_{ijk}$ is associated to the control point P_{ijk}.

We obtain the following equation :

$$Vol(M) = \sum_{k=0}^{p-1} Surf_k(M)B_k^{p-1}(z)$$

In this way, the control points $\{P_{mjp}\}_{0\leq j\leq n}$ and $\{P_{inp}\}_{0\leq i\leq m}$ are not taken in account during the deformation. As this seems to us non intuitive, we choose the first solution.

In this following section, we will explain the way these tools are combined into our "Multidimensional deformation" tool and the goal on defining it as a space-time tool.

4 Multidimensional deformation tool

As pointed out by Brandel[5] and Turk[18], it is easy to create animations with topological changes by working in higher dimensions. The three tools we defined offer control on 4D shapes and can be used to create topological changes in an intuitive way; plates m–x illustrate the continuous merging of two spheres and of two tori that successfully

appear.
We will only explain how the first animation was created; the second was created in the same way. We created a sphere embedded in the yzt space, then we extruded it along the x axis. Finally we applied an axial deformation on the object. The tool (of degree 3) was constructed in order to send the points having their abscissa different to 0 and 1 to the future and to deform as less as possible the other points. In the present instance, the control points were set as $P_0 = (0,0,0,0)$, $P_1 = (1/3,0,0,1)$, $P_2 = (2/3,0,0,1)$ and $P_3 = (1,0,0,0)$ and the handles S_i (resp T_i) were set to be equal to the vector $(0,1,0,0)$ (resp $(0,0,1,0)$). The sequences were created by displaying constant time sections of the 4D objects.

In order to create an easy to visualize and manipulate tool, we represent complex deformations by a graph of elementary deformations. In this kind of graph, an edge $A \to B$ means that the tool A deforms the object B.

We use the graph to compute all the deformations. The algorithm consists in sorting the graph topologically. And for each node B of the graph, if there are $n + 1$ incoming edges $A_0 \to B \ldots A_n \to B$, the deformation undergone by a vertex of B is the average of the deformations induced by each of the $n + 1$ tools. This technique to combine deformations can be found in several articles [17, 9, 3, 2].

To generate continuous surface animations and to ease the definition of new tools, we enriched our graph by defining aggregates of tools. An aggregate represents the set of deformations an object undergoes during an animation.

If an aggregate is composed of $l + 1$ tools $Element_i$, the deformation algorithm associated consists in applying each tool $Element_i$ separately and saving the result in a point P_i. Finally, the P_i's are interpolated using De Casteljau's scheme with respect with time; the result is the deformed point by the aggregate. Actually we use the Bezier Basis of functions to interpolate because our tools are built over this basis but any other basis can be used.

$$Aggregate(M) = \sum_{i=0}^{l} Element_i(M)B_i^l(t)$$

With this aggregate we propose a new way to animate deformations different to the one proposed by Coquillart [8]. They propose to animate tools independantly of the way the associated objects are animated, while we propose a space-time deformation tool : animation and deformation algorithms are unified.

Conclusion

By following the generalization idea, tools defined by curves, surfaces and volumes are unified. Before they were separated by the techniques used to freeze points. For instance, the freezing process associated to the axial tool Axdf [13] is based on the computation of frenet frames while for the EFFD it is based on solving numerical equations.

Another advantage and consequence of this unification is that an explicit formulation of deformations and so of animations can always be found.

These tools have been combined in two different ways so as to satisfy the needs of deformations as a simple modeling tool and the needs of animation. The fact of using space-time objects is not an obstacle in using this model in a classical key frame animation system. Of course the interaction with tools will only remain 3D and hence a class of metamorphosis studied in [5] may not be attained.

We are going to complete our work by exploring non linear aggregates, by generalizing tools based on other interpolation schemes like BSplines [15], integrating 0-dimensional tools like Dogme [4], and defining specific 4D operations, ...

References

1. D. Bechmann, Y. Bertrand, and S. Thery. Continuous free-form deformation. *Compugraphics'96 and a Special Issue of Computer Networks and ISDN Systems*, 1996.
2. Dominique Bechmann and Hubert Peyré. Deformation multi-tool combining existing deformation tools. *Poster Presentation in solid modeling*, 2001.
3. Carole Blanc. *Techniques de modélisation et de déformation de surfaces pour la synthèse d'images*. PhD thesis, 1994.
4. Paul Borrel and Dominique Bechmann. Deformation of n-dimensional objects. *International Journal of Computational Geometry & Applications*, 1(4):427–453, September 1991.
5. S. Brandel, D. Bechmann, and Y. Bertrand. Stigma: a 4-dimensional modeller for animation. *Computer Animation and Simulation '98*, August 1998.
6. Yu-Kuang Chang and Alyn P. Rockwood. A generalized de casteljau approach to 3d free-form deformation. *Proceedings of SIGGRAPH 94*, pages 257–260, 1994.
7. Sabine Coquillart. Extended free-form deformation: A sculpturing tool for 3d geometric modeling. *Computer Graphics*, 24(4):187–196, 1990.
8. Sabine Coquillart and Pierre Jancène. Animated free-form deformation: An interactive animation technique. *Computer Graphics*, 25(4):23–26, 1991.
9. B. Crespin. Implicit free form deformation. *Fourth International Workshop on Implicit Surfaces*, pages 17–23, 1999.
10. Feng Jieqing, Ma Lizhuang, and Peng Qunsheng. A new free-form deformation through the control of parametric surfaces. *Computers & Graphics*, 20(4):531–539, 1996.
11. F. Klok. Two moving coordinate frames for sweeping along a 3d trajectory. *Computer Aided Geometry Design*, 3:217–229, 1986.
12. F. Lazarus, S. Coquillart, and P. Jancene. Axial deformation: An intuitive deformation technique. *Computer-Aided Design*, 26(8):607–613, 1994.
13. F. Lazarus, S. Coquillart, and P. Jancène. Axial deformations : An intuitive technique. *Computer-Aided Design*, 26(8):607–613, 1994.
14. Ron MacCracken and Kenneth I. Joy. Free-form deformations with lattices of arbitrary topology. *Proceedings of SIGGRAPH 96*, pages 181–188, 1996.
15. Marek Mikita. Free-form deformation: Basic and extended algorithms. *12th Spring Conference on Computer Graphics*, pages 183–191, June 1996.
16. Thomas W. Sederberg and Scott R. Parry. Free-form deformation of solid geometric models. *Computer Graphics*, 20(4):151–160, 1986.
17. Karan Singh and Eugene Fiume. Wires: A geometric deformation technique. *Proceedings of SIGGRAPH 98*, pages 405–414, 1998.
18. Greg Turk and James F. O'Brien. Shape transformation using variational implicit functions. *Proceedings of SIGGRAPH 99*, pages 335–342, 1999.

Editors' Note: see Appendix, p. 197ff. for colored figure of this paper

Mixing Triangle Meshes and Implicit Surfaces in Character Animation

Antoine Leclercq [†], S. Akkouche [‡] and E. Galin [††]

[†]Infogrames
82-84 rue du 1 Mars 1943
69628 Villeurbanne Cedex
aleclercq@fr.infogrames.com
http://www710.univ-lyon1.fr/~leclercq/

[‡]L.I.G.I.M
Ecole Centrale de Lyon
B.P. 163, 69131 Ecully Cedex
samir@ec-lyon.fr

[††]L.I.G.I.M
Université Claude Bernard Lyon 1
69622 Villeurbanne Cedex
egalin@ligim.univ-lyon1.fr

Abstract. This paper presents a technique for mixing implicit surfaces and mesh models in character modeling and animation. Implicit surfaces provide an organic aspect to standard triangle meshes and are used to add specific features. We propose a method for generating a smooth mesh from both a coarse triangle mesh and implicit primitives. The final model may be animated and displayed in real time.

Keywords: mesh models, implicit surfaces, character animation.

1 Introduction

Implicit surfaces form a very interesting model for modeling and animating organic shapes. They have been successfully used in the design of complex sea shell models [9], and for animating soft substances [4] and virtual human characters [16, 19, 12].

Let us recall that an implicit surface is mathematically defined as a set of points in space $\mathbf{x}$ that satisfy the equation $f(\mathbf{x}) = 0$. Therefore, vizualizing implicit surfaces typically consists in finding the zero-set of f, which is difficult to perform.

Polygonization algorithms provide a fast representation of the surface that may be rendered with the now democratized graphic hardware. Polygonal meshes tend to become the standard representation for surface geometry in many computer graphics applications. Although many accelerated polygonization schemes using spatial and temporal coherence [10] have been proposed, experience shows that visualising complex implicit models in real time is still difficult.

Another advantage of polygonal models is their ability to be smoothed using subdivision techniques [7, 8, 22, 3]. Subdivision algorithms proceed in two steps. The control mesh is first refined to create new vertices using a dyadic scheme, i.e. new vertices are inserted at the center of the edges. The vertices are then elevated by weighting the influence of their neighbors. The overall process is recursively applied to generate the final mesh.

Other smoothing techniques perform an iterative N-adic decomposition of the triangles [18, 17] that split triangles into n^2 sub-triangles. In contrast to subdivision techniques, those methods need not explore the neighborhood of the vertices of the mesh to compute the elevation map but rely on the normals at the control vertices only. The results are visually as convincing as subdivisions.

Tentatives to mix implicit surfaces and the polygonal model have been performed. The underlying idea is to keep the best of both worlds. Implicit surfaces may provide a smooth organic look to mesh models, accelerate collision detection and fake physically based deformations. Triangle meshes are versatile and can model any kind of shape at different levels of detail. Moreover, triangle meshes can be rendered in real time using the graphic hardware. Existing mixed models focus on the following two objectives: accelerating and improving collisions, and skinning skeletal models.

Parent[13] has proposed to embed a meshed object into a set of implicit primitives approximating the general shape of the object to perform collision detection and propagate better deformations over the mesh. The mesh is deformed according to the modification of the potential field defined by the implicit primitives. This method relies on the implicit contact model proposed by Gascuel[11].

Shen[14] has proposed to attach skeletal implicit primitives to an animation skeleton to create virtual actors. Implicit surfaces are used to skin a polygonal skeleton. The surface is created by finding the polygonal intersection between the implicit surface and cross sections located along the skeleton. The vertices of the resulting polygonal contours are used as control points to define B-Spline patches that skin the model.

In this paper, we use implicit primitives to create and animate organic features on animated character models that are represented by a triangle mesh. The original mesh model comes from an animation modeler providing an animation skeleton and a coarse mesh. Implicit primitives are inserted only in some areas of interest where we aim at adding features. The other are let free of implicit primitives if they already provide sufficiently fine detail or out of efficiency.

Our method generates a global smoothed mesh on the fly during the animation of the character in real time. In the section 2, we present an overview of the edition of the implicit surface and control mesh models. In section 3, we address the smoothing algorithm used to create the final mesh. We show how to obtain smooth blending between regions where implicit primitives deform the control mesh and ordinary mesh areas. Section 4 presents some results and timings.

2 Overview

In our animation system, the designer first creates an esquisse of a coarse mesh attached to an animation skeleton. In general, the mesh is characterized by many small triangles in the regions of interest of the shape, and may also feature large triangles in flat or slightly curved regions. For instance, video-game designers often create fine details for the head of animated character, whereas the body is characterized by a coarser mesh. The overall model is split into different regions that are in general the principal parts of the animated character.

The second step of the method aims at adding or modifying the shape of the model in some specific regions. Features are added by inserting skeletal implicit primitives wherever needed. Implicit surfaces help adding an organic look to the mesh model in some regions. For instance, muscles lend themselves to implicit modeling. Implicit surfaces are created by blending skeletal primitives. In our implementation, we use ellipsoidal primitives characterized by a center and three axes out of efficiency. The skeletal primitives are also attached to the animation skeleton so that they may be animated later. During this modeling step, the control mesh may be smoothed at each step so that the designer can modify the model interactively.

Eventually, the animation of the model only start when editing has been finished. At each step of the animation, the position and orientation of the primitives of the animation skeleton are updated. The control mesh follows the animation skeleton accordingly as in standard animation systems. The implicit primitives attached to the skeleton also follow the animation skeleton. The control mesh is refined and smoothed on the fly

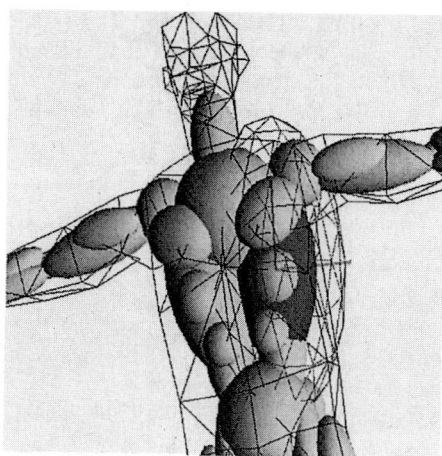

Fig. 1. Inserting implicit primitives in the control mesh model.

during the animation as the implicit primitives constantly move which results in some deformations of the surface in their region of influence.

Smoothing is performed in two steps. First, the mesh is refined using a N-adic refinement scheme. Then, the elevations of vertices are computed as follows. The new vertices of triangles outside regions of influence are moved using a N-adic smoothing algorithm [17, 18]. If a triangle fully lies inside the region of influence of f, the vertices are relocated on the implicit surface using a projection scheme that resembles the seed migration proposed by Desbrun [5]. The vertices inside triangles that straddle the regions of influence are moved using a weighted combination of both previous techniques. We address the details of the smoothing process in the next section.

3 Smoothing process

In this section, we address the computation of a smooth triangle mesh generated by the control mesh and the implicit primitives. Our algorithm proceed in two steps. First, we refine the whole control mesh using an N-adic scheme. Then, we move the vertices of the subdivided mesh to create a smooth model. The overall algorithm may be outlined as follows.

1. Refine all the triangles of mesh T using the N-adic subdivision scheme.
2. For each vertex p of the refined mesh, let T its parent triangle in the control mesh :
   - 2.1 If T lies in the region of influence of the field function f, evaluate the direction of projection, project p onto the implicit surface and compute its normal as the normalized gradient of f.
   - 2.2 If T lies outside the region of influence of the field function f, evaluate the new position of p and its normal following a smoothing technique.
   - 2.3 Otherwise, T straddles the region of influence, relocate p and compute its normal by weighting the results obtained in the two previous cases.

The first step aims at creating a refined mesh. The refinement is controlled by a refinement-depth parameter that balances the level of detail and the number of generated triangles which directly affects the overall performance. We use the same refinement depth for all the triangles of the control mesh which guarantees a consistent topology all over the refined mesh.

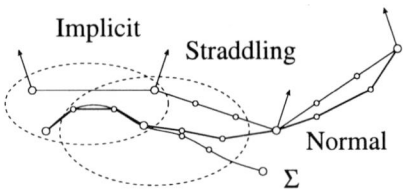

Fig. 2. Smoothing process used for implicit, straddling and normal triangles

The second step moves the vertices of the refined mesh in order to smooth the general shape of the character. As outlined in the algorithm, three cases arise, depending whether a triangle is fully inside, outside or straddling the region of influence of the implicit primitives. Those triangles will be referred to as *implicit, normal* and *straddling* triangles respectively. Figure 2 illustrates the smoothing process invoked for neighboring implicit, normal and straddling triangles. We address the three specific smoothing algorithms in the next paragraphs.

3.1 Smoothing implicit triangles

Let us recall that given vertices **p** on a control mesh, we aim at moving those vertices to an implicit surface created by blending implicit primitives. Let us first detail the implicit primitives we use. In our implementation, the implicit surface is created by blending several skeletal primitives organized in a blending graph. The blending graph [21, 4] enables us to avoid unwanted blending between parts of the character model that should not melt, for instance the forearms and the torso. The final field function f is obtained by computing the sum and sometimes the maximum of field functions f_i of the primitives.

The evaluation of the field functions f_i is critical for real-time animation. Many evaluations of f_i are often needed to project a point in space onto an implicit surface. Field functions f_i are defined as $f_i = g_i \circ d_i$ where g_i denotes the potential function and d_i the distance to a skeleton. In our implementation we use spheres and ellipsoids which are very efficient to compute and produce convincing organic shapes. Spheres are the fastest to compute, whereas ellipsoids are implemented as spheres transformed by an affine transformation matrix. The ellipsoids are not only aligned to the animation skeleton axis, but may have any orientation. We use the following simple quadratic potential function, in normalized form $g(r) = (1 - r^2)^2$ which is the fastest to compute [15].

Let **T** be a triangle inside an implicit region. The vertices of the refined triangles are to be projected onto the implicit surface. Our projection algorithm is inspired by different methods presented in the literature. Desbrun [4] has proposed to project seeds that are defined on the bounding box of each primitive along a predefined direction. The main advantage of this method is it speed, while its main drawback lies in the fact that the mesh is built separately for each primitive. The piecewise generated mesh can't be easily closed in areas where many primitives blend which results in cracks in the polygonization. Although Crespin [2] has presented a method for closing the mesh, too many triangles are required for performing this crack-fixing step, which makes this approach too expensive in our application which should perform on the fly and in real-time.

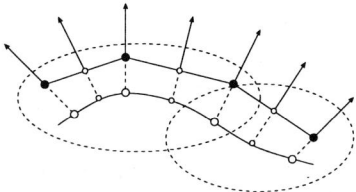

Fig. 3. Mesh smoothing for implicit triangles. The regions of influence of primitives have been dashed.

Our algorithm will take the good part of Desbrun's method. We project the vertices of the refined mesh along predefined direction onto the implicit surface. New vertices and normal are computed as a barycentric combination of the three vertices and vertex normals of their parent triangle.

The projection of **p** is defined as the first intersection between the implicit surface and a ray whose origin is the vertex **p**, and whose direction follows the vertex normal if $f(\mathbf{p}) > 0$ and the opposite direction of the normal if $f(\mathbf{p}) < 0$. This projection step is crucial as it is invoked for the vertices of each implicit and straddling triangle. Implementation details are addressed in section 4.

3.2 Normal triangles

Triangles of the control mesh that do not intersect the region of influence of f also need to be smoothed. Let us recall that those triangles have been refined during the refinement step, so we need to compute a displacement map for the vertices of the refined triangles. It is interesting to point out that any smoothing algorithm may be used at this point. In our implementation, we use the N-Patch smoothing process [17]. This algorithm will be implemented in hardware in the next generation of 3D accelerators chipsets on graphic cards. Although we haven't been able to take advantage of such hardware acceleration up to now, we expect to increase the performance of our method soon.

This smoothing algorithm deals with each triangle of the control mesh independently. Each vertex inserted in the refined triangle is elevated according to the vertices position and normal of the refined triangle.

Fig. 4. Triadic smoothing using N-Patches

The topological refinement involved in this algorithm is a simple n^2 decomposition.

Let us recall that we use the same refinement rule, with the same depth, for the implicit regions and the straddling regions so as to obtain a mesh with a consistent topology all over the character.

3.3 Straddling triangles

We invoke a specific process to obtain a smooth transition between the refined implicit triangles and normal triangles. Straddling triangles are characterized automatically in a pre-processing step, and defined as triangles that share at least one edge with an implicit triangles and a normal triangles.

Straddling triangles are processed by combining the previous two methods. Let ABC a refined triangle, we assign weight to its vertices, referred to as ω_A, ω_B and ω_C, and defined as 1 if the vertex is inside the region of influence and 0 otherwise. Let (α, β, γ) the barycentric coordinates of a vertex $\mathbf{p}$ inserted in the triangle ABC. We compute a final parameter denoted as ω that weights the influence of the implicit region and the mesh only region.

$$\omega = \alpha \omega_A + \beta \omega_B + \gamma \omega_C$$

Let $\mathbf{p}_{Implicit}$ and $\mathbf{p}_{Normal}$ denote the vertices obtained with the implicit projection and the N-Patch elevation algorithms respectively. The final vertex position is defined as follows:

$$\mathbf{p}' = \omega \mathbf{p}_{Implicit} + (1 - \omega) \mathbf{p}_{Normal}$$

The same process is applied to the normals that need to be eventually normalized.

4 Implementation details

Let us recall that we need to compute the smooth triangle mesh skinning the animated skeletal model on the fly in real time. Although the topological refinement of the coarse mesh may be performed as a pre-processing step, the computation of the elevations of the inserted vertices is to be performed at each time step. Normal triangles are smoothed into N-Patches in real time [17]. Straddling and implicit triangles require more computations as the inserted vertices need to be projected onto the implicit surface.

Projecting a vertex $\mathbf{p}$ onto the implicit surface can be thought of as computing the first intersection between a ray with origin $\mathbf{p}$ and a given normal. We have implemented and compared two methods to project vertices on the implicit surface. The first one uses an analytic ray intersection scheme presented derived from [20] whereas the second one uses a binary search inside an interval.

4.1 Analytic scheme

Wyvill [20] first proposed analytic techniques for ray tracing blobs created with sphere and ellipsoid primitives. Let $\mathbf{x}(t) = \mathbf{p} + t\vec{\mathbf{n}}$ the parametric equation of the ray where $\vec{\mathbf{n}}$ refers to the mesh normal at vertex $\mathbf{p}$. The squared Euclidean distance of a point along the ray to the center of the sphere may be written as a second degree polynomial of variable t. As we use quartic potential functions, the field function along the ray $f(t)$ is a piecewise quartic polynomial whose roots may be computed analitically. The general algorithm may be written as follows:

1. For each primitive i, compute its field contribution $f_i(t)$ along the ray over the interval $[t_i^-, t_i^+]$ if the ray intersects the region of influence of primitive i, otherwise set $f_i(t)$ to null.

2. Compute the overall field function along the ray $f(t)$, which is a piecewise polynomial in t formed after substituting the ray equation into the polynomial equations of the different regions of space the ray traverses.
3. Search the roots of the polynomial equation $f(t) = T$ over the sub-intervals, where T is fixed threshold.

In practice, this method requires the quite expensive computation of the closed form expression of $f(t)$ before any root finding process may be invoked.

4.2 Ray sampling

In our case, we can easily find an interval where the ray does intersect the implicit surface. The direction of the ray no longer follows the vertex normal $\vec{n}$. Instead, we use a precomputed direction. For each vertex $\mathbf{p}$ of the refined mesh, we can compute a corresponding anchor point denoted as $\mathbf{q}$ on the animation skeleton. The anchor points are computed only once during initialisation. They are defined as points on the animation skeleton the closest to the mesh vertices we want to project. The anchor point is animated using the animation skeleton so that it should always lie on the animation skeleton. Since the body of the character is built around the animation skeleton, the potential of the anchor point is always positive.

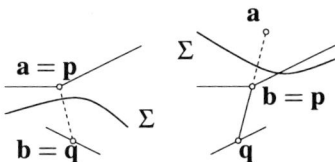

Fig. 5. Computation of the line segment intersecting the implicit surface

The algorithm proceeds in two steps. First, we define a line segment $[\mathbf{ab}]$ intersecting the implicit surface, with $f(\mathbf{a}) < 0$ and $f(\mathbf{b}) > 0$ respectively. Two cases appear. If the mesh vertex $\mathbf{p}$ is outside the implicit surface, then set $\mathbf{a}$ to $\mathbf{p}$ and $\mathbf{b}$ to its corresponding anchor point $\mathbf{q}$. Otherwise, set $\mathbf{b}$ to $\mathbf{p}$ and locate $\mathbf{a}$ as shown in Figure 5.

The second step performs a simple iterative binary search over the line segment $[\mathbf{ab}]$. Experiments show that less than eight steps are necessary to approximate the intersection. In order to speed up the computation of $f(\mathbf{x})$ during the binary search, we first cull primitives that do not intersect $[\mathbf{ab}]$.

4.3 Back face culling

In general, back-facing triangles need not be displayed. Therefore, another improvement consists in eliminating back facing triangles before performing the projection of the vertices of the refined triangle mesh. A classic backface culling algorithm is not satisfying though, as the triangles of the control mesh are refined and deformed during the smoothing process. Thus, refined triangles may appear at the silouhette edges even if their parent triangle were facing backwards.

In our implementation, we only eliminate triangles whose three vertex normals are pointing backwards. As the vertex normals represent the way a triangle deforms, this criterion enables us to preserve triangles that may modify silouhette edges. This results in significant accelerations as show in Table 1.

5   Results

The refinement and smoothing algorithms have been implemented and linked with the animation system developed at Infogrames. The following timings have been performed on a Pentium III-733 with a GeForce-1 graphic card.

Technique	Analytic ray tracing		Binary search	
Subdivision	Normal	Face culling	Normal	Face culling
2^2	104	123	141	165
3^2	54	67	76	92
4^2	33	43	47	59
5^2	22	30	31	40
6^2	15	21	22	29
7^2	11	16	17	22

Table 1. Frame rates obtained using analytic ray tracing and binary search

Table 1 compares the frame rates obtained using analytic ray tracing and binary search. In both cases, we have reported the frame rate with and without back face culling. Timings show that the binary search technique performs significantly faster than the analytic ray tracing method. One reason for this is that we take advantage of the known location of primitives around the animation skeleton. Therefore, the interval where the ray surface intersection is searched is very small, and only a few iterations are needed to converge to the surface.

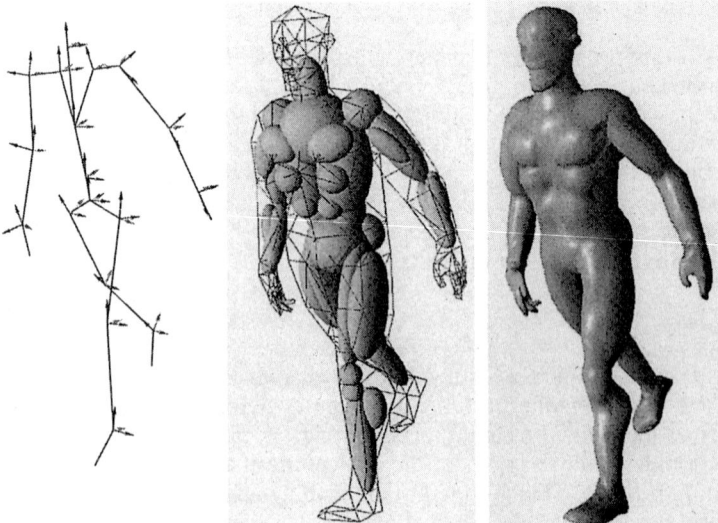

Fig. 6. Walking humanoid model, from left to right, animation skeleton, mesh model and implicit primitives, final smooth mesh model

Refinement	2^2 subdivision		3^2 subdivision		4^2 subdivision		5^2 subdivision	
Model	N	Fps	N	Fps	N	Fps	N	Fps
Humanoid	2368	165	5328	92	9472	59	14800	40
Horse	1648	197	3708	133	6592	86	10300	60

Table 2. Frame rate (labeled as Fps) and number of refined triangles (denoted as N) for the humanoid and horse models at increasing subdivision depths

The back face culling pre-processing step also speeds up the overall process. As one could expect, the higher the subdivision depth, the greater the accelerations.

Table 2 reports the number of frames per second obtained with the humanoid and the horse models. The control meshes involve 592 and 412 triangles respectively. 41 implicit primitives have been added to the humanoid model that are mostly located on the torso, whereas the horse model only involves 24 evenly located over the body. Without implicit primitives, both models may be rendered at 212 frames per second.

Fig. 7. Unblended implicit primitives and resulting horse model

Timings show that adding implicit primitives considerably reduces the overall rendering speed. Experiments show that using a subdivision level greater than 5 does not provide any significant visual improvement. The frame rate obtained at this depth is still real time. In general, the subdivision depth adapts to the size of the overall model on the screen so as to provide sufficient level of detail. Unless the character model fills the screen, the subdivision depth is in general set to 2 or 3 which proves to be acurate enough.

Although mapping textures onto general implicit surfaces remains a challenging problem, our method handles texture mapping in a natural way. In our technique, we rely on the coarse mesh to attach the texture map to the model. The uv-coordinates of the vertices of the refined triangles in the texture map are simply computed using their barycentric coordinates in the parent triangle (see section 3.3). Experiments performed with a GeForce-1 graphic card show that the frame rate is almost insensitive to the use of textures.

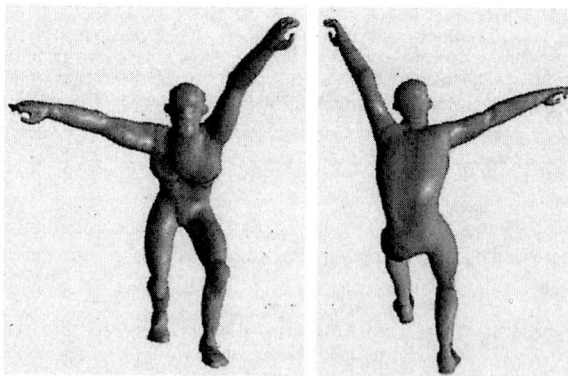

Fig. 8. Dancing character

6 Conclusion and future work

Triangle meshes provide a fast and versatile geometric representation of surfaces that can be rendered in real time with existing hardware. Implicit surfaces lend themselves for the creation of smooth organic shapes. In this paper, we have combined the best of both worlds. We have show that implicit primitives can be inserted in the character creation process to add organic features to mesh models. Our shape editor has been tested by designers at Infogrames who easily created the humanoid and the horse models.

We did not take advantage of temporal and spatial coherence to speed up computations. For instance, the projection of the vertices for implicit and straddling triangles could be improved as the previous projection point could be used to define a smaller research interval.

In the future, we plan to use more complex implicit primitives such as cone-spheres, cylinders or spline skeletal elements. Moreover, the parameters of the implicit primitives could be modified during the animation to create more realistic deformations.

References

1. J. Bloomenthal, C. Bajaj, J. Blinn, M. P Cani-Gascuel, A. Rockwood, B. Wyvill and G. Wyvill. *Introduction to Implicit Surfaces*, Morgan Kaufmann 1997.
2. B. Crespin, P. Guitton, C. Schlick. Efficient and accurate tessellation of implicit sweeps. *Proceedings of CSG'98*, 1998.
3. T. DeRose, M. kass, and T. Truong, Subdivision Surfaces in Character Animation. *Computer Graphics (Siggraph 1998 Proceedings)*, 85-94, July 1998.
4. M. Desbrun and M. P. Gascuel. Animating soft substances with implicit surfaces. *Computer Graphics (Siggraph 1995 Proceedings)*, 287-290, August 1995.
5. M. Desbrun, N. Tsingos and M. P. Gascuel. Adaptive Sampling of Implicit Surfaces for Interactive Modeling and Animation. *Computer Graphics Forum*, **15**(5): 319-325, December 1996.
6. M. Desbrun and M. P. Cani. Active Implicit Surface for Animation. *Graphics Interface'98*, 143-150, June 1998.
7. D. Doo and M. Sabin. A subdivision algorithm for smoothing down irregularly shaped polyhedrons. *Computer Aided Design*, 157-175, 1978.

8. D.Doo and M. Sabin. Analysis of the behaviour of recursive division surfaces near extraordinary points. *Computer Aided Design*, **10**(6) : 356-360, 1978.
9. C. Galbraith, P. Prusinkiewicz and B. Wyvill. Modeling Murex Cabriti Seashell with a Structured Implicit Surface Modeler. *Proceedings of Computer Graphics International 2000*, 2000.
10. E. Galin and S. Akkouche. Incremental Polygonization of Implicit Surfaces. *Graphic Models and Image Processing*, **62** : 19-39, 2000.
11. M. P. Gascuel. An Implicit Formulation for Precise Contact Modeling. *Computer Graphics (Siggraph 1993 Proceedings)*, 313-320, August 1993.
12. P. Kalra, N. Magnenat-Thalmann, L. Moccozet, G. Sannier, A. Aubel, D. Thalmann. Real-time Animation of Realistic Virtual Humans. *IEEE Computer Graphics and Applications*, **18**(5) : 42-55, 1998.
13. R. Parent. Implicit function based deformations of polyhedral objects. *Proceedings of Implicit Surfaces'95*, 113-128, April 1995.
14. J. Shen and D. Thalmann. Interactive shape design using metaballs and splines. *Proceedings of Implicit Surfaces'95*, 187-196, April 1995.
15. A. Sherstyuk. Kernel functions in convolution surfaces : a comparative analysis. *The Visual Computer*, **15**(4) : 171-182, 1999.
16. D. Thalmann, J. Shen, E. Chauvineau. Fast Realistic Human Body Deformation for Animation and VR Applications. newblock*Computer Graphics International*, Korea, 166-174, June 1996.
17. A. Vlachos, J. Peters, C. Boyd and J. L. Mitchell. Curved PN Triangles. *ACM Symposium on Interactive 3D Graphics*, 159-166, March 2001.
18. P. Volino and N. Magenat Thalmann. The Spherigon : a simple polygon patch for smoothing quickly your polygonal meshes. *Computer Animation 98 Proceedings*, 72-79, 1998.
19. J. Wilhelms and A. Van Gelder. Anatomically Based Modeling. *Computer Graphics (Siggraph 1997 Proceedings)*, 173-180, 1997.
20. G. Wyvill and A. Trotman. Ray Tracing Soft Objects. *Computer Graphics International'90*, 469-476, 1990.
21. A. Guy and B. Wyvill. Controlled blending for implicit surfaces using a graph. *Proceedings of Implicit Surfaces'95*, 107-112, 1995.
22. D. Zorin, P. Schröder and W. Sweldens. Interpolating subdivision for meshes with arbitrary topology. *Computer Graphics (Siggraph 1996 Proceedings)*, 189-192, 1996.

3

Natural Phenomena

Visual Simulation of Smoke and Fire

Jos Stam

Alias | wavefront
Seattle, USA

The visual simulation of complex natural phenomena such as smoke and fire is a challenging and important problem in computer graphics. Applications range from adding special effects to movies to enhancing the look and feel of video games. In this talk I will present different techniques to simulate the motion and appearance of smoke and fire. My approach is based on the physics of fluid flow, namely the Navier-Stokes Equations. I will present a stable numerical technique which solves these equations. Stability allows the simulation to be advanced at any time step, which results in faster animations. Using these techniques animators can, for the first time, interact in real time with smoke and fire.

The algorithm combines linear system solvers and semi-Lagrangian techniques to achieve stability. The linear system arises both in the implicit treatment of the viscosity and diffusion terms and in the solution of a Poisson equation necessary to keep the flows mass-conserving. We solve these linear systems efficiently using a standard conjugate gradient solver. A semi-Lagrangian technique is used to resolve the non-linear advection term that appears in the Navier-Stokes equation. The method accounts for the transport of both mass and momentum within the fluid. These quantities are transported by tracing paths (characteristics) backwards from each computational cell through the flow. We then interpolate both momentum and mass at the endpoint of this path and transfer these values back to the computational cell. This technique is very easy to implement as it only requires a good interpolator and a particle tracer.

Stability, however, introduces artificial numerical dissipation into the flows, thus increasing their effective viscosity. Although the overall motion looks fluid-like small scale vortices typical of smoke vanish too rapidly. Therefore, I will present some techniques which can counteract this dissipation at very little additional cost. One such technique is borrowed from the computational fluid's literature and is known as "vorticity confinement". The basic idea is to inject the energy lost due to numerical dissipation back into the flow using a forcing term. The force is designed specifically to increase the vorticity of the flow. Visually this keeps the smoke alive over time.

In addition, I will present some techniques to "dress up" the flows using advected texture maps that add more realistic detail to the flows. This is achieved by moving the texture coordinates of a fractal-like map through the flow. This technique adds convincing wispy detail to otherwise smooth flows.

To illustrate the algorithms, I will give live demonstrations in two and three dimensions and will show several high quality animations.

References

- Jos Stam, "Stable Fluids", SIGGRAPH 1999 Proceedings, 121-128.
- Jos Stam, "Interacting with smoke and fire in real time", Communications of the ACM, Volume 43, Issue 7, 2000, 76-83.
- Ronald Fedkiw, Jos Stam and Henrik Wann Jensen, "Visual Simulation of Smoke", SIGGRAPH 2001 Proceedings, 1-8.

Phenomenological Simulation of Brooks

Fabrice Neyret   Nathalie Praizelin
Fabrice.Neyret@imag.fr   NathaliePraizelin@wanadoo.fr
iMAGIS-GRAVIR/IMAG-INRIA

Abstract. The goal of our work is to simulate the shape and variations of the water surface on non-turbulent brooks both efficiently and at very high resolution. In this paper, we treat only the shape and animation. We concentrate on the simulation of quasi-stationary waves and ripples in the vicinity of obstacles and banks, and more particularly, shockwaves. To achieve this, we rely on phenomenological laws such as the ones collected over the last two centuries in the field of hydrodynamics: most of the visually interesting phenomena (apart from turbulence) are known qualitatively and characterized in reasonably simplified situations. It is thus wasteful to run a full-range Navier-Stokes simulation for quiet flows when only qualitative results are needed. The complexity of the velocity field along the streambed and around the obstacles is taken into account by solving a simple Laplace equation, assuming a stationary irrotational non-compressible ideal 2D flow. We obtain a stationary solution of the surface waves, that we perturb in order to get a quasi-stationary brook simulation. This yields a real-time simulation of the fluid visible features.

Keywords: natural phenomena, fluids, phenomenological simulation, interactive simulation.
URL: http://www-imagis.imag.fr/Membres/Fabrice.Neyret/brooks/

1   Introduction

Computer Graphics researchers and artists have been interested in reproducing the natural look and natural phenomena for a long time. However, objects resulting from fluid motion such as clouds, smoke, fire, wind, ocean waves, rivers or cascades are particularly difficult to simulate; especially from the engineering point of view that corresponds to the current trend for CG fluids.

These simulations are difficult as the physics is complex (and the parameters are not always known); its numerical solving is very expensive (which gets worse very quickly with spatial resolution); the needed spatial range is large (landscape scale); the visible characteristics are only emerging phenomena (*i.e.,* they are not explicitly modeled). While every human observer has a common knowledge about how a cloud, a brook or the ocean should look, and expects to see details as small as its retinal resolution allows. Moreover, as an element of a movie or a game, the artist needs to have control of some of the visible features of the fluid.

Our long term goal is the visually realistic efficient simulation of a brook, if possible in real time. For the moment, we only deal with non-turbulent brooks (in particular, without hydraulics jumps). In the scope of this paper, we concentrate only on shape and animation.

Water is a continuous (and transparent) medium, thus the motion of particles cannot be seen, except if an object (*e.g.,* a leaf) is carried with the flow. The only feature that can be seen is the air-fluid interface, mainly through its reflection of the sky and its refraction of the brook bottom. Therefore, the only useful problem is the determination of the fluid surface. In a perfectly regular flow, the surface is indeed stationary, even if the fluid velocity is large. This surface can be calculated from the 2D velocity field by the geometric construction of stationary waves. In this paper, we deal only with shockwaves and ripples, which are very salient features (having high frequency), as illustrated on Fig. 1. In reality, instabilities make the flow oscillating: a realistic brook is only quasi-stationary, and this beating effect is an important part of our intuition of alive water flow. Therefore, our simulation has to take this aspect into account.

The paper is structured as follow: we review in section 2 the various methods introduced in CG to produce simulations of fluids and in section 3 the physics we rely on. This yields to the principles and structure of our method, exposed in section 4, which we detail in the following sections: we describe the numerical solving yielding the stationary velocity field in section 5; the geometric construction of stationary shockwaves in section 6; the field perturbation process yielding quasi-stationarity in section 7; the complete shockwave structure allowing quasi-stationarity in section 8; results in section 9. As the current stage is only a first step in a long term project, we give some milestones for future work in section 10.

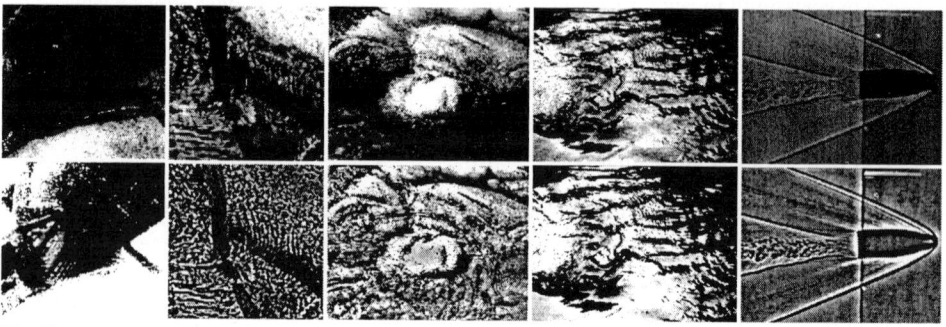

Fig. 1. The shockwaves and ripples features we are interested in (the bottom images are contrast enhancement of the top images). NB: the fluid in the right image (courtesy N.T. Clemens, University of Texas at Austin) is air: it shows front and back shockwaves, a wake, and thin ripples along the object, as for water. However it doesn't show the ripples in front of shockwaves that exist on water, due to surface tension.

2 Previous Work

The various CG approaches aiming at simulating fluids divide into 3 families:
- CFD (Computational Fluid Dynamics) inspired simulations corresponding to the current trend in CG [11, 6, 7, 22, 9]. They generate very rich visual results, reproducing the complexity of running fluids at the price of high computation costs; except for [9] which deals with 2D fluids and [22] that introduces a scheme allowing stability even out of the time step range required by the physical simulation.
- Signal processing approaches [19, 21, 4, 13, 24], also based on intensive calculations (far less than CFD, however), can be qualified as 'phenomenological' in that they aim at reproducing the effects (spatio-temporal shape or force field) without looking at the causes, oppositely to CFD. The problem is that statistical models tend to lose persistent features (*e.g.*, eddies) and that a good model accounting for static distribution (*e.g.*, for clouds density) doesn't trivially yield a good animated model. Among the mentioned papers, only [13, 24] deal with water (ocean waves).
- Empirical or phenomenological animations [8, 15, 27, 28, 10] rely on simplified analytical models: trochoids for ocean waves [8, 15, 10]; Laplace fields for wind [27]; hydraulics for rivers [28]. Some were introduced in early CG at a time where CFD wasn't affordable. New models are also proposed regularly since they offer a good appearance/cost ratio.

Note that spectrum-controlled signals such as Perlin noise [16, 17] are a useful ingredient for empirical animations: they are used in this spirit for cloud density in [4] and for random waves on rivers in [25]. It can also be used to account for small scale (*i.e.*, subgrid) animation in physical simulations, e.g. for fluids in [23] (stochastic interpolation) and for brooks in [26] (noise following the streamlines).

Note also that among all the mentioned papers, very few can deal with brooks:
- CFD can model turbulent running water very well, but cannot easily account for shockwaves and surface tension ripples. This would require very high resolution and dedicated solvers;
- Signal processing approaches give great results on wide areas (*e.g.*, ocean, wind) but cannot easily apply to narrow streams with obstacles since the statistics change at every location;
- Empirical models have been used for some aspects of brooks but not for visual features as crucial as shockwaves and ripples. BTW, these features have never been accounted for in CG.

Looking for information to develop our phenomenological model, we found specialized matter about hydraulics, waves theory, shockwaves and ripples in [12, 1, 2, 18]. We also looked into general fluid mechanics textbooks such as [5, 14]. We got very nice illustrations of real fluids features in [20, 3].

3 Tools from the physics

3.1 Waves theory

Propagation of waves on water surface corresponds to displacement waves and has strong similarities with sound waves in air, which are compression waves. The most important difference is velocity: the velocity of sound is constant in standard conditions (temperature, density), while water waves are *dispersive, i.e.,* their velocity depends on their wavelength λ: capillary waves ($\lambda < 1.7cm$) and gravity waves ($\lambda > 1.7cm$) go faster than intermediate waves ($\lambda = 1.7cm$ corresponds to the slowest waves, which have a 23 cm/s velocity). As compared to air, this means that whatever the fluid velocity (in a range), a stationary wave can exists (*i.e.*, having an adequate wavelength).

'Dispersive' means that a focused packet of waves tends to spread out. This implies that the energy doesn't travel at the same speed as waves in deep water: the *group velocity* is $\frac{1}{2}$ of the *phase velocity* for gravity waves and $\frac{3}{2}$ for capillary waves. This has numerous consequences, from the typical shape of ship waves to the location of stationary waves according to their wavelength. However, when the wavelength is greater than the fluid layer depth h (the *shallow water* case), this dispersive behavior disappears and the waves' velocity becomes constant, equals to $\sqrt{gh}$ with g the gravity acceleration.

When dynamic instabilities are negligible a stationary flow triggers only stationary waves. By construction, stationary waves have fronts whose propagation exactly opposes the flow velocity $\vec{V}$. If the propagation angle of this front, relative to upstream, is θ its velocity is thus $\|\vec{V}\|.cos\theta$. Note that since the energy does not propagate at the same speed as waves it is carried along by the flow, at a speed of $\frac{V}{2}$ for gravity waves, thus showing energy in a cone of aperture $19.5°$ downstream (for ships... and ducks!). For the same reason capillary waves can propagate upstream but they dissipate quickly.

The case of brooks corresponds to shallow water, so gravity waves are not dispersive: we can tell about a constant wave velocity c as in air (although it depends on the layer depth). This is why the main wave features (*e.g.*, shockwaves) are similar to the soundwave experiments in air (see Fig. 1.5). However, the smallest waves remain dispersive; this is why there are ripples on water surface, *e.g.*, upstream of shockwaves.

56

3.2 Geometric properties of shockwaves

The *Froude number* $F_r = V/c$ is equivalent to the *Mach number* for sound, *i.e.*, shockwaves occur when the flow runs faster than $Froude = 1$. Brooks are generally supercritical (*i.e.*, $Froude > 1$). In an homogeneous velocity field, the shockwave generated by a small object (*e.g.*, a stick) is a 2D cone (*i.e.*, 2 lines, which we call *left* and *right* Froude lines, streamwise), whose aperture α is equal to $arcsin(\frac{c}{V})$, as for a supersonic bang cone (see Fig. 2.1). Note that the slope α is very sensitive to V: it is $\frac{\pi}{2}$ for $F_r = 1$; $\frac{3\pi}{8}$ for $F_r = 1.08$; $\frac{\pi}{4}$ for $F_r = 1.4$. If the field is not homogeneous, the shockwave curves so that it locally fits to this angle relative to $\overrightarrow{V}$ (same if c varies, due to a change in depth), see Fig. 2.2. A consequence is that left lines (resp. right lines) originary from different locations never intersect.

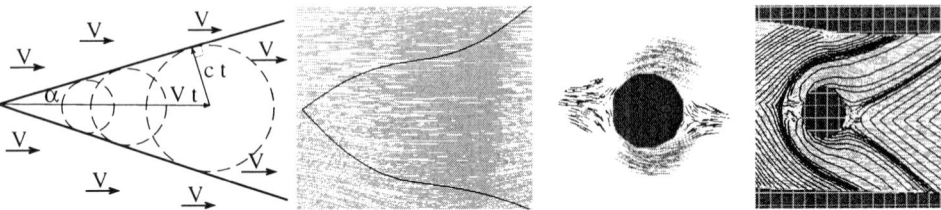

Fig. 2. *Left:* shockwave 'cone', consisting of 2 Froude lines having a slope α. *Middle left:* the lines' slope changes with flow velocity. *Middle right:* flow around an obstacle. The flow, coming from the left, is globally supercritical. It is slowed down upstream and downstream of the obstacle inducing subcritical areas (*i.e.*, $Froude < 1$, in dark); it is accelerated on the obstacle sides (grey areas correspond to $Froude > 2$). *Right:* convergence or divergence of Froude lines and accumulation on shockwaves location. The 3 images were generated using our simulator.

Note that as for supersonic air flows, the water surface is potentially covered with slight shockwaves called *Froude waves*, triggered by every small disturbance of the flow. The previous remark implies that in an area with decreasing velocity the upstream lines tend to converge towards the downstream lines, which have a greater aperture. Conversely, for an increasing velocity the downstream lines tend to converge towards the upstream lines. An extreme case occurs if a line starts orthogonally to the flow (*i.e.*, on a location with $F_r = 1$): it constitutes the asymptote for all the Froude waves around. This accumulation of perturbations is a geometric interpretation of shockwaves (see Fig. 2.4).

The stream runs around obstacles in the flow (*e.g.*, stones) but it is slowed down in the areas immediately upstream and downstream of an obstacle and accelerated on the sides (see Fig. 2.3). For this reason, there are always several critical transitions around an obstacle where shockwaves are triggered (see Fig. 5). A shockwave is orthogonal to $\overrightarrow{V}$ at the location where $Froude = 1$ then it curves as it enters areas with faster velocity.

The surface flow traversing a shockwave suddenly slows down to $Froude < 1$. But it progressively retrieves its velocity thus possibly triggering another (small) shockwave. This cycle can repeat several times. The regular patterns of ripples on the sides of obstacles (as well as along gutters) and of herringbones on fast areas in the stream (see Fig 1.4), are probably linked to this phenomenon.

4 Our Method

The arguments in section 3.1, in the case of brooks, lead us to solve the flow as if it were non-dispersive and then to 'dress' the solution to add the details (*i.e.*, ripples) coming from the dispersive part of the flow. Section 3.2 contains all the necessary ingredients to geometrically build the shockwaves in the non-dispersive case. We will turn the stationary velocity field precalculated by CFD into a real-time quasi-stationary flow using perturbations in the spirit of [27]. This yields the following pseudo-algorithm, containing the various tasks to be solved:

Velocity field construction:
- we first need to build the stationary velocity field corresponding to a given brook, taking into account banks, obstacles and depth variations (see section 5).

Shockwaves construction:
- Next, we need to determine the starting point of shockwaves: as suggested, they are on the most upstream location on the isovalue curves of $F_r = 1$. Since areas of $F_r < 1$ are immediately upstream and downstream of obstacles, we can check for the departure of these isocurves along the obstacle boundary then follow these curves in the water up to the targeted location. It is the location where the Froude waves, orthogonal to the flow, are tangent to the curve: we choose for characterizing criterion $\overrightarrow{V} \perp iso_{F_r=1}$. If this location does not exist on the curve (*e.g.*, if the area is along a bank) then the starting location is the upstream end of the curve.
- Once a starting point is obtained, we have to draw the left and right lines of the shockwave. Each line is drawn simply by tracing successive segments whose slope relative to the local $\overrightarrow{V}$ is $arcsin(\frac{c}{V})$.

Ripples construction:
- Ripples are drawn at the same time immediately upstream the shockwave and parallel to it. As they fade quickly, we simply draw 4 of them with a given offset.
- The other type of ripples, looking like Froude waves starting at the obstacle sides, have to be drawn. As suggested before, we assume that they are caused by repeated weak shockwaves. We look for the supercritical areas on the boundaries (*i.e.*, obstacles and banks) in which we launch Froude wave lines separated by a given offset.

5 Stationary Velocity Field

This section deals with the CFD precomputation of the stationary velocity field.

5.1 Physical modelisation

We assume that brooks are quasi-stationary, which we will simulate by perturbing a stationary solution (moreover, the stationary field is a precalculation, while its perturbation is real-time). We assume that the flow is 2D, *i.e.*, that it is not qualitatively different within a vertical column. If we want to account for variable depth, we simply have to weight $\overrightarrow{V}$ with depth in the equations, *i.e.*, to consider the rate of flow instead of the velocity. Water is incompressible in common situations. As we only need a qualitative velocity field, we assume for simplicity that the fluid is ideal (invisible)[1] and irrotational. With these hypothesis, the fluid is represented by a Laplace equation:

---

[1]The introduction of viscosity can change the field by triggering the separation of the boundary layer. As solving is a precalculation, we could afford to solve a more comprehensive stationary fluid model. But it would probably show dynamic instabilities, while we want to rely on a stationary field, introducing instability in a separate stage. However, separation points can also be predicted and injected as boundary conditions in the ideal fluid model.

$\Delta\phi = 0$, with $\vec{V} = grad\phi$ (ϕ is called the potential) [2]. A typical solution is figured in Fig. 3. If we want to account for variations of the depth h, the equation changes to $h\Delta\phi + \nabla h.\nabla\phi = 0$.

Boundary conditions are Neumann kind on banks and obstacles ($\vec{V}.\vec{N} = 0$ turns to $\nabla\phi.\vec{N} = 0$, with $\vec{N}$ the normal to the boundary) and Dirichlet kind on the two brooks ends: we choose $\phi = \phi_0$ on the upstream end and ϕ_1 on the downstream end. Since there is an extra degree of freedom, we can fix $\phi_0 = 0$. We get ϕ_1 from the brook average velocity estimated by the Chézy formula[3] $V_{av} = C\sqrt{ih}$, where h is the brook depth and i its slope. The constant C depends on the nature of the brook bottom: we choose $40\ m^{1/2}s^{-1}$, corresponding to a low slope mean width river with a bottom made of small stones. If l is the length of the brook segment and z_0, z_1 are the altitude at the two ends, we have $V_{av} = \frac{\phi_1-\phi_0}{l}$, thus $\phi_1 = C\sqrt{(z_1 - z_0)lh}$.

The user provides an image representing the brook with banks and obstacle in dark (the depth variation in the brook being represented by grey levels) and absolute lengths (size of the image in meters, and the difference of altitude). Note that this image could also come from MNT data, or from a procedural tool.

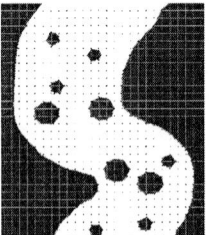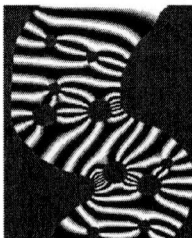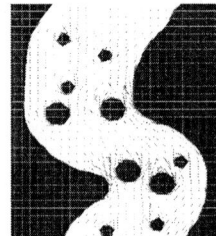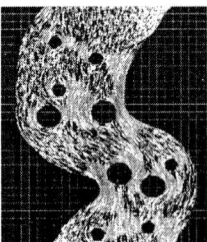

Fig. 3. *From left to right*: the brook painted by the user. The discretization is done using the 32×32 figured grid with a special care for the boundary (*i.e.*, extra nodes); the nodes are the small squares. The potential ϕ resulting of the system solving (interpolated). The corresponding velocity field, at the nodes, and interpolated (supercritical areas are marked in grey).

5.2 Discretization

We use a Finite Difference scheme on a quasi-regular grid, containing the regular grid nodes, plus nodes at the intersection of obstacles boundary with the grid lines (see Fig. 3.1 and Fig. 4). This allows for a better representation of boundary conditions at the price of a more complex discretization scheme: a grid cell can have 3, 4 or 5 corners. We rely on centered schemes for the discretized differential operators. Near the boundary some of the nodes are displaced (see Fig. 4), so we use a quasi-centered scheme with weights $\left(\frac{1}{h_1\frac{h_1+h_3}{2}}, \frac{1}{h_2\frac{h_2+h_4}{2}}, \frac{1}{h_3\frac{h_1+h_3}{2}}, \frac{1}{h_4\frac{h_2+h_4}{2}}, -\left(\frac{2}{h_1h_3} + \frac{2}{h_2h_4}\right)\right)$ instead of $\left(\frac{1}{h^2}, \frac{1}{h^2}, \frac{1}{h^2}, \frac{1}{h^2}, -\frac{4}{h^2}\right)$ for the Laplacian (see Fig. 4 for notations).

The system solving is sensitive to boundary conditions discretization, so we have to settle them carefully. The Neumann condition $\nabla\phi.\vec{N} = 0$ tells that ϕ doesn't variate along the direction $\vec{N}$ so we translate it by linking the ϕ value at the boundary node to

---

Remark: the existence of a slow boundary layer implies that an iso$_{F_r=1}$ lies along the boundary when the nearby fluid is supercritical, which explains the starting of shockwaves in these locations.

[2] $rot(\vec{V}) = 0$ (irrotational flow) implies that we can derivate $\vec{V}$ from a potential ϕ, *i.e.*, $\vec{V} = grad\phi$. $div(\vec{V}) = 0$ is thus equivalent to $\Delta\phi = 0$.

[3] The Chézy formula is largely used in hydraulics; it allows estimation of the velocity of a river in functions of various practical global parameters.

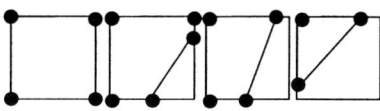 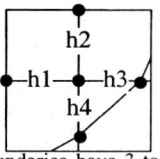 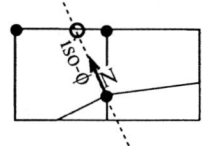

Fig. 4. *From left to right:* grid cells covering boundaries have 3 to 5 nodes. Quasi-centered differential operator discretization scheme. Discretization scheme for the Neumann boundary condition.

its value on the location obtained by projecting this node on the cell sides parallel to $\vec{N}$ (there are 2 candidate cells for each boundary node and at least 2 candidate borders per cell; see Fig. 4,right)). The value on the projected location also being defined by the interpolation of the 2 closest fluid nodes, this yield one equation per boundary node.

5.3 System solving and use of the solution

We solve this system using a standard solver and we compute $\vec{V}$ at each node. At the end of this precalculation we have a data structure encoding the quasi-regular grid, with ϕ, $\vec{V}$ and V values at each node (that we can store on disk). These values have to be interpolated when needed inside a given cell. For regular cells, this is a bilinear interpolation. For boundary cells it is less simple: bilinear interpolation can be used for trapezoid 4 corner cells and linear interpolation for 3 corner cells. Finding a continuous interpolation for 5 corner cells is far from trivial: for interpolating values we preferred cutting these cells into 2 parts of 4 corners.

6 Stationary Shockwaves

This section deals with the geometric construction of the stationary shockwaves. As explained in section 4, we have to find the ends of the iso$_{F_r=1}$ curves on the obstacles boundaries, follow them in order to find the locations where $\vec{V} \perp iso_{F_r=1}$ then to draw the 2 parts of each shockwave.

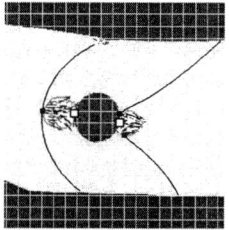 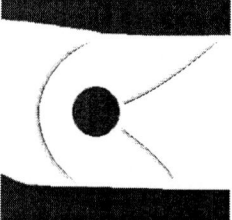 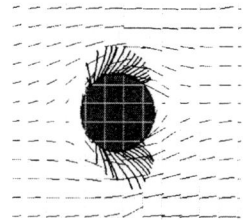

Fig. 5. *Left:* the various geometric constructions calculated in real-time by our simulator. The brook is designed by the user using a classical painter. The velocity field is solved on the 32×32 grid (the flow is coming from the left; the light grey vectors correspond to supercritical flow, the dark grey to subcritical areas). The stop points are figured (the 2 white squares). The curves iso$_{F_r=1}$ are traced in black. The starting locations of shockwaves found on the curves are marked as black squares. The upstream and downstream shockwaves (corresponding to four Froude lines) are shown in dark. *Middle:* the visible features obtained (*i.e.*, the shockwaves and their associated ripples). *Right:* ripples along the sides.

6.1 Finding the iso$_{F_r=1}$ curves extremities

Note that with ideal fluid assumption (no viscosity) the fluid velocity is 0 on the most upstream and downstream locations of the obstacles (called *stop points*). Since the areas $F_r < 1$ are in the vicinity this gives a clue to find the curve: an end should exist on each side of the stop point (see Fig. 6). Thus, we test every pair of boundary nodes until obtaining opposite conditions for them (*i.e.*, $F_r < 1$ for one node and $F_r > 1$

60

for the other). We estimate the exact end location (where $F_r = 1$) by interpolating. Inside the initial cell (the one containing the stop point) we have to consider this point as a node for interpolation, since the variations of V are non convex in this cell. This allows us to find a curve even in very high velocity fields, for which every grid node is supercritical: the extra 'nodes' corresponding to stop points are the only subcritical ones so the surrounding isocurve is extremely small (see Fig. 6). The fact it exists is sufficient to trigger a shockwave so it is important not to miss it. On the banks there are generally no stop points so we simply have to check every boundary segments.

6.2 Finding the shockwave start point on the iso-curve

We follow the obtained curves in the same spirit as we follow the boundaries: we test the criterion by looking for cells for which $\vec{V_0}.\vec{l}$ and $\vec{V_1}.\vec{l}$ have opposite signs (with $\vec{l}$ the current curve segment and $\vec{V}$ the velocity at segment ends; see Fig. 6,right for notations) or segment ends for which $\vec{V}.\vec{l_0}$ and $\vec{V}.\vec{l_1}$ have opposite signs. The exact location is obtained again by interpolating. Note that for the isocurve downstream of an obstacle, this location is usually at the 2 ends of the curve (see Fig. 5). We have to deal with special cases for narrow $F_r < 1$ areas which can yield more than 2 intersections of the isocurve with some cells (see Fig. 6). Following the isocurves counter-clock wise (*i.e.*, the $F_r < 1$ area lies on the left), we can discriminate the right path. Note that some isocurves can connect to 2 obstacles and thus might be followed twice. A consequence is that since the curve wouldn't be closed in such case, we have to follow the isocurves from both ends. However this would mean following them twice in the case they are closed. So we mark the end cells of treated isocurves in order to avoid redundancy.

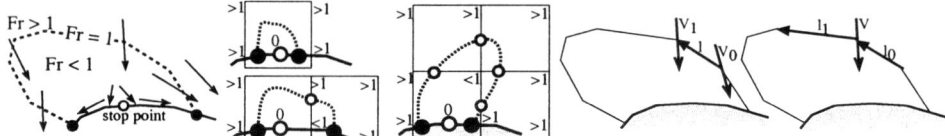

Fig. 6. *Left:* general situation upstream an obstacle. *Middle:* various cases of the iso$_{F_r=1}$ tracking from the Froude value on nodes. *Right:* search for the most upward point on the isocurve, where $V \perp isocurve$.

6.3 Tracing the shockwaves

At this point, we can launch the 2 Froude lines constituting the shockwave. We displace the starting point slightly upstream to avoid the line falling immediately in the subcritical area (where no Froude wave can exist). Then we interactively create segments having a slope α relatively to $\vec{V}$ and a given length dl, with α given in section 3 (see Fig. 2). This segment is obtained by $\frac{dl}{V} \cos \alpha \, \vec{V} + \frac{dl}{V} \sin \alpha \, \vec{V^\perp}$, with $\vec{V^\perp}$ oriented left to $\vec{V}$ for left lines and right to $\vec{V}$ right lines. Note that no trigonometric function need to be calculated as $\sin \alpha = \frac{c}{V}$ and $\cos \alpha = \sqrt{1 - (\frac{c}{V})^2}$. We stop the lines' construction if an obstacle or a subcritical area is hit. In reality, the energy of the shockwave probably dissipates before this. Since we couldn't find a physical criterion, we have to rely on an arbitrary distance criterion if we want to avoid creating too long shockwaves.

6.4 Drawing the ripples

As suggested in section 3, we draw the associated ripples at the same time as shockwaves. These consist of 4 parallel lines with a given offset and intensity fading with the distance upstream. The Froude ripples on the obstacle sides are generated in the same spirit as above: on the boundary areas in contact with supercritical flow we emit Froude lines with regular offsets.

7 Making the field Quasi-Stationary

To obtain the stationary solution we solved a Laplace equation with boundary conditions. Since it is linear, linear combination of solutions also obey the Laplace equation. In the same spirit as [27], we choose incompressible perturbations (*i.e.,* obeying the Laplace equation) having a small support (being null farther from a given radius, boundary conditions are thus automatically matched). We choose sources and vortices as perturbations to be added to the stationary velocity field, tuned to obey $\nabla \vec{V} = 0$ (sources can be seen as the above view of horizontal vortex rings). These perturbations correspond to upstream instabilities carried with the flow. We drop randomly, at the upstream end of the brook, particles following the flow associated with a perturbation (see Fig. 7). The velocity used for the visible features construction at a given location is then the sum of the stationary flow and of the various nearby perturbations (for optimization, we set in each cell a list of the perturbations covering it).

Note that, in addition to random perturbations, we can also create regular perturbations (*e.g.,* vortex pairs behind obstacles in order to create von Karman wakes) or perturbations associated to events (*e.g.,* extra obstacles, possibly moving).

8 Quasi-Stationary Shockwaves

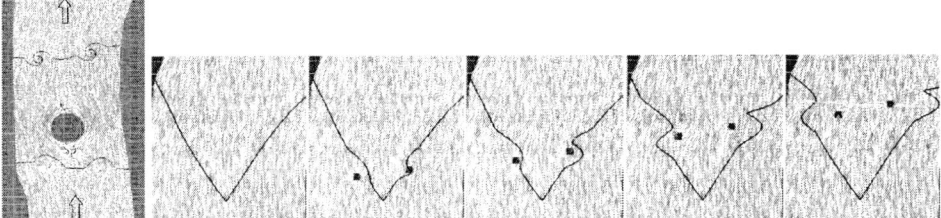

Fig. 7. *Left:* perturbations dropped in the flow in order to make it quasi-static. To visualize the effects, we launched 2 lines of passive particles (linked floaters). Top: vortices. Bottom: sources (*i.e.,* horizontal vortex rings). The perturbations are associated to particles carried with the flow, figured by the small squares. *Right:* Effects of the perturbations on Froude waves. Left particle: source. Right particle: vortex.

8.1 Consequences of quasi-stationarity on shockwaves

The shockwave geometric construction of section 6 is purely static. If we change the value of $\vec{V}$ at a given location the shockwave drawing would change instantaneously, which is not physically correct (and worse, not realistic). We have to take into account the speed of information transport along a Froude wave which is different to the flow velocity both in value and in direction. If the velocity changes at a given location, this locally changes the slope of the Froude wave, which yields an offset in the whole wave downstream, even if the velocity is unchanged there (see Fig. 7). There is thus 2 causes of change at a given location: local slope change due to local velocity change and change due to upstream change in the line location. Note that other events can perturbate the shockwave: a change in velocity can also change the shape of the curve iso$_{F_r=1}$ and thus the starting location of the shockwave. The appearance of a subcritical area on the path of a shockwave or the sweep of a shockwave up to an obstacle or a subcritical area, will stop its downstream propagation (but the downstream part separated by the interruption will persist, carried with the flow, as illustrated on the animations).

8.2 Structure and simulation of evolving shockwaves

Since we have to update the visible features instead of re-creating them at each time step, we have to store all the vertices of each Froude line. Each vertex is re-evaluated from the local and upstream conditions (*i.e.,* local velocity and previous vertex location). We have to take into account the speed of the information transport along a Froude wave, which is $V_F = \sqrt{V^2 - c^2}$: if the distance between 2 vertices along the line is dl, the time for the perturbation of the first vertex to reach the second is $\frac{dl}{V_F}$, *i.e.,* $\lambda = \frac{dl}{dt V_F}$ times steps. If $\lambda > 1$, more than 1 time step should be necessary to transmit the information to the next vertex. If $\lambda < 1$, the information should be transported farther than this vertex. This is classically simulated using relaxation: in the first case we only transmit $\frac{1}{\lambda}$ of the perturbation to the next vertex, *i.e.,* $P_2^{t+dt} = (1 - \frac{1}{\lambda})P_2^t + \frac{1}{\lambda}(P_1^t + dl\,\overrightarrow{slope}_1)$. In the second case, we immediately transmit the information to all the $\text{int}\,(\frac{1}{\lambda})$ next vertices, and we do a $\text{frac}\,(\frac{1}{\lambda})$ relaxation on the next one.

To account for vertices entering in subcritical areas, we add an *invalid* flag to mark such vertices. The flag information is transmitted the same way. This avoids generation of separate vertex lists for orphan Froude line segments, knowing that the line will probably reappear in the near future. For newly created Froude lines, new vertices are created at the downstream end at a rate $\frac{1}{\lambda}$. To avoid visual discontinuities we fade the line intensity close to the open ends of a line segment.

9 Results

Our brook simulator runs in real time. Classically, the simulation time step dt is matched to the measured calculation duration during the previous steps in order to guarantee the true real-time.

The user provides a grey-level image of a brook, encoding in black the outside, and in grey the depth (see Fig. 8). This image can come either from a MNT, procedural tools, or a regular painter (we used *xpaint* for our tests). The user also provides the required grid resolution (32×32 or 64×64 in our tests), the size of the corresponding terrain in meter, the brook depth and the difference of altitude between the brook ends. In our tests, this was generally $32m \times 32m$ for the terrain, $80cm$ for the altitude decrease and $8cm$ for the brook depth.

Our implementation allows the storage of the precalculated stationary velocity field; to modify the Froude number (which is equivalent to changing the global velocity or the brook depth); to visualize the velocity field, the potential ϕ; to drop active (*i.e.,* perturbating) or passive particles in the flow (points, lines or circles); to put and displace 'needles' triggering shockwaves (see animations). Most of these features are for tests but several could be used to interface the simulation with objects or events.

There is no realistic rendering for the moment: the result consists of the drawing of the visible features. In section 10 we evoke possible ways of making realistic rendering.

We have implemented all the features treated in the paper (see Fig. 9 to 11 in Appendix). The limitations have also been mentioned: for the moment we use arbitrary offsets for the ripples, and end criteria to determine where the features should vanish are lacking, yielding too persistent Froude lines (see Fig. 10).

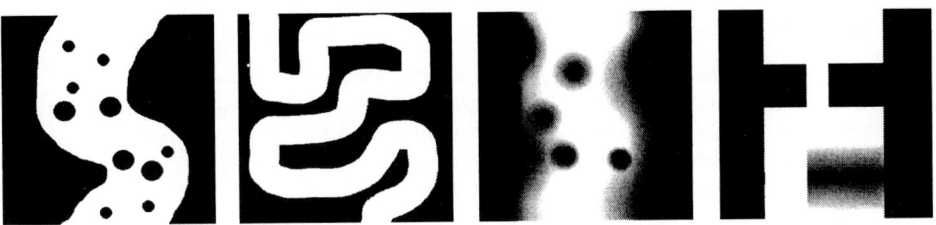

Fig. 8. Various brooks drawings.

10 Conclusion and Future Work

Our long term goal is the real-time detailed realistic rendering of brooks. We have achieved a first step: we have shown how to calculate animated geometric constructions of some important visible features existing on the water surface of brooks by combining simplified precalculated CFD and phenomenological hydraulics laws (accounting for shockwaves and ripples had never be done before in CG). The fact that we obtain geometric constructions (to be used as a skeleton defining the surface) and not a series of velocity and height fields, provides a resolution-independent features: the choice of visual resolution now depends purely on rendering criteria. Moreover, our primitives are very compact, and can be built in real-time by the simulator.

Remaining work to be done is twofold:

- realistic rendering, and more generally, 3D rendering: the main problem is to construct a surface from our geometric primitives. Since they represent waves (or parallel waves, for ripples) on a flat surface, we propose building mesh bands along the lines. Once the surface is defined, reflection and refraction maps should be sufficient to render the water aspect in a real-time framework.

- Improving the features and accounting for more effects: at first, we need criteria for fading and stopping the shockwaves and for tuning the wavelength of ripples. Beyond shockwaves and ripples, we would like to generate herringbones, von Karman wakes, hydraulics jumps, foam, etc... The first is very similar to the ones we treated, except that shockwaves don't occur in the vicinity of obstacles. The second could be achieved by launching regularly vortex particles and associating a visual effect to them, *e.g.,* smooth noise [26]. The third are subject to specialized literature [1] that could be adapted to our framework as well. The fourth are more difficult, but real observation shows that a threshold can separate states with or without air bubbles mixed to the water.

In conclusion, we hope to have illustrated how phenomenological approaches can very efficiently generate interesting features that would be rather expensive to obtain by numerical approaches. These 2 approaches can be combined to benefit from the strength of both: efficiency, resolution, controllability for the first and adaptability to spatial conditions of the second.

Acknowledgments:
We wish to thank Andreas Ruff and Pauline Jepp for proofreading this paper. We also would like to thank François Charru of IMFT, Mark Cramer of Virginia Polytechnic Institute, and Noel Clemens of University of Texas at Austin, for their valuable discussions on fluids and waves.

References

[1] M. Carlier. *Hydraulique générale et appliquée*. Eyrolles, 1980.

[2] P. Chassaing. *Mécanique des fluides. Eléments d'un premier parcours*. Cepadues éditions, 1997.

[3] M.S. Cramer. Gallery of fluid dynamics. http://www.eng.vt.edu/fluids/msc/gallery/gall.htm.

[4] David Ebert, Kent Musgrave, Darwyn Peachey, Ken Perlin, and Worley. *Texturing and Modeling: A Procedural Approach*. Academic Press, October 1994.

[5] R. Feynman. *Lectures on physics*. Addison-Weisley Publishing Compagny, 1977.

[6] Nick Foster and Demitri Metaxas. Realistic animation of liquids. In Wayne A. Davis and Richard Bartels, editors, *Graphics Interface '96*, pages 204–212. Canadian Information Processing Society, Canadian Human-Computer Communications Society, May 1996.

[7] Nick Foster and Dimitris Metaxas. Modeling the motion of a hot, turbulent gas. In Turner Whitted, editor, *SIGGRAPH 97 Conference Proceedings*, Annual Conference Series, pages 181–188. ACM SIGGRAPH, Addison Wesley, August 1997.

[8] Alain Fournier and William T. Reeves. A simple model of ocean waves. In David C. Evans and Russell J. Athay, editors, *Computer Graphics (SIGGRAPH '86 Proceedings)*, volume 20, pages 75–84, August 1986.

[9] Manuel Noronha Gamito, Pedro Faria Lopes, and Mário Rui Gomes. Two-dimensional simulation of gaseous phenomena using vortex particles. In Dimitri Terzopoulos and Daniel Thalmann, editors, *Computer Animation and Simulation '95*, pages 2–15. Eurographics, Springer-Verlag, September 1995.

[10] Jean-Christophe Gonzato and Bertrand Le Saëc. A phenomenological model of coastal scenes based on physical considerations. In D. Thalmann and M. van de Panne, editors, *Computer Animation and Simulation '97*, Eurographics, pages 137–148. Springer-Verlag Wien New York, 1997.

[11] Michael Kass and Gavin Miller. Rapid, stable fluid dynamics for computer graphics. In Forest Baskett, editor, *Computer Graphics (SIGGRAPH '90 Proceedings)*, volume 24, pages 49–57, August 1990.

[12] J. Lighthill. *Waves in fluids*. Cambridge University Press, 1978.

[13] G. A. Mastin, P. A. Watterberg, and J. F. Mareda. Fourier synthesis of ocean scenes. *IEEE Computer Graphics and Applications*, 7(3):16–23, March 1987.

[14] L.M. Milne-Thomson. *Theoretical Hydrodynamics*. MacMillan & Co LTD, 1968.

[15] Darwyn R. Peachey. Modeling waves and surf. In David C. Evans and Russell J. Athay, editors, *Computer Graphics (SIGGRAPH '86 Proceedings)*, volume 20, pages 65–74, August 1986.

[16] Ken Perlin. An image synthesizer. In B. A. Barsky, editor, *Computer Graphics (SIGGRAPH '85 Proceedings)*, volume 19(3), pages 287–296, July 1985.

[17] Ken Perlin and Fabrice Neyret. Flow noise: textural synthesis of animated flow using enhanced Perlin noise. In *SIGGRAPH 2001 Technical Sketches and Applications*, August 2001.

[18] Jean-Pierre Petit. *Le mur du silence*. Belin. http://www.chez.com/jppetit/mhd.html.

[19] M. Shinya and A. Fournier. Stochastic motion-motion under the influence of wind. *Computer Graphics Forum*, 11(3):119–128, 469, 1992.

[20] Japan society of mechanical engineers. *Visualized flow*. Pergamon Press, Oxford, 1988.

[21] Jos Stam. Stochastic dynamics: Simulating the effects of turbulence on flexible structures. *Computer Graphics Forum*, 16(3):159–164, August 1997. Proceedings of Eurographics '97.

[22] Jos Stam. Stable fluids. In Alyn Rockwood, editor, *Proceedings of the Conference on Computer Graphics (Siggraph99)*, pages 121–128, N.Y., August8–13 1999. ACM Press.

[23] Jos Stam and Eugene Fiume. Turbulent wind fields for gaseous phenomena. In *Proceedings of SIGGRAPH '93*, pages 369–376. ACM SIGGRAPH, 1993.

[24] Sebastien Thon, Jean-Michel Dischler, and Djamchid Ghazanfarpour. Ocean waves synthesis using a spectrum-based turbulence function. In *Computer Graphics International Proceeding*, 2000.

[25] Sebastien Thon, Jean-Michel Dischler, and Djamchid Ghazanfarpour. A simple model for visually realistic running waters. In *Eurographics UK*, 2000.

[26] Sebastien Thon and Djamchid Ghazanfarpour. A semi-physical model of running waters. In *Eurographics UK*, 2001.

[27] Jakub Wejchert and David Haumann. Animation aerodynamics. In Thomas W. Sederberg, editor, *Computer Graphics (SIGGRAPH '91 Proceedings)*, volume 25, pages 19–22, July 1991.

[28] Yingqing Xu, Cheng Su, Dongxu Qi, Hua Li, and Shenquan Liu. Physically based simulation of water currents and waves. *Computers & Graphics*, 21(3):277–280, May 1997.

Editors' Note: see Appendix, p. 201 for colored figures of this paper

An interactive forest

Thomas Di Giacomo

iMAGIS-GRAVIR (joint project CNRS-INRIA-INPG-UJF)

Stéphane Capo

Infogrames Interactive SA

François Faure

iMAGIS-GRAVIR (joint project CNRS-INRIA-INPG-UJF)

Abstract. We present a prototype of a forest in which a video game player can move and interact physically with the trees.

The trees are procedurally built on-the-fly at each redraw. Two animation approaches are combined: a procedural method which handles most of the trees efficiently, and a physically-based method which allows user interaction with the trees. The physically-based method is dynamically applied only where needed. Physical data is computed only where the physical method is applied, and deleted afterwards. Smooth transitions between animation methods are performed.

Levels of detail are used for rendering and for procedural animation. Our method allows the display and the animation, including user action, of a 256-tree forest at interactive rates.

1 Motivation

We address the problem of displaying and animating large scenes with vegetation in the context of a collaboration with a video game company namely Infogrames. More specifically, our aim is to model a forest in which the player can move and interact with the scene, e.g. grab a branch and shake the tree. Such an application has been a challenging problem in computer graphics due to geometric and dynamic complexity. Rendering and animating a single tree may require thousands of polygons and degrees of freedom, or more. The complexity of a forest may thus be practically intractable. However, level-of-detail (LOD) approaches can help us adapt the complexity of the elements according to their visual importance. A tree in the foreground may be modeled using ten thousands polygons, while a tree in the background may be modeled using only a few hundred polygons.

In applications with a fixed point of view, the geometric and dynamic elements can be modeled offline, provided that we are able to refine them according to their visual contribution. The scene is then rendered and animated using standard techniques. The problem is more difficult when the point of view changes over time, because the LODs have to be dynamically adapted. We thus have to perform smooth transitions between LODs to avoid "popping" effects. This applies to geometry as well as animation.

When using standard graphics hardware acceleration, rendering complexity mainly depends on the number of polygons and the amount of texture data. In contrast, animation complexity is not only a function of the number of degrees of freedom in the model, it also depends on the method used. Procedural methods can be fast but do not guarantee physical plausibility, especially when interactions occur. In contrast, physically-based methods generate more realistic motion and allow interactions but they are generally compute-intensive.

In this paper, we present our approach for animating and rendering a forest. We mainly focus on animation. The geometric model is procedurally computed on-the-fly at each refresh using a small set of parameters which entirely define each individual tree. This results in a very compact geometrical data set. A procedural method is used to animate the trees at different levels of detail to model the action of wind. A simplified dynamic model of tree is used to handle user interaction. Both animation methods are closely related to well-known approaches. Our main contribution is to combine them so that physically-based animation is used only where needed. Physical data is dynamically generated to handle interaction and deleted thereafter. Transitions between procedural and physical animation are performed to avoid popping. Combined with our procedural LODs, the method allows the animation of an interactive forest made of a few hundreds of trees with industrial video game quality (textures, lights, high frame rates).

The remainder of the paper is organized as follows. In section 2 we present previous work on related topics. In section 3 we outline our geometric modeling method. In section 4 we present our animation method. Results are shown in section 5. We finally conclude and discuss future work in section 6.

2   Related Work

2.1   LOD for animation

As for geometry, animation techniques can be adapted and simplified in certain cases i.e., when motions are too fast, too far away, or too numerous for human sight, [Ber97], or when motions are of low interest and do not need complex calculations. Though [GCB95] applied this idea to procedural animation by decreasing sampling frequency of motions, and degrees of freedom of human articulated figure, it seems more appropriate to apply it to physically-based animation because of its high cost in computations. To simplify or refine motions, adaptive models must be created, and smooth transitions between their levels of detail ensured [Val99].

One can mix different models, or construct a single multiresolution model. Multiple models are used by [CH97] to simulate monopodes with three different models, dynamic, kinematic and single particle motion, where transitions are possible only at certain times. [PC01] also simulates a prairie with three models, 3D blade of grass, texels and 2D textures, by interpolating 3D motions to match the texel when needed.

Methods working on a single multiresolution model are mainly physically-based approaches : [HPH96] and [HH98] refine mass-spring networks, [DDBC99] and [DDCB01] proposed a multiresolution FEM, the dynamic multiresolution response is compared to other models, to simulate deformations of a liver.

In this paper we present a hybrid method which uses two different models, the procedural part being multiresolution.

2.2   Wind, trees

Forests with blowing winds have been studied by [SF92] and [Sta96], both using stochastic vector fields for the wind, and a modal analysis of beams vibrations for the response of the trees. However, [Sta96] overrides the integration by directly synthetising the motions. We could not apply such a method because of our need for interactions.

We generate wind with the same kind of primitives as [PC01], that is to say 2D masks containing a vector field, with velocity and influence area.
We also make simplifying assumptions similar to [Ono97] on the dynamics of the tree : the density of the tree is uniform, no collisions occur between branches or leaves, branches move by bending, not torsion.

3 Geometric model

Our trees are made of skeleton nodes defining topology and meshes defining geometry. Skeleton nodes define the topology, lengths and angles of the branches. Figure 1 shows the geometric parameters (h, θ, ϕ) used to define the position of a branch with respect to its parent. The reference frame of the child is first translated by h and rotated by θ along the z axis of the parent. A rotation of angle ϕ along the axis y of the child is then applied. Meshes define branch shapes and textures. In order to reduce the geometric

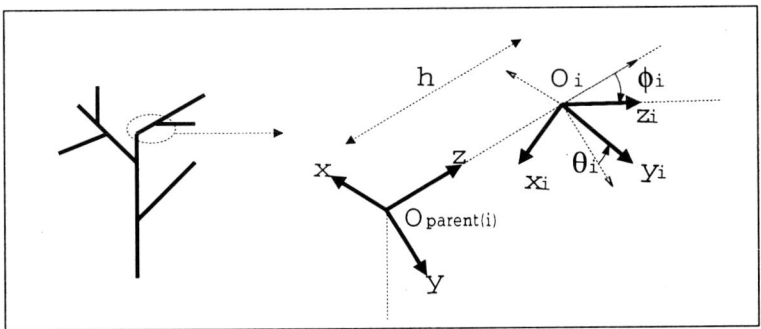

Fig. 1. A branch i positioned with respect to its parent.

data set, skeleton nodes and meshes are recomputed procedurally at each screen refresh using small sets of parameters which model seeds. The set of seeds totally defines the forest and is the only permanent data. Compared with progressive mesh approaches used in other applications, our approach has the following advantages:

- we can generate a whole forest, with all different trees, at a very low memory cost;
- the topological and geometrical information allows us to simplify topology as well as shape;
- smoothness is not limited by a reference model and can be arbitrarily high.

The additional computation cost is partially balanced by the reduction of data flow. Moreover, an increasing number of platforms (Playstation 2, recent PC cards) use specialized processors for mesh generation, which saves a lot of computation time.

Our goal is to generate visually convincing trees for games rather than botanical applications. We have thus made the following choices :

- The skeleton generation is controlled by parameters given by the game designer through a graphic interface (size, number of children, number of leaves,...).
- Simple rules found from real tree observation are used by the system and can not be altered. For example, the maximum angle between a branch and its mother is a function of their relative diameters.

- The number of parameters is as small as possible. This makes modeling easier and reduces the data needed to model an entire unique tree to less than one kilobyte.
- Perlin noise is used to obtain a more natural look.

We adjust the LODs according to the size of the elements projected to the screen. The LODs are modulated by a global factor which is a function of the total complexity of the scene at the previous frame. This feedback mechanism allows us to approximately set the global complexity to an arbitrary level.

4 Tree animation

We animate the trees by controlling the angles θ and ϕ (see fig. 1) for each branch. In this section, we first present the procedural animation method, then the physically-based method, and finally the combined method.

4.1 Procedural animation

Our procedural motion is a function of wind primitives traversing the scene. We first describe the wind primitives, the equations of motion, and how we apply levels of detail to procedural motion.

Wind. A wind primitive (see fig. 2) is defined by an area of influence (disk (C, r)), a force vector F and a pulsation ω. Each branch of a tree inside the area of influence

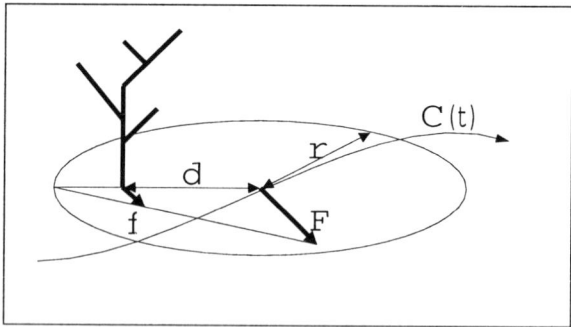

Fig. 2. A wind primitive applied to a tree.

undergoes a force f given by:

$$f = \frac{r - d}{r} sin(\omega t) F$$

if $d < r$, zero elsewhere. Phase angle is omitted for simplicity. The disk can move along a given trajectory $C(t)$. Such primitives allow us to test our framework. In future work we will implement more sophisticated functions.

Response to wind. Our procedural method is not physical since it is not based on the time integration of an acceleration. However, it is designed to ease the transitions to the physically-based method. Each wind force applied to a branch creates a torque at its base, which is responsible for angular motion. We approximate the torque by:

$$\tau(t) = Lz \times f(t)$$

where L is the length of the branch and z its axis. The torque is then projected to the rotation axes to obtain a rotation amplitude. The motion due to a wind primitive is thus given by

$$\theta = \theta_0 + \frac{1}{m}\tau(t)z_{parent}$$
$$\phi = \phi_0 + \frac{1}{m}\tau(t)y$$

where z_{parent} and y are the axes of rotation of the branch with respect to its parent (fig. 1). The term m is an approximation of the inertia of the branch(see section 4.2). The action of the wind thus acts as a force integrated twice. By summing the motions due to all the primitives applied to a given branch we obtain:

$$\theta = \theta_0 + \frac{1}{m}z_{parent}\sum_i \tau_i(t) \tag{1}$$

$$\phi = \phi_0 + \frac{1}{m}y\sum_i \tau_i(t) \tag{2}$$

Angles are directly set to the value of the torque applied. The wind direction is taken into account by torque projections, along with force magnitude and pulsation.

Levels of detail. The animation LODs have been developed independently of rendering. For now, the level of detail is related to recursion depth rather than screen size, this corresponds to the transition between dark and light grey levels of the fig. 3. Branch joints beyond the given level are fixed. This level can be dynamically set for each tree independently, according to eye distance and to the presence of wind. Transitions are implemented by linear interpolation over a time interval $[t_0, t_1]$ as follows:

- fixed to mobile : $\theta = \alpha\tilde{\theta}$ with $\alpha = \frac{t-t_0}{t_1-t_0}$
- mobile to fixed : $\theta = \alpha\tilde{\theta}$ with $\alpha = \frac{t_1-t}{t_1-t_0}$

where $\tilde{\theta}$ is the response to wind actions and θ the angle actually applied. At any time during the transition, we can switch back to the previous LOD by reversing the evolution of α.

4.2 Physically-based animation

Physically-based animation uses physical data such as force, mass and stiffness. Though the procedural model is not designed to generate such data, we build it using the geometrical data available. Here we first briefly explain how to build a physical model using the procedurally generated geometrical data. We then present a simplified method for the physical animation.

Physical model. As previously mentioned, no physical data is kept permanently. We derive on-the-fly mass, stiffness and damping using geometrical data. The forces involved are caused by the wind, by the user's action and by the joints.

In contrast to procedural animation, we now consider wind action as a real force. To vary continuously from procedural to physical animation, we apply the second time derivative of wind action. Using our current wind primitives, we get:

$$\tau_{physical} = -\omega^2 \frac{r-d}{r} sin(\omega t) Lz \times F$$

The motion due to the wind is thus theoretically the same as the motion computed procedurally. In practice, due to explicit time integration, divergence would eventually occur if joint damping were not applied.

User action is modeled as an external force applied to a branch. This force is handled similarly to wind force.

The torques applied by the joints are modeled using linear damped angular springs. The stiffness k and damping ν are estimated from branch diameter and length. In the theory of linear elasticity, stiffness is related to the inverse of the section area. For a given force, the displacement at the end of a branch is proportional to its length. We thus set k proportional to d^2/l where d is the average branch diameter and l the length. We make the common assumption that damping is proportional to stiffness. The torque generated by a given joint is given by:

$$(k\theta + \nu\dot{\theta})z_p + (k\phi + \nu\dot{\phi})y$$

Mass is closely related to volume. We thus set the term m proportional to ld^2. In future work we will investigate the use of $l^3 d^2$, which models the inertia of a bar.

Equations of motion. In order to save computation time, we apply simplified dynamics and consider only rotations. The laws of dynamics give:

$$\begin{aligned} \tau &= J\dot{\Omega} + \Omega \times J\Omega \\ &\simeq m\dot{\Omega} \end{aligned}$$

where τ is the net torque applied to a body, Ω its angular velocity in world coordinates, $\dot{\Omega}$ its angular acceleration and J its inertia matrix. The second equation is derived using the simplifying assumption $J \simeq mI$ where I is the identity matrix.

The net torque applied to a given branch is the sum of the actions of the wind and joint forces:

$$\begin{aligned} \tau = &- \sum_{i \in winds} \omega_i^2 \tau_i \\ &- (k\theta + \nu\dot{\theta})z_p - (k\phi + \nu\dot{\phi})y \\ &+ \sum_{j \in children} (k_j\theta_j + \nu_j\dot{\theta}_j)z - (k_j\phi_j + \nu_j\dot{\phi}_j)y_j \end{aligned}$$

where subscript p denotes the parent of the branch. We then project the angular acceleration of the body with respect to its parent to the two rotation axes to obtain the angular joint accelerations:

$$\dot{\Omega}_{rel} = \frac{1}{m}\tau - \dot{\Omega}_p$$
$$\ddot{\theta} = z_p\dot{\Omega}_{rel}$$
$$\ddot{\phi} = y\dot{\Omega}_{rel}$$

Time integration is performed using the standard Euler method:

$$\dot{\theta}(t+dt) = \dot{\theta}(t) + \ddot{\theta}(t)dt$$
$$\theta(t+dt) = \theta(t) + \dot{\theta}(t)dt$$

and similarly for ϕ. Note that position and velocity must be stored frame to frame to perform time integration. This results in a temporary memory overhead of four values per branch animated physically.

4.3 Hybrid animation

We use hybrid animation to combine wind influence and user action such as branch grabbing. We first show how the two methods can coexist within the same tree. We then explain how transitions are performed.

Coexistence of the two methods. Procedural animation is computed by applying equations (1) and (2), which do not depend on how the other branches are animated. Procedural animation can thus be trivially applied within a mixed animation. Physically-based animation is based on net force computation. Spring forces depend on object positions and velocities. For each branch animated physically, we thus need to know the position and velocity of the neighboring branches. If a neighboring branch is animated physically, then its velocity is a part of its dynamic state as well as position. If it is animated procedurally, we compute its velocity by finite differentiation $\Delta x/\Delta t$. Figure 3 illustrates how methods coexist within a tree.

Transitions between the two methods. Transition from procedural to physical animation is done instantaneously using the positions computed procedurally and the velocities deduced. However, an instantaneous transition from physical motion to procedural would generate a popping effect since position is procedurally computed as a function of time, without considering previous position and velocity. We thus compute both motions and perform a smooth blending during a time interval, typically one and half a second. Transition starts at time t_0 and ends at time t_1. We use a parameter α smoothly varying from 0 to 1 during the given time interval:

$$u(t) = \frac{t - t_0}{t_1 - t_0}$$
$$\alpha(t) = 3u^2 - 2u^3$$
$$\theta(t) = (1-\alpha)\bar{\theta}(t) + \alpha\tilde{\theta}(t)$$
$$\phi(t) = (1-\alpha)\bar{\phi}(t) + \alpha\tilde{\phi}(t)$$

where the tilde denotes motion computed procedurally and the bar denotes motion computed physically. At any time, we can switch back to physically-based motion by reversing the evolution of α.

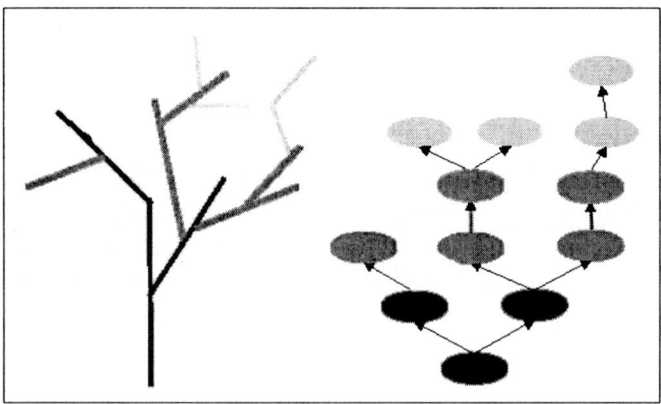

Fig. 3. Hybrid animation. The branches at the bottom (black) are animated physically. The intermediate levels (dark grey) are animated procedurally. The higher levels (light grey) are fixed.

5 Results

The experiments were made on a PIII 800MHz with 512MO RAM computer, with a NVIDIA GeForce256 board using OpenGL.

- Procedural animation of a tree with level of details. The motion of the tree is computed with respect to the direction, the magnitude and its position in the area of influence of the winds (these areas are the red circles of fig. 4a). We can simplify or refine the depth level in which branches are animated (red branches on fig. 4a), ensuring smooth transitions (shown in green). The transitions can be adapted to gain smoothness by increasing their durations.
- Procedurally animated forest (fig. 4b, 4c). We choose the following criteria for individual LODs : if the tree is not under any wind influence, its level is set to zero and the tree does not move. Levels are refined depending on the number of influent windfields, the distance to the camera and the position of the tree in the area of influence. Fig. 4c shows that we obtain interactive frame rates (27fps) using LODs, while it was not the case without LODs (around 1fps on the same scene).
- Physically-based animation of a single tree. All branches are physically handled, showing that they come back to their original positions after a gust of wind. This experiment is mainly done to calibrate our physic parameters to respond to the wind.
- Hybrid animation of a tree. We combine the two method : the multiresolution procedural method and the physically-based method. Continuity is achieved when switching the motion of a branch from procedural to physics, and from physics to procedural.
- Force and wind applied to a tree. The user applies an external force to a selected branch (yellow branch on fig. 4d at rest, and 4e pulled) which is pulled to the right while the tree is influenced by the wind. The physical LOD is then set, at least, at the same depth level as the branch grabbed. The motion is therefore the combination of the action of the wind and the applied force.

- Full forest. Finally, we animate a forest including 256 trees (fig. 4f), in which physics is applied where needed. We can select any branch of the scene and interact with it.

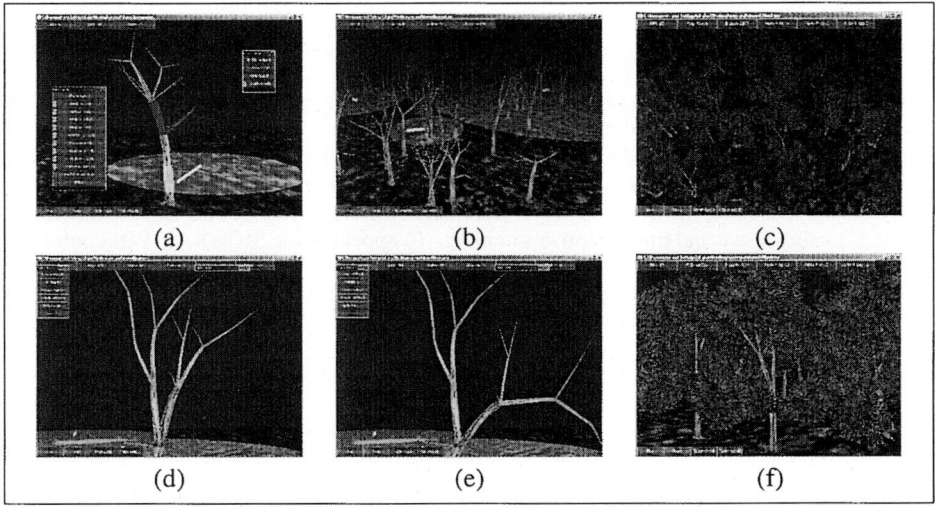

(a) (b) (c)

(d) (e) (f)

Fig. 4. Results.

6 Discussion

We have presented a prototype of an interactive forest. It is made of trees built on-the-fly at each redraw using a small set of parameters defining position, topology and shape. This method reduces memory requirements and allows the fine tuning of the levels of detail. We have developed a new animation method well-suited for this approach. It combines a fast procedural method including levels of detail with a physically-based model used to handle interactions. Transitions between the animation methods can be performed at any time. The physical method is dynamically applied only where needed. As a result, high frame rates are obtained as well as interactivity.

Additional development is necessary for practical use. The partitioning of the tree according to the animation method applied needs be more finely tuned than our current level-based approach. We will enhance the procedural and physically-based animation methods. More sophisticated wind primitives will be implemented. Implicit integration will be applied to stiff objects. We also plan to investigate noise functions to treat leaf animation in addition to branches. Collision detection will also be included.

From a more fundamental point of view, we will further investigate how procedural and physically-based methods can coexist. In our current implementation, physical branches are parents of procedural branches. The opposite would be useful also, e.g. if a bird lands on a small branch we may not need to animate all parent branches physically, but only those really influenced by the bird. More generally, we need a criterion to determine which branch needs to be animated physically. We also plan to apply LODs to the physically-based animation, probably using sub-tree clustering.

This work is partly funded by the PRIAMM project called "Modèles multi-échelles de végétation animée et interactive pour le jeu vidéo".

References

Ber97. R. Berka. Reduction of computations in physic-based animation using level of detail. In *Spring Conference of Computer Graphics*, 1997.

CH97. D. Carlson and J. Hodgins. Simulation levels of detail for real-time animation. In *Graphics Interface*, 1997.

DDBC99. G. Debunne, M. Desbrun, A. Barr, and M.-P. Cani. Interactive multiresolution animation of deformable models. In *Computer Animation and Simulation*, Sep. 1999.

DDCB01. G. Debunne, M. Desbrun, M.-P. Cani, and A. Barr. Dynamic real-time deformations using space and time adaptive sampling. To appear in the SIGGRAPH'01 conference proceedings, 2001.

GCB95. J. P. Granieri, J. Crabtree, and N. I. Badler. Production and playback of human figure motion for visual simulation. *Modeling and Computer Simulation*, 5(3):222–241, 1995.

HH98. P. Howlett and W. T. Hewitt. Mass-spring simulation using adaptive non-active points. *Computer Graphics Forum*, pages 345–354, 1998.

HPH96. D. Hutchinson, M. Preston, and T. Hewitt. Adaptative refinement for mass-spring simulations. In *Eurographics Workshop on Animation and Simulation*, pages 31–45, Sep. 1996.

Ono97. H. Ono. Practical experience in the physical animation and destruction of trees. In *Eurographics Workshop on Animation and Simulation*, pages 149–159, Sep. 1997. Industrial Light and Magic.

PC01. F. Perbet and M.-P. Cani. Animating prairies in real-time. In *Symposium on Interactive 3D Graphics*, 2001.

SF92. M. Shinya and A. Fournier. Stochastic motion-motion under the influence of wind. *j-CGF*, 11(3):C119–C128, C469, sept 1992.

Sta96. J. Stam. Stochastic dynamics: Simulating the effects of turbulence on flexible structures. Technical Report RR-2847, INRIA Rocquencourt, March 1996.

Val99. Bernard Valton. *Gestion de la complexite de scenes animees et interactives : contributions a la conception et a la representation*. PhD thesis, Univ. de Rennes(FR), 1999.

Meshes on Fire

Haeyoung Lee[†]   Laehyun Kim[†]   Mark Meyer[‡]   Mathieu Desbrun[†]

[†]U. of So. Cal. - [‡]Caltech

Abstract.
We present a new method for the animation of fire on polyhedral surfaces. Using the notion of *discrete straightest geodesics*, we evolve fire fronts *directly on the surface* of arbitrarily complex objects. Animator control and motion complexity is achieved by driving the fire motion using multi-scale turbulent wind fields and geometric quantities. Our model also supports adaptivity of the fire fronts, multiple simultaneous fires, and merging of multiple fires. This new technique produces convincing simulations at interactive rates even on a low-end PC, greatly increasing the productivity of the animation design process.

1 Introduction

Fire is a common, yet mysterious entity used in widely varying areas such as entertainment and training. The physical use of fire can however be both costly and dangerous. Computer simulation of fire offers many benefits including increased control, reduced expense and danger, and reproducibility. However, most previous work has been focusing on fire rendering, while we propose to concentrate our effort on *fire propagation*.

1.1 Previous Work

Fire simulation has been extensively researched in computer graphics [9, 10, 2, 6, 11, 4, 1]. The earliest computer graphics fire model was presented by Reeves [9]. The model used a large number of particles to animate a fire engulfing a planet. Although particles can easily represent fuzzy objects, representing well defined boundaries is more problematic and many particles are required to represent the fire.

Stam and Fiume [11] discretize the flammable object using a texture that represents fuel density, temperature, etc at every point on the object. A finite difference scheme is used to simulate the resulting fire. A turbulent wind field [10] is simulated and interacts with the fire to produce complex animations. The method is computationally expensive and requires a fine discretization to accurately represent the fire boundary.

Perry and Picard [6] and Beaudoin et al. [1] represent the boundary of the fire directly using several connected sample points. This results in far fewer particles being required to adequately animate the evolving fire boundary. Our model most closely resembles this work, with several important extensions including adaptivity, multiple simultaneous fires, and fire merging.

Our work also formalizes the use of geodesic flow to simulate the evolution of the fire boundary over a polyhedral object. Polthier et al. [7, 8] recently used geodesic flow to investigate surface properties. However, as our intended application area is different, several modifications were required to produce an appropriate geodesic flow algorithm, such as an appropriate handling of swallow tails created by conjugate vertices.

1.2 Overview

In this paper, we present a technique for modeling fires over polygonized objects (see Appendix Figure 5(a)). Our system represents a fire as an evolving front (also known as the *inception boundary*) and a system of particle-based flames. Since the front should only propagate on the object's surface, we use discrete straightest geodesics as defined in [7, 8] to evolve the fire front's motion directly on the surface itself. Using the formalism of geodesics we can guarantee that the front evolves correctly and always remains on any triangulated 2-manifold, regardless of its complexity.

To create rich, complex motion for the front, as well as to allow for general animation control, we drive the front motion using dynamic wind fields [10]. This multi scale technique allows the animator to describe large scale motions while a stochastic process creates the visually rich, small scale, turbulent motions.

As the front moves across the objects' surface it deposits particle-based *flames*. These flames evolve as standard fire particles [11] - flickering in the wind and even flying off the surface given a large enough wind field. These flames are rendered as blobs and leave a charred residue on the burnt surface.

Our system also incorporates advanced effects such as multiple, simultaneous flame fronts, merging of multiple fronts, fire ignition due to flying flame particles, and adaptivity for accurate fronts at minimal computational cost. Even with these complex features our system runs at interactive rates on a standard PC - extremely useful when designing a fire animation. Higher quality renderings [11, 1] can then be produced offline.

The remainder of the paper is organized as follows. The basics of geodesics for both continuous and discrete surfaces are described in detail in section 2. Our fire propagation model is introduced in section 3. Results are presented in section 4 followed by conclusions in section 5.

2 Front Propagation on Meshes

Under the assumption of no external factors (i.e., no wind field, uniform fuel density, etc.) a fire front on a flat surface would propagate out equally in all directions, creating concentric fronts as shown in figure 1(a). Each point on the front travels in a (euclidean) straight line. Therefore, we can determine the next front by simply advancing each point on the front along its respective propagation line. To extend this technique to curved surfaces, we must extend the notion of straight lines from the euclidean plane onto the surface. In this section, we review and extend a technique originally defined by Polthier and Schmies [7].

2.1 Geodesics on Polyhedral Surfaces

Geodesic curves are the extension of euclidean straight lines to a surface and are defined for a smooth surface as:

Definition 1: Let S be a smooth 2-dimensional surface. A smooth curve $\gamma \subset S$ is a geodesic curve if any of the following equivalent properties hold:

- γ is a locally shortest curve
- γ is a straightest curve (has zero geodesic curvature)

Using definition 1, we can now solve for the evolution of a front moving on a smooth surface by simply moving all points on the front appropriately. Given a point **p** on the

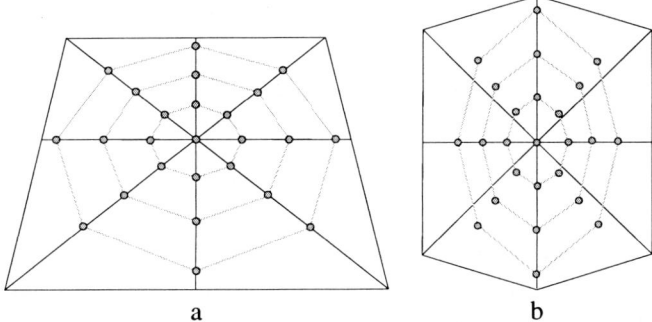

Fig. 1. *(a) Evolving a front on a flat plane. All points on the front move along euclidean straight lines. (b) Evolving a front on a polyhedral surface. All points on the front move along discrete straightest geodesics.*

front and the direction (in the tangent plane of S) of front motion $\mathbf{d}(\mathbf{p})$ at $\mathbf{p}$, move $\mathbf{p}$ along the geodesic γ at $\mathbf{p}$ in the direction $\mathbf{d}(\mathbf{p})$.

Although definition 1 allows one to update a front on a smooth surface, we often need to work with discrete polyhedral meshes. While geodesic curves on smooth surfaces are both straightest and locally shortest, on polyhedral meshes these two concepts *differ*. In fact, shortest geodesics on polyhedral meshes are not necessarily unique while the straightest geodesic given a point and direction on the polyhedral mesh is uniquely defined. As our original motivation was to determine how to move straight in a given direction on a polyhedral mesh, we require only the definition of straightest geodesics on polyhedral meshes, as introduced in [7]:

Definition 2: Let M be a polyhedral 2-dimensional surface. A curve $\gamma \subset M$ is a straightest geodesic curve if for every point $\mathbf{p} \subset \gamma$ the left and right curve angles, θ_l and θ_r are equal - where θ_l and θ_r measure the angle to the left or right of the curve at $\mathbf{p}$ *within the surface*.

Definition 2 then allows one to advance a front on a polyhedral mesh by uniquely solving the following initial value problem:

Discrete straightest geodesic initial value problem: Given a polyhedral mesh M, a point $\mathbf{p} \subset M$, and a polyhedral tangent vector $\mathbf{d}$ at $\mathbf{p}$, there exists a unique straightest geodesic $\gamma \subset M$ solving the initial value problem:

$$\begin{aligned} \gamma(0) &= \mathbf{p} \\ \gamma'(0) &= \mathbf{d} \end{aligned}$$

where the set of all *polyhedral tangent vectors* at a point $\mathbf{p} \subset M$ is defined to be all vectors within the faces of M adjacent to $\mathbf{p}$.

Advancing a front on a polyhedral surface now amounts to advancing each point on the front along a unique straightest geodesic. This can be accomplished by a simple Euler integration. Given a point $\mathbf{p}(t_i)$, and a polyhedral tangent direction $\mathbf{d}(t_i)$ to follow, the next point $\mathbf{p}(t_i + \Delta t)$ is found as:

$$\mathbf{p}(t_i + \Delta t) = \mathbf{p}(t_i) + \mathbf{d}(t_i)\Delta t \tag{1}$$

For each pair of vertices $\mathbf{p}(t_i)$ and $\mathbf{p}(t_i + \Delta t)$ three cases must be considered (see figure 2):

- $\mathbf{p}(t_i)$ and $\mathbf{p}(t_i + \Delta t)$ lie on the same face - since the surface is locally flat, this case is trivial to handle. Tangent values for $\mathbf{p}(t_i)$ and $\mathbf{p}(t_i + \Delta t)$ are the same.
- $\mathbf{p}(t_i + \Delta t) - \mathbf{p}(t_i)$ first crosses an edge - using the intersection with the edge $\mathbf{q}$, we must rotate $\mathbf{d}(t_i)$ around the edge by the angle between the two normal vectors of two neighboring surfaces. Using this rotated vector as the new polyhedral tangent, we continue on towards $\mathbf{p}(t_i + \Delta t)$, possibly crossing more edges on the way.
- $\mathbf{p}(t_i + \Delta t) - \mathbf{p}(t_i)$ first crosses a vertex - we calculate the polyhedral tangent vector $\mathbf{d}(\mathbf{q})$ at the intersected point $\mathbf{q}$ such that the resulting curve through $\mathbf{p}(t_i)$, $\mathbf{q}$, and $\mathbf{q} + \mathbf{d}(\mathbf{q})$ will have equal left and right curve angles. Using this new tangent, we continue on from $\mathbf{q}$.

Every single particle update will be a succession of any of these three simple cases. Propagation on arbitrary meshes, even with a very irregular connectivity, is therefore handled robustly.

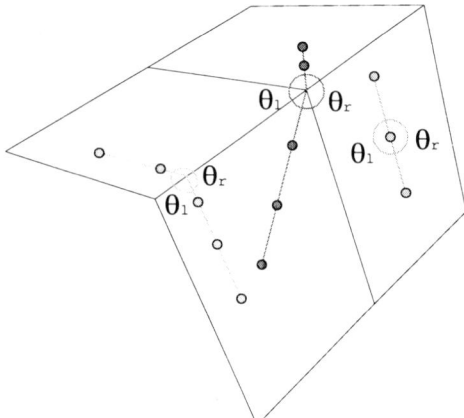

Fig. 2. *Three cases for integrating straightest geodesics: (green) both points on the same face, (blue) path between points intersects an edge, (red) path between points intersects a vertex. In each case, the two angles θ_r and θ_l are equal.*

Notice that evolving the front using discrete straightest geodesics guarantees a unique solution to the problem. This method correctly handles even the case when a point on the front evolves directly through a vertex. There is however a problem when the front passes through a hyperbolic point (a point where gaussian curvatue is negative) or a conjugate point (a point where the gaussian curvature is positive): a swallow tail effect appears (see Figure 4 and Appendix Figure 8(a)), after a conjugate point, creating a front interference. Our fire propagation model modifies the initial approach [7] to correctly deal with this case, as described next.

2.2 Continuous Fire Front

Although the original work [7] was designed to handle swallow tails, our fire propagation method should not contain these features. Since the fire burns the surface as it moves, front interferences (corresponding to double burning) should not occur. To remedy this problem, we first describe how we can keep the front ordered and uniformly sampled.

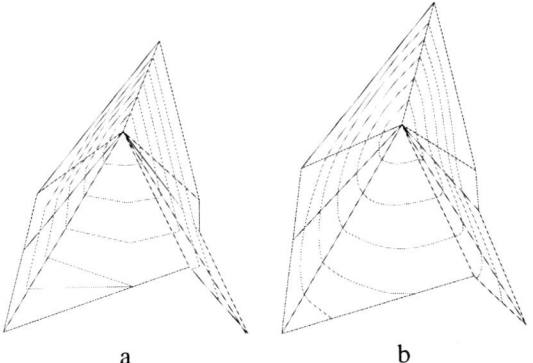

Fig. 3. *(a) No adaptive sampling: Many points must be created at the start in order to ensure an adequate discretization. (b) Adaptive sampling: Starting with a small number of points (eight) a smooth curve is created by adaptively refining where necessary.*

Adaptive, Ordered Front. To represent the continuous fire front, we maintain an ordered list of the front particle emitters allowing each particle access to its immediate neighbors. Often, as the front progresses, our original sampling becomes inadequate — especially after a hyperbolic vertex with negative gauss curvature, neighboring flame particles will diverge excessively.

In order to provide a smooth description of the front, at each time step, new front particle emitters are deposited dynamically between the diverged particle emitters. If the distance between two consecutive particles becomes too large compared to the bounding box of the object (or any other geometry-driven criteria), we insert a new particle in between. To find the position and direction of the inserted particle, we tested two methods. In the first method, we start a new particle on the initial starting point of the front, with a tangent direction equal to the average of the 2 particles, and we compute its path up to the current time. However, after a hyperbolic vertex, this first method fails since there is always a "shadow" cone that will never be reached.

To suppress this issue, we use a second method that uses the current positions and tangents of the two consecutive particles apart and simply adds a particle in between. When the consecutive particles are either on the same face or on adjacent faces, the insertion is easy to do. In the rare cases (for a mesh extremely irregular and non uniform) when the particles are too far away, we first find the faces lying inside a small bounding box of the segment we want to split, then project the midpoint of the segment to the closest face in the bounding box. The new tangent vector is simply the average of the two consecutive tangent vectors. This technique also has the advantage of being significantly faster than the first method since it doesn't have to start from the original position and simulate to the current time.

Inversely, we destroy particles in highly sampled regions when they become too close. This adaptive refinement of the front as illustrated in Figure 3.

Using this adaptive sampling, the initial front can be sampled with a small number of points. This greatly reduces the memory and computational requirements for evolving smooth fronts on complex objects. As explained in the next paragraph, this ordering of the front also helps us to remove the undesirable interferences that may appear during propagation.

Suppressing Swallow Tails. Using this notion of an ordered front, we propose a simple technique to detect and handle these swallow tail effects. Since these tails develop large tangent discontinuities around the interference (see Figure 4(a)), we simply remove particles that have a large tangent difference with their immediate neighbor. As shown in Figure 4(b), this alleviates the interference problem, and leads to a smooth evolving front as desired.

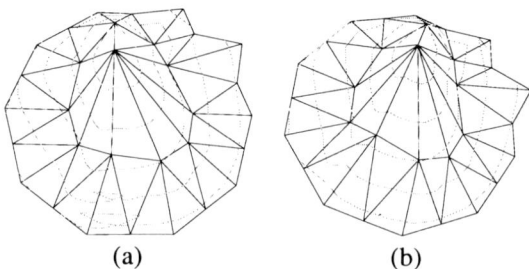

(a)   (b)

Fig. 4. *Swallow tail effect: (a) after crossing a point, a front can develop a swallow-tail-like inteference. (b) By simply removing points with wildly different tangent directions, the front is fixed.*

2.3   Discussion

We have described in detail how to propagate fronts on a triangulated surface, regardless of mesh discretization. We have also described how every front particle follows a geodesic path at an arbitrary speed. Therefore, in the next section, we show how to use these different features to animate a realistic fire propagation on a 2-manifold.

3   Fire on Meshes

In this section we discuss in detail the process of animating fire propagation on meshes. In particular we discuss our wind field and front propagation models, effects of terrain slope, flame particles, avoiding double burning, and multiple fronts.

3.1   Wind Field Model

Using the front propagation and straightest geodesics described in the previous section we can propagate a fire front over our polyhedral model. However, using solely the geodesic flow to evolve the front results in extremely uniform and simple motion. This is due to the fact that we evolve the front using a constant geodesic velocity while the speed of fire propagation should depend on several complex factors including wind, fuel density, and terrain slope. Additionally, we currently have no mechanism to allow for animator control over the fire.

   To add both animator control and visual complexity to the front propagation, we drive the front velocity using a multi scale turbulent wind field model proposed by Stam et al.[10]. The wind field models wind velocity as a sum of two terms: a large scale term, $\mathbf{w}_l(\mathbf{x},t)$, used to describe global wind motion, and a small scale term, $\mathbf{w}_s(\mathbf{x},t)$, used to describe local turbulence (see Appendix Figure 6):

$$\mathbf{w}(\mathbf{x},t) = \mathbf{w}_l(\mathbf{x},t) + \mathbf{w}_s(\mathbf{x},t) \qquad (2)$$

The large scale field can be specified by the animator or built by combining several wind field primitives. The small scale field is created using stochastic techniques to model turbulence. By separating the field this way, the animator has high level control and is not burdened with the specification of small, complex motions such as turbulence.

In order to reduce runtime computation the wind field is precomputed and stored in a 4D grid. During the simulation, the wind velocity at any point and time can be obtained by a 4D linear interpolation of the nearest grid points. Since the wind field can be constructed to have periodic boundaries, the grid can be tiled in both space and time. Additional wind fields can be combined with the precomputed field at runtime to allow for interactive wind field modifications (eg. mouse interaction).

3.2 Front Propagation

Given the wind field and the surface, we must now evolve the front in a plausible, visually complex way. We represent the front as a set of sample points, **p**, each with an associated direction of propagation, **d**, as explained in Section 2. The velocity of propagation for one of these points is given by:

$$\mathbf{v}(t) = \mathbf{d}(t)(1 + k_{wind}\, \mathbf{d}(t) \cdot \mathbf{w}(\mathbf{p},t)) \tag{3}$$

where k_{wind} is a coefficient specifying how strongly the wind influences the fire velocity and the term $(1 + k_{wind}\, \mathbf{d}(t) \cdot \mathbf{w}(\mathbf{p},t))$ is clamped to zero when it is less than zero. Note that this formulation reduces to the uniform geodesic flow in the absence of external wind. Using this velocity, we update the particle position using the geodesic flow technique of section 2 updating the tangential $\mathbf{v}(t)$ and $\mathbf{d}(t)$ when crossing edges and vertices.

We initialize the fire by placing a sampled front on the surface with the initial directions of the samples in the direction normal to the front. It is also possible to allow the user to specify the starting position of a fire by just clicking somewhere on the mesh. Given this starting position, we simply place several front samples at this location each with a different initial radial direction. The system then evolves the fire naturally and automatically.

3.3 Effects of Terrain Slope

In the absence of external wind the fire front should propagate up a vertical wall more quickly than across a horizontal floor. This is due to the upward convection of the air near the combustion area. We can simulate this by adding a wind-like term that opposes gravity. The velocity equation is then:

$$\mathbf{v}(t) = \mathbf{d}(t)(1 + k_{wind}\, \mathbf{d}(t) \cdot \mathbf{w}(\mathbf{p},t) - k_{slope}\, \mathbf{d}(t) \cdot \mathbf{g}) \tag{4}$$

where k_{slope} is a coefficient specifying how strongly the slope affects the velocity and **g** is the gravity vector.

Using this new velocity formulation the front is updated as described in the previous section. Our current implementation uses only the wind field and terrain slope to modulate the front velocity. However, it is possible to modify the velocity function to account for other factors including fuel density and fuel thickness. The animator can for instance spray-paint directly on the surface fuel densities, to direct the fire propagation at her will. However, our simple model using only wind and slope factors already leads to visually complex and realistic propagation over a mesh without any user interaction.

3.4 Flame Particles

In order to visualize the fire, flame particle emitters are deposited on the surface as the the front evolves. These emitters are deposited in the small area swept out by the front samples (see Appendix Figure 7). They can have values determined by local surface properties such as temperature, fuel density, and front velocity. These emitters then emit flame particles according to their internal state. These flame particles are standard particles as defined in [11]. Their motion is determined by a combination of advection due to the wind field, diffusion and decay, to simulate the integration of the PDE defining fire motion. Additionally, the size, transparency and color (from red when hot to dark grey for the smoke) of each flame particle can vary over time. After a period of time the particles and emitters die off.

3.5 Blackening of Burnt Regions

Once a region has burnt down, we must change its color accordingly. In order to implement a smooth color change in the burnt area, the color of each vertex is darkened according to the distance to the fire front (to simulate the alteration due to the heat of the flames). Each time a particle is advanced in a triangle (or across a triangle during its integration step), we increase the darkness of the vertices of the current triangle depending on the distance from the particle. To do so, we use a simple color lookup table to compute a luminance; if the current luminance of the vertex is higher than this new luminance, we change the color accordingly. When the three vertices of a triangle have been completely burnt, the whole triangle will be completely dark. If, however, only a corner has been burnt, the Gouraud shading used to display the mesh will provide a smooth ramping of the color. This effect can be seen in Appendix Figure 7(c), where we voluntarily reduced the number of flame emitters to clearly show the blackening.

3.6 Multiple Fronts

An important characteristic of fire propagation is that a flame can ignite another fire at a remote location. For instance, if a fire flame reaches an overhanging part of the object not yet burnt, a new fire front can develop at this point. In order to simulate this remote fire ignition, we should know how close to the surface each flame particle is. Computing the distance to the closest surface triangle at runtime would be prohibitive as the number of particles can be significant. Instead, we employed an implicit representation of the object's surface through a regular grid approximation. We used the closest point transform [5] to store the distance to the burning object on a coarse, regular grid, as a pre-process (Appendix Figure 9(a) shows the grid nodes around the object). We can then keep track of whether a particle penetrates the object by checking the interpolated distance from grid points near the particle. In addition, in order to quickly find the position where to start the new fire, an index of the closest vertex as well as the distance value will be assigned at each grid point before the simulation.

Once an interpenetration is detected during the animation, we proceed as follows: we first move the flame particle out of the object (the flame will therefore "lick" the object's surface), and then, if this particle is still hot enough, we start another fire front at this very location on the surface. This new fire front is initialized and assigned a unique front ID (we use a simple integer counter that we increment each time a new front is created) for further distinction between fronts. This behavior is illustrated in Appendix Figure 9 (b) and (c).

3.7   Fire Front Merging

Although we already solved the interference problem in the previous section (as depicted, this time for a real fire front, in Appendix Figure 8), there is another issue that needs to be dealt with: a fire front can/will eventually collide with itself or another fire front at some point during the propagation. The front must then to stop, since the area it is entering has already been burnt.

This case of "double burning", when two different fire fronts are to be merged into one fire front as shown in Appendix Figure 10(c), can easily be avoided. Although it would be easy to keep a pointer on each triangle to the list of the front IDs currently propagating over it, and then find the exact intersection(s) within the triangle, we opted for a simpler procedure. Whenever a triangle becomes completely burnt, we simply declare the front particles on it as dead: they will no longer move or emit flame particles. As demonstrated in Appendix Figure 10, this is sufficient to deal with both self-intersection and collision of different fronts. Notice that this procedure does *not* change the fact that we still have an ordered description of every front: some parts are simply no longer moving, but they still form the contour of the whole front. If one was to set fires at different points on the mesh, the final contours of the fronts (once everything has burnt) would be the Voronoï regions of these starting points, if no wind and slope effects are taken into account.

3.8   Rendering

Our simulation is visualized in real time using the OpenGL library. We used glPoint to render our evolving particles. A particle can be displayed as a transparent disk using the GL_POINT_SMOOTH mode and the GL_BLEND mode of the OpenGL library, generating automatic billboards for the blobby particles. To ensure correct transparency, we have to order the points in decreasing depth value. The transparency of each particle is determined mainly by the distribution of mass, decay constant and size. The size is changed over time to account for diffusion [10]. The color of the flames changes with temperature which decreases with time, as does its mass. We assume that the color of a flame is a function of its distribution of mass and its size.

Obviously, our implementation uses only one of the many possible rendering techniques. Other more sophisticated renderings of flames [11, 1] could be used instead. However, our simple rendering method allows for real-time display, which is very convenient for rapid design of an animation.

4   Results

The interactivity of our technique allowed us to test fire propagation on arbitrary meshes very quickly. Appendix Figure 10 (a) illustrates a typical session, where the animator clicks on a point on the mesh to start near the top of the model: the flame front then propagates on the surface instantaneously. The shape, speed, and the direction of the front flames are influenced by wind, geodesic flow, and terrain slope, and the result has a natural look of real fire propagation. Blackening of burnt regions are also spreading as the front flames evolve. Other examples, like the heightfield on Appendix Figure 5 (b) or the complex shape in Appendix Figure 9 demonstrates that we can handle any boundary or genus too, as long as the mesh is a 2-manifold.

5   Conclusion

In this paper, we developed a fire propagation technique designed for arbitrary triangle meshes. We define the fire propagation as a set of front particles following simple geodesics on the mesh, with a velocity depending on external wind and/or forces, slope, and other possible attributes. Contrary to previous methods, we define an lazy, adaptive front description, and handle conjugate points, front merging, and remote ignition to mimic real fire behavior. We also offer control to the animator by describing the wind field as a sum of a small scale and a large scale field. We demonstrated that our approach leads to complex and visually realistic fire front propagation. We used [10] for rendering of the flame, but this technique is open to other good offline rendering techniques if necessary.

Merging geometric properties of the meshes and physical properties of the wind contributes to the realism of this natural phenomenon simulation. This combination of geodesics and random wind fields can also be applied directly to other complex simulations such as spreading liquids on meshes or for the visualization of heat distribution. Future work includes the handling of non-manifold meshes, which should be done by keeping track of bifurcations in the fire fronts happening at each non-manifold edge/vertex.

Acknowledgements

Many thanks to Eitan Grinspun for initial discussions and support. This work has been partially supported by the Integrated Media Systems Center, a NSF Engineering Research Center, cooperative agreement number EEC-9529152.

References

1. P. Beaudoin, S. Paquet, and P. Poulin. Realistic and controllable fire simulation. *Graphics Interface 2001*, 2001.
2. N. Chiba, S Ohkawa, K. Muraoka, and M Miura. Two-dimensional visual simulation of flames. *The Journal of Visualization and Computer Animation*, 1994.
3. A. C. Fernandez-Pello. Flame spread modeling. *Combustion Science and Technology*, 1983.
4. W. W. Hargrove. Simulating fire patterns in heterogeneous landscapes. *Ecological modeling 2000*, 2000.
5. Sean Mauch. Closest point transform. http://www.ama.caltech.edu/ŝeanm/software/cpt/cpt.html, 2000.
6. C. H. Perry and R. W. Picard. Synthesizing flames and their spreading. *Eurographics Workshop on Animation*, 1994.
7. K. Polthier and M. Schmies. Straightest geodesics on polyhedral surfaces. *Mathematical Visualization*, pages 135–150, 1998.
8. K. Polthier and M. Schmies. Geodesic flow on polyhedral surfaces. *Proceedings of Eurographics-IEEE Symposium on Scientific Visualization '99*, 1999.
9. W. T. Reeves. Particle systems-a technique for modeling a class of fuzzy objects. *ACM Transactions on Graphics*, pages 91–108, 1983.
10. Jos Stam and Eugene Fiume. Turbulent wind fields for gaseous phenomena. *Computer Graphics Proceedings, ACM SIGGRAPH*, pages 369–376, 1993.
11. Jos Stam and Eugene Fiume. Depicting fire and other gaseous phenomena using diffusion processes. *Computer Graphics Proceedings, ACM SIGGRAPH*, 1995.
12. F. A. Williams. Mechanisms of fire spread. *Sixteenth Simpomsium on Combustion*, 1976.

Editors' Note: see Appendix, p. 202f. for colored figures of this paper

4

Physically-based Animation

Continuous deformation energy
for Dynamic Material Splines
subject to finite displacements

O. Nocent and Y. Remion

LERI-MADS
E-mail: nocent@leri.univ-reims.fr, yannick.remion@univ-reims.fr
http://www.univ-reims.fr/Leri

Abstract. This paper presents some improvements of a previous continuous parametric model for dynamic animation of curvilinear objects called Dynamic Material Splines (DMS). It begins with the replacement of the previous "parametric density" function by an actually "per unit length density" function. It then shows how continuous deformation energy can be used to model internal strains for DMS according to the classical theory of elasticity. After these theoretical developments, numerical results are given to point out the advantages of continuous deformation energy versus discrete springs.

1 Introduction

Let's briefly remind of the modelling scheme for curvilinear objects presented in our previous papers [8,9]. The dedicated dynamic animation engine had been built with a simulation objective (and specifically, simulation of knitted cloth at a mesoscopic or yarn scale). Our long-term goal had always consisted in performing as few methodological approximations as permitted, while providing as much versatility as possible concerning the objects shapes and material behaviour.

The first step towards this goal concerned the continuous modelling of the curvilinear objects. The unified and generic parametric 3D-curve model was built using a succession of ns curves called "spline segments" defined as functional combinations of a common set of n time-dependant 3D control points $\mathbf{p}^i(t)$ weighted by a set of parametric functions $b_i^j(\omega)$. The absolute 3D position of a point belonging to the spline segment j, of parametric coordinate ω at time t, was given by:

$$\mathbf{p}(j,\omega,t) = \sum_{i=1}^{n} b_i^j(\omega) \cdot \mathbf{p}^i(t) \qquad 1 \le j \le ns, \omega \in [0,1] \tag{1}$$

According to lagrangian formalism [1,4], control points $\mathbf{p}^i(t)$ had been considered as DMS generalised coordinates, or degrees of freedom. A specific derivation of Lagrange equations yielded a formally accurate yet numerically computable and solvable ODE system governing the evolution of the control points of the continuous curve. Classical numerical integration techniques were then used to obtain global animations from this ODE system.

This global overview exhibits two main methodological approximations, which we yet believe inescapable and, thus, won't discuss for long. Primarily, the necessary numerical integration implies a time "slicing" that could only be avoided if the studied system were simple enough to provide a formally solvable ODE system. Secondly, the geometrical (and kinematical) modelling of the curvilinear objects has to be defined with a finite (and ideally small) number of degrees of freedom. This unavoidable kinematic reduction implies configuration or shape restrictions for the modelled object. Even if one can consider that the unified spline model is quite rich as it encompasses many different configuration spaces and may be parameterised by increasing the number of control points and curve segments, once a model has been chosen, the shape restriction does hold.

Obviously, for the relevance of the physical model, inertial properties as well as internal and external strains had been supposedly defined and used to "fill in" the different ODE terms. Among these properties or strains, some (as inertia, gravitation and internal strains) are modelled in physics by scalar, vector or tensor fields over the object particles. Our simulation goal pushes us towards similar continuous modelling schemes for our DMS. The purpose of this paper is to extend the previous model in this direction concerning mass repartition and internal strains.

If mass repartition (which governs both inertia and gravitation) had already been modelled as a continuous scalar field, its definition had been chosen for its formal convenience in regard of the particle identification scheme used in the kinematic modelling and is not "user-friendly". In fact, it consists of a parametric density (mass per parametric unit ω) function and not a usual density (mass per unit length) function. Section 2 will present how the needed parametric density function can be obtained from user-friendly data such as per unit length density function defined for a predefined rest state of the curve.

Concerning internal strains, our previous choice was even farther from our objectives as these internal strains were temporarily approximated by discrete springs attached between consecutive material points. Although discrete modelling of internal strains is still popular [2,3,5] and provides some advantages, we are eager to study an actually continuous mechanical model for deformable curves. Consequently, we naturally came to define a continuous deformation energy based on the "finite displacements" theory of linear elasticity, since the usual assumption of "small perturbations" is irrelevant for rather highly deformable objects. Section 3 will remind the concerned physics entities and laws, apply those to the specific case of the DMS, and finally expose how the animation engine handles the related strains.

Section 4 will present numerical results to exhibit efficiency and accuracy of continuous deformation energy compared to succession of springs.

2 "Improved" mass repartition

The mass repartition inside the curvilinear object, has been conveniently modelled by a continuous parametric density function since this function shares the particle identification scheme of the kinematical model (Eq. (1)). It was defined as:

$$\mu : \begin{cases} \{1, \cdots, ns\} \times [0,1] \times \mathbb{R} \to \mathbb{R} \\ (j, \omega, t) \mapsto \mu(j, \omega, t) \end{cases} \tag{2}$$

We state that mass repartition is actually time invariant and we thus simplify the definition of Eq. (2) as $\mu(j, \omega)$. This assumption means that matter is tied to its parametric position ω and is not gliding along the DMS. It is important to notice that, even if the parametric mass density $\mu(j, \omega)$ remains invariant, the corresponding mass density per unit length $\rho(j, \omega, t)$ varies according to the DMS local elongation. This property further justifies the use of the parametric density in the "internal stages" of the engine.

Obviously, the relation between these two density functions involves the DMS arc length $l(j,\omega,t)$ which one cannot suppose equal to the parameter ω :

$$\partial_\omega l(j,\omega,t) = \left\|\partial_\omega \mathbf{p}(j,\omega,t)\right\| \quad ; \quad l(j,\omega,t) = \int_0^\omega \left\|\partial_u \mathbf{p}(j,\omega,t)\right\| du \tag{3}$$

From the definitions of the density functions, the expression of the infinitesimal mass of a small material segment $d\omega$ around a particle (j,ω), gives the following relation (see Fig. 1):

$$\mu(j,\omega)d\omega = \rho(j,\omega,t)\partial_\omega l(j,\omega,t)d\omega \tag{4}$$

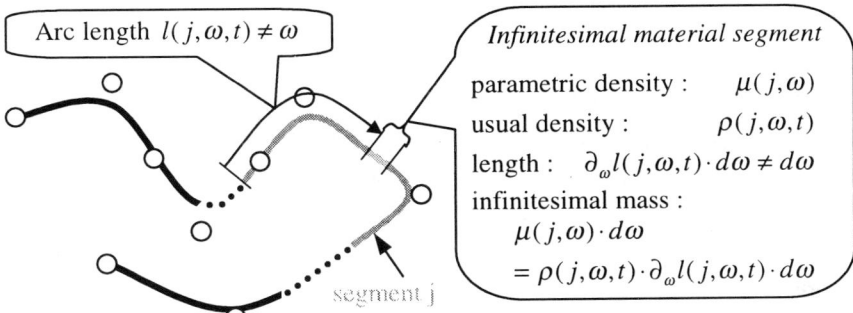

Fig. 1. Mass density per parametric unit vs. mass density per unit length.

The first improvement proposed by this paper consists of defining the parametric density function $\mu(j,\omega)$ equivalent to any user-predefined mass repartition per unit length $\rho^0(j,\omega)$ for a given DMS rest state defined by a specific set of control points $\mathbf{p}^{0i}$.

For the sake of simplicity, the rest state is chosen as a rectilinear DMS whose spline segments have the desired rest lengths (Fig. 2).

We furthermore choose to align this rectilinear "curve" with the referential first axis, leading to the following rest position definition:

$$\mathbf{p}^0(j,\omega) = \left(\sum_{i=1}^n b_i^j(\omega)\cdot \mathbf{p}_1^{0i} \quad 0 \quad 0\right)^T \quad 1\le j \le ns, \omega \in [0,1] \tag{5}$$

Since this rest state is a valid DMS configuration, relations similar to Eq. (3) and (4) hold:

$$\partial_\omega l^0(j,\omega) = \left\|\partial_\omega \mathbf{p}^0(j,\omega)\right\|, \quad \mu(j,\omega)d\omega = \rho^0(j,\omega)\partial_\omega l^0(j,\omega)d\omega \tag{6}$$

Making the additional assumption that $\partial_\omega \mathbf{p}_1^0(j,\omega) > 0$ (this can practically be achieved by choosing $\mathbf{p}_1^{0\,i+1} > \mathbf{p}_1^{0\,i}$ for $1\le i < n$). We thus state:

$$\partial_\omega l^0(j,\omega) = \partial_\omega \mathbf{p}_1^0(j,\omega)$$

and, thanks to Eq. (5) and (6), finally obtain:

$$\mu(j,\omega) = \rho^0(j,\omega)\partial_\omega \mathbf{p}_1^0(j,\omega) = \rho^0(j,\omega)\sum_{i=1}^n \partial_\omega b_i^j(\omega)\cdot \mathbf{p}_1^{0i} \tag{7}$$

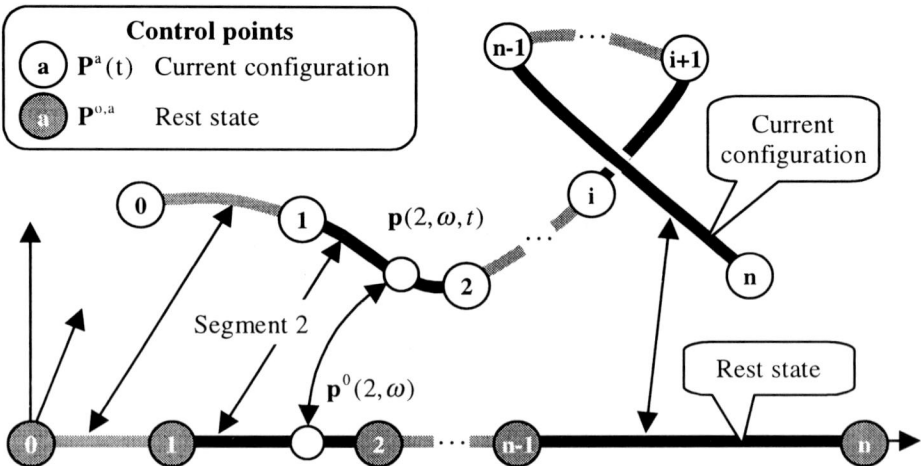

Fig. 2. Definition of Dynamic Material Spline rest state.

Most of the time, we are dealing with polynomial blending functions. Considering a constant or even polynomial mass density per unit length $\rho^0(j,\omega)$, we are able, during the initialisation step, to compute accurately integral terms involving the resulting polynomial parametric mass density $\mu(j,\omega)$ (Eq. (7)) such as generalised mass matrix and gravitational energy.

3 Continuous elastic internal strains

The second and major improvement proposed for DMS is the introduction of a continuous model for elastic internal strains. Since mass repartition and gravitational energy have already been modelled as continuous quantities, the definition of continuous deformation elastic response is a large step towards continuous modelling of deformable elastic curves.

The theory of elasticity is based upon the assumption that the deformations undergone by the material are reversible and induce a response stress that can be conveniently modelled by an energy function of the deformation. Many possibilities arise in order to express both the deformations measuring scheme and the corresponding energy. Some of these models imply a "small displacement" assumption that does not hold in the case of highly deformable objects such as the DMS. Hence, we are driven to the "finite displacements" theory to express our deformation elastic energy.

From this theoretical framework, we have chosen the Green-Lagrange tensor to express deformations and the classical Piola-Kirchhoff law [6] to express the function giving the elastic energy density from this deformation tensor. This arbitrary choice has mainly been driven on account of the implied non-linear response to elongation (i.e. a third order response, see section 4 for details) that is convenient for many curvilinear objects and in particular for the yarns in knitted cloth simulation. We start this section with a short overview of the required mathematical entities and definitions. We then apply these developments to the specific case of DMS and present how this DMS continuous elastic energy is handled by the lagrangian animation engine.

3.1 Theoretical background

In the classical continuum mechanics [10], the chosen Green-Lagrange tensor is introduced under lagrangian formalism. This formalism is based on the study of particle trajectories $\chi(\mathbf{x}^0, t)$, assuming that each particle is identified by a reference position $\mathbf{x}^0$. As a convention, one calls $\mathbf{x}^0$ and t the lagrangian variables and $\mathbf{x}(t) = \chi(\mathbf{x}^0, t)$ the lagrangian unknowns.

The deformation study begins with the definition of the transformation gradient tensor allowing to express the direction of a material fibre in the current configuration around a particle $\mathbf{x}^0$, from this same fibre direction in the reference configuration:

$$\mathcal{F}(\mathbf{x}^0, t) = \partial_{\mathbf{x}^0} \chi(\mathbf{x}^0, t) \tag{8}$$

Then, the Cauchy-Green tensor, also called dilatation tensor, models local dilatation and sliding of fibres identified by their directions expressed in the reference configuration, around a particle $\mathbf{x}^0$ in the current configuration:

$$\mathcal{C}(\mathbf{x}^0, t) = \mathcal{F}(\mathbf{x}^0, t)^T \mathcal{F}(\mathbf{x}^0, t) \tag{9}$$

Finally, the Green-Lagrange tensor, or deformation tensor, characterises local deformation around a particle $\mathbf{x}^0$ in the current configuration ($\mathcal{I}$ is the identity tensor):

$$\mathcal{E}(\mathbf{x}^0, t) = \tfrac{1}{2}(\mathcal{C}(\mathbf{x}^0, t) - \mathcal{I}) \tag{10}$$

As part of the "finite displacements" linear elasticity theory, the chosen Piola-Kirchhoff law expresses the elastic energy density per lagrangian (i.e. reference) volume unit $e_v(\mathbf{x}^0, t)$ as a quadratic function of the deformation measures encompassed in the Green-Lagrange tensor:

$$e_v(\mathbf{x}^0, t) = \frac{\lambda}{2} \operatorname{tr}\left(\mathcal{E}(\mathbf{x}^0, t)\right)^2 + \mu \operatorname{tr}\left(\mathcal{E}(\mathbf{x}^0, t)^2\right) \tag{11}$$

where λ and μ are Lamé constants, defined from Young modulus E and Poisson coefficient v as:

$$\lambda = Ev / (1 - 2v)(1 + v) \qquad \mu = E / 2(1 + v) \tag{12}$$

An equivalent formulation of the same Piola-Kirchhoff law introduces the "pseudo-stress" second Piola-Lagrange tensor $\mathcal{S}(\mathbf{x}^0, t)$:

$$\mathcal{S}(\mathbf{x}^0, t) = \lambda \operatorname{tr}\left(\mathcal{E}(\mathbf{x}^0, t)\right) \mathcal{I} + 2\mu \mathcal{E}(\mathbf{x}^0, t), \quad e_v(\mathbf{x}^0, t) = \frac{1}{2} \operatorname{tr}\left(\mathcal{S}(\mathbf{x}^0, t) : \mathcal{E}(\mathbf{x}^0, t)\right) \tag{13}$$

3.2 Application to DMS

DMS have been defined like ideal curvilinear objects without any thickness. This mathematical assumption leads to build objects without any physical existence. In order to be able to apply the previous theoretical results that are strongly based on the 3 dimensional aspect of continuous medium, we now consider that DMS have infinitesimal thickness.

Around each DMS point, we consider a material section orthogonal to the curve in rest state. Moreover, we suppose this material section remains orthogonal to the curve at any instant (Fig. 3). This assumption is conceivable since the DMS thickness is negligible. For any DMS point $\mathbf{p}(j, \omega, t)$, we thus build an orthonormal referential $(\mathbf{u}^1(j, \omega, t), \mathbf{u}^2(j, \omega, t), \mathbf{u}^3(j, \omega, t))$ with the first axis tangential to the curve at $\mathbf{p}(j, \omega, t)$.

92

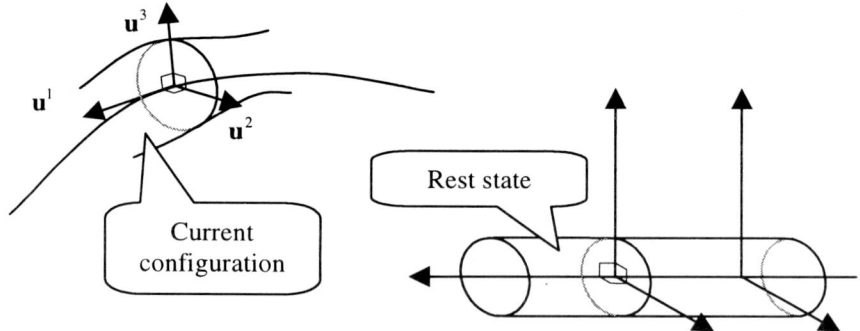

Fig. 3. Section of a "thick" DMS with its associated local referential.

Finally, the position of a particle in this "thick" DMS, identified by a segment number j and a multi-index $\mathbf{w} = (\omega_1 \equiv \omega, \omega_2, \omega_3)$, is given by:

$$\chi(t) = \mathbf{p}(j,\omega_1,t) + \omega_2 a_2(j,\omega_1,t)\mathbf{u}^2(j,\omega_1,t) + \omega_3 a_3(j,\omega_1,t)\mathbf{u}^3(j,\omega_1,t)$$

where $a_2(j,\omega_1,t)$ and $a_3(j,\omega_1,t)$ represent linear dilatation factors in the material section respectively along $\mathbf{u}^2(j,\omega_1,t)$ and $\mathbf{u}^3(j,\omega_1,t)$. The existence of these factors is crucial as it allows the necessary constriction in the section plane.

Using the notations defined in section 2 for the DMS rest state, the reference position is expressed as:

$$\mathbf{x}^0 = \left(\mathbf{p}_1^0(j,\omega_1) \quad \omega_2 \quad \omega_3\right)^T = \left(\sum_{i=1}^{n} b_i^j(\omega_1)\cdot\mathbf{p}_1^{0i} \quad \omega_2 \quad \omega_3\right)^T$$

As each particle is identified by its parametric coordinates $\mathbf{w}$ and not directly by its reference position $\mathbf{x}^0$, we have to introduce partial derivation according to $\mathbf{w}$ for the gradient tensor calculation (Eq. (8)).

$$\mathcal{F}(\mathbf{x}^0,t) = \partial_{\mathbf{x}^0}\chi(t) = \partial_{\mathbf{w}}\chi(t)\partial_{\mathbf{x}^0}\mathbf{w} = \partial_{\mathbf{w}}\chi(t)\left(\partial_{\mathbf{w}}\mathbf{x}^0\right)^{-1}$$

with $\quad \partial_{\mathbf{w}}\chi(t) = \left(\partial_{\omega_1}l\mathbf{u}^1 + \omega_2\partial_{\omega_1}\left(a_2\mathbf{u}^2\right) + \omega_3\partial_{\omega_1}\left(a_3\mathbf{u}^3\right) \quad a_2\mathbf{u}^2 \quad a_3\mathbf{u}^3\right)$

and $\quad \left(\partial_{\mathbf{w}}\mathbf{x}^0\right)^{-1} = \begin{pmatrix} \partial_{\omega_1}l^0(j,\omega_1)^{-1} & & \\ & 1 & \\ & & 1 \end{pmatrix}$

Since we assume infinitesimal thickness, parameters ω_2 and ω_3 are negligible according to $\partial_{\omega_1}l(j,\omega_1,t)$. From now on, we will consider that $\omega_2 = \omega_3 = 0$. As a consequence, previously defined terms depend on only one scalar parameter $\omega = \omega_1$. This leads to the following simplified expression of the tensor:

$$\mathcal{F}(\mathbf{x}^0,t) = \mathcal{U}(j,\omega,t)\mathcal{A}(j,\omega,t)$$

where $\mathcal{U}(j,\omega,t) = \left(\mathbf{u}^1 \quad \mathbf{u}^2 \quad \mathbf{u}^3\right)$, $\mathcal{A}(j,\omega,t) = \begin{pmatrix} \gamma & & \\ & a_2 & \\ & & a_3 \end{pmatrix}$, $\left.\begin{array}{c} \\ \\ \\ \\ \end{array}\right\}$ (14)

and $\gamma(j,\omega,t) = \partial_\omega l(j,\omega,t)/\partial_\omega l^0(j,\omega)$

One should note that $\gamma(j,\omega,t)$ expresses the local axial relative dilatation factor.

According to the classical tensors' definitions (Eq (9) and (10)) and since the vector basis $\left(\mathbf{u}^1, \mathbf{u}^2, \mathbf{u}^3\right)$ is orthonormal and $\mathcal{A}(j,\omega,t)$ is a diagonal matrix, we finally express the deformation tensor as follows:

$$\mathcal{E}(\mathbf{x}^0,t) = \tfrac{1}{2}\begin{pmatrix} \gamma(j,\omega,t)^2 - 1 & & \\ & a_2(j,\omega,t)^2 - 1 & \\ & & a_3(j,\omega,t)^2 - 1 \end{pmatrix}$$

At this point of the derivation, one should notice that both radial dilatation factors $a_2(j,\omega,t)$ and $a_3(j,\omega,t)$ are unknowns and must be balanced for by two new equations.

Following a classical mechanical modelling scheme (used, for instance for the thin shell theory construction), we consider that no forces are applied upon the object surface [7]. This leads to the nullity of the two radial pseudo-stress components at the DMS surface, properties that, according to the infinitesimal DMS thickness, can be extended to any inner point $\mathbf{x}^0$, thus providing the two expected equations:

$$S(\mathbf{x}^0,t)_{22} = S(\mathbf{x}^0,t)_{33} = 0 \qquad (15)$$

Applying the second Piola-Lagrange tensor expression (Eq. (13)) and Lamé constant definitions (Eq. (12)) to Eq. (15), we obtain, after some calculations, the following results:

$$\mathcal{E}(\mathbf{x}^0,t)_{22} = \mathcal{E}(\mathbf{x}^0,t)_{33} = -v\mathcal{E}(\mathbf{x}^0,t)_{11}, \quad S(\mathbf{x}^0,t)_{11} = E\mathcal{E}(\mathbf{x}^0,t)_{11}$$

This gives simplified expressions of the deformation and pseudo-stress tensors:

$$\mathcal{E}(\mathbf{x}^0,t) = \frac{1}{2}\left(\gamma(j,\omega,t)^2 - 1\right)\begin{pmatrix} 1 & & \\ & -v & \\ & & -v \end{pmatrix}, \quad S(\mathbf{x}^0,t) = \frac{E}{2}\left(\gamma(j,\omega,t)^2 - 1\right)\begin{pmatrix} 1 & & \\ & 0 & \\ & & 0 \end{pmatrix} \qquad (16)$$

The deformation tensor $\mathcal{E}\left(\mathbf{x}^0,t\right)$ exhibits an interesting structural property. In fact, an axial elongation is coupled with a radial contraction involving the Poisson coefficient v which is the natural constriction measurement.

From Eq. (11) or (13), applied to Eq. (16) we find the expression of the deformation energy density per lagrangian (i.e. reference) volume unit:

$$e_v(\mathbf{x}^0,t) = \frac{E}{8}\left(\gamma(j,\omega,t)^2 - 1\right)^2$$

The global deformation energy is then obtained by summation:

$$e(t) = \int e_v(\mathbf{x}^0,t)\,dv^0 = \int e_v(\mathbf{x}^0,t)\,dx_1^0 dx_2^0 dx_3^0$$

Denoting s, the area of the infinitesimal reference section supposed constant, and using the coordinates substitution $x_1^0 = \mathbf{p}_1^0(j,\omega_1)$, $x_2^0 = \omega_2$, $x_3^0 = \omega_3$, leads to the result:

$$e(t) = \frac{E s}{8} \sum_{j=1}^{ns} \int \left(\gamma(j,\omega,t)^2 - 1\right)^2 \partial_\omega l^0(j,\omega)\,d\omega \qquad (17)$$

3.3 Internal energy handling in the animation engine

According to the lagrangian formalism underlying the DMS animation engine, forces are expressed by using their virtual power ratings for virtual movements instilled by each degree of freedom η_d. Classically, if the intended forces are conservative, these virtual power ratings may be derived from the associated potential energy as:

$$W^d(t) = -\partial_{\eta_d} e(t) \qquad (18)$$

Remembering that the degrees of freedom η_d of the DMS are the coordinates of the control points $\mathbf{p}_k^i$, we apply Eq. (18) to the potential deformation energy (Eq. (17)) and, thanks to Eq. (14), (4), and (1), obtain the needed virtual power ratings:

$$W_k^i(t) = -\frac{\partial e}{\partial \mathbf{p}_k^i}(t) = \frac{E\,s}{2}\sum_{m=1}^{n}\mathbf{p}_k^m(t)\left[\mathcal{B}_{im} - \sum_{p,q=1}^{n}\mathcal{B}_{impq}\left\langle \mathbf{p}^p(t)\middle|\mathbf{p}^q(t)\right\rangle\right] \qquad (19)$$

with:

$$\mathcal{B}_{impq} = \sum_{j=1}^{ns}\int\frac{b_i^{j}{}'(\omega)\,b_m^{j}{}'(\omega)\,b_p^{j}{}'(\omega)\,b_q^{j}{}'(\omega)}{\partial_\omega l^0(j,\omega)^3}\,d\omega\,, \quad \mathcal{B}_{im} = \sum_{j=1}^{ns}\int\frac{b_i^{j}{}'(\omega)\,b_m^{j}{}'(\omega)}{\partial_\omega l^0(j,\omega)}\,d\omega \qquad (20)$$

Even if we consider polynomial blending functions as in section 2, scalars $\mathcal{B}_{im}$ and $\mathcal{B}_{impq}$ correspond to rational function integrals and cannot be computed accurately. But, since these terms remain constant and are calculated once during the initialisation step, we are able to use high order numerical integration methods to compute them.

According to Eq (19), the computation of the virtual power ratings of internal strains seems to exhibit unaffordable complexity ($o(n^4)$, n being the number of control points). However, in practical cases, the underlying spline definition often holds the "locality" property. This ensures that every spline segment depends upon a finite (and usually small) number δ of consecutive control points:

$$b_i^j(\omega) = 0, \quad i < j \text{ or } i \geq j+\delta, 1 \leq j \leq ns, \omega \in [0,1]$$

In such a case, it is convenient to switch the summations in Eq. (19) and (20) as:

$$W_k^i(t) = \frac{E\,s}{2}\sum_{j=\max(1,i-\delta+1)}^{\min(ns,i)}\sum_{m=j}^{j+\delta-1}\mathbf{p}_k^m(t)\left[\mathcal{B}_{im}^j - \sum_{p,q=j}^{j+\delta-1}\mathcal{B}_{impq}^j\left\langle \mathbf{p}^p(t)\middle|\mathbf{p}^q(t)\right\rangle\right] \qquad (21)$$

with:

$$\mathcal{B}_{impq}^j = \int\frac{b_i^{j}{}'(\omega)\,b_m^{j}{}'(\omega)\,b_p^{j}{}'(\omega)\,b_q^{j}{}'(\omega)}{\partial_\omega l^0(j,\omega)^3}\,d\omega\,, \quad \mathcal{B}_{im}^j = \int\frac{b_i^{j}{}'(\omega)\,b_m^{j}{}'(\omega)}{\partial_\omega l^0(j,\omega)}\,d\omega \qquad (22)$$

The computations expressed in Eq (21), may be obtained in $o(ns \cdot \delta^4)$ complexity with a loop over the ns segments j that fills the 3δ appropriate $W_k^i(t)$ (for $i \in [j, j+\delta[$) with the convenient terms from Eq. (21), assuming that the δ^4 $\mathcal{B}_{impq}^j$ and δ^2 $\mathcal{B}_{im}^j$ terms of Eq. (22) (for $i, m, p, q \in [j, j+\delta[$) have been pre-computed for each segment during the initialisation step. As δ is a constant of the model, the achieved asymptotic complexity is $o(ns) = o(n)$.

4 Evaluation and results

4.1 Equivalent elongation spring law

In order to compare continuous deformation energy with succession of springs, we have to give the equivalent local spring law definition, which expresses how the elastic stress is related to a given elongation. We classically introduce the usual Cauchy stress tensor $\sigma(\mathbf{x}(t))$ as follows:

$$\sigma(\mathbf{x}(t)) = \det\left(\mathcal{F}(\mathbf{x}^0,t)\right)^{-1}\mathcal{F}(\mathbf{x}^0,t):\mathcal{S}(\mathbf{x}^0,t):\mathcal{F}(\mathbf{x}^0,t)^T \qquad (23)$$

Let $\mathbf{n}$ be a normal vector of an infinitesimal surface element dS. The force $\mathbf{F}$ resulting from internal strains, applied on dS is given by $\mathbf{F} = dS\,\sigma : \mathbf{n}$. We now apply this formula to a DMS actual section area $s' = a_2 a_3 s$ with normal vector $\mathbf{n} = \pm \mathbf{u}^l$. As we only deal with internal strains along the curve direction, the formula becomes:

$$\lambda \mathbf{u}^l = \pm s' \sigma : \mathbf{u}^l \tag{24}$$

where λ corresponds to the algebraic stress intensity which, thanks to Eq. (24), (23), (16) and (14), can be expressed as a third order polynomial of the local relative dilatation factor γ:

$$\lambda = \pm a_2 a \, s \left\langle \mathbf{u}^l \middle| \sigma : \mathbf{u}^l \right\rangle = \pm \frac{E\,s}{2} \gamma \left(\gamma^2 - 1 \right) \tag{25}$$

In order to validate both the theoretical development yielding this formula (Eq. (25)) and the computer implementation, we propose a static virtual experiment consisting of a traction reaction measure. To remain "static" this experience must insure that internal strains are homogeneous in the object. This is achieved by choosing a null gravity and a starting still state homothetical to the rest state (see result below ; Eq. (27)). Hence our DMS will start with control points defined as:

$$\mathbf{p}^i(0) = \alpha \mathbf{p}^{0i} \tag{26}$$

Considering Eq. (14), (6) and (3), these control points definition (Eq. (26)) imply:

$$\mathbf{p}(j,\omega,0) = \alpha \mathbf{p}^0(j,\omega) \Rightarrow \gamma(j,\omega,0) = \alpha \quad 1 \le j \le ns, \omega \in [0,1] \tag{27}$$

Constraining both end points of the curve to remain motionless then insures that the object remains still over time. Furthermore the constraint enforcing strains, applied on the DMS "end faces", must balance internal strains on those faces. These enforcing strains are introduced in the evolution equations as unknown Lagrange multipliers λ_0, λ_1 that accurately correspond to their intensities and must be resolved for by the engine. Hence those computed Lagrange multipliers should match the internal strain law (Eq. (25)) on the corresponding end faces:

$$\lambda_0 = \pm \frac{E\,s}{2} \gamma \left(\gamma^2 - 1 \right), \quad \lambda_1 = \mp \frac{E\,s}{2} \gamma \left(\gamma^2 - 1 \right) \tag{28}$$

The numerical results of this experiment for different relative elongation factors $\gamma - 1$ are shown in Fig. 4 along with the expected theoretical law (Eq. (28)):

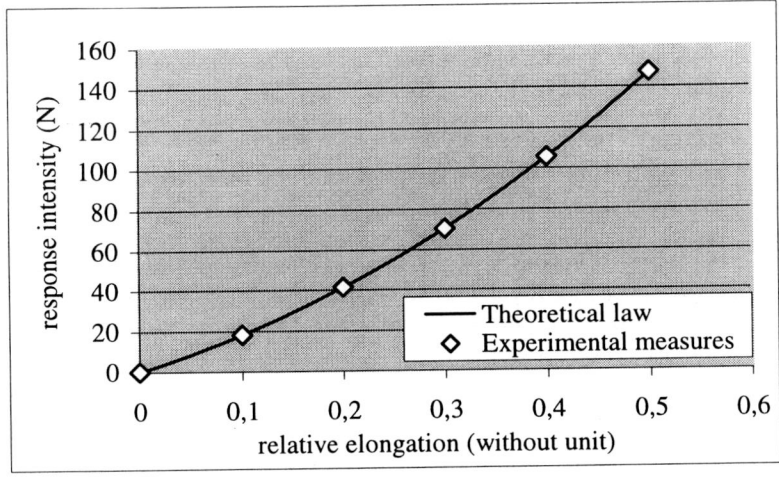

Fig. 4. Virtual traction experimental results.

The previous development clearly demonstrates that, with the chosen model, any rectilinear segment with homogeneous elongation behaves like a spring with an elastic law defined as:

$$f = \tfrac{1}{2} E s (l/l_0)\left((l/l_0)^2 - 1\right) \tag{29}$$

Thus, if one assumes that the curve segment between two particles remains approximately rectilinear and with homogeneous elongation, its internal strains may globally approximated by a spring, following the Eq. (29) law, and attached between those two particles. This is the basic assumption underlying the approximation of internal strains by series of consecutive springs.

4.2 Dynamic comparison

These comparison experiments are rather simple as they correspond to physical simulations of similar DMS whose sole differences lie in their different internal strain models (one uses the described continuous elastic energy, while the others use different number per segment of consecutive springs sharing the same elastic law expressed by Eq. (29)).

Table 1 below shows the numerical results of two such experiments while pictures drawn from these animations are shown in Appendix A and B. The "error" terms stand for the mean over time of the square root of the mean square distance between the studied DMS particles and their homologues from a reference DMS simulation. We have chosen this reference simulation as the "continuous" one on account of its greater modelling relevance. The "Time" results correspond to the global CPU time required for a 5 s simulation on a processor AMD Athlon 1.2 GHz.

Table 1. Numerical results corresponding to simulations of hanging ropes.

Springs per segment	Rope hanging from one end		Rope hanging from both ends	
	Error	Time	Error	Time
2	0.2721 m	2.120s	0.0976 m	4.110s
5	0.0459 m	3.300s	0.0814 m	5.310s
10	0.0234 m	5.290s	0.0825 m	7.280s
15	0.0133 m	7.260s	0.0825 m	9.260s
20	0.0107 m	9.250s	0.0825 m	11.240s
Continuous elasticity	-	6.230s	-	8.250s

These results and the corresponding simulations (see Appendix A and B) clearly demonstrate that few springs per segment yields unacceptable errors and that the continuous elastic energy model is as costly as a "medium accuracy" spring solution.

5 Conclusion

We proposed two main improvements to our Dynamic Material Splines model. First, we showed how to build a parametric mass density function, which is the natural expression of mass repartition for DMS, equivalent to a more user-friendly mass density per unit length function defined for a given rest state. Then, in order to improve the model homogeneity, we modelled internal strains by using continuous deformation energy.

This continuous internal energy modelling has been built within the "finite displacements" framework of the theory of linear elasticity and more specifically with the Piola-Kirchhoff law using the Green-Lagrange deformation tensor. This deformation tensor is a quadratic polynomial measure of the more usual local deformation expressions such as elongation or dilatation. Hence, the "linear" elasticity based on this "quadratic" tensor yields a "quartic" energy that, in turn, implies "cubic" elastic strains.

This energy modelling is quite restrictive compared to discrete springs whose elastic laws can easily be chosen or defined by the end user. In fact, the definition of the continuous elastic law is deeply embedded in the mathematical developments yielding the computational model. We are eager to point out that many other choices are proposed by the theory of elasticity, including more "linear" laws. Each of these available laws could be developed as in this paper to yield a new continuous internal elastic strain for DMS. This seems awful at first glance, but we are already studying if a generic or abstract development of such continuous elastic models could permit to model one's own elastic law, choosing by this way at the modelling level (and not the software design level) its "usual" order. Nevertheless, the presented development is operational and greatly improves our previous yarn model for knitted cloth simulation. Moreover, the greater theoretical accuracy of this model yields an improved quality of the produced simulations. Another side advantage of the continuous modelling is a drastic simplification of the modelling step for the end user : he(she) "only" has to specify the Young modulus and Poisson coefficient, and, no more, to take complex structural decisions such as setting the number and organisation of the discrete springs.

On account of the reasonable computation cost, the great simplification of the modelling stage and, overall, the enhanced theoretical and practical accuracy implied for the produced simulations, we think that this study proves the utility and feasibility of continuous internal elastic energy handling for DMS.

References

1 V. I. Arnold. Mathematical Methods of Classical Mechanics, 2nd Edition. Springer-Verlag, New York, 1989.

2 D. Baraff and A. Witkin. Large steps in cloth animation. In *Computer Graphics Proceedings*, pages 43-54. Addison Wesley, 1998.

3 D. Bourguignon and M.P. Cani. Controlling Anisotropy in Mass-Spring Systems. In *Proceedings of the 11th Eurographics Workshop on Computer Animation and Simulation*. Springer-Verlag, Aug. 2000.

4 M.G. Calkin. Lagrangian and Hamiltonian mechanics. River Edge, NJ:World Scientific, Singapore, 1996.

5 B. Eberhardt, O. Etzmuβ. Implicit-Explicit Schemes for Fast Animation with Particle Systems. In *Proceedings of the 11th Eurographics Workshop on Computer Animation and Simulation*. Springer-Verlag, Aug. 2000.

6 J. Garrigues. Mécanique des milieux continus en déformations finies. http://esm2.imt-mrs.fr/gar/gd.html, Dec. 2000.

7 L. Landau and E. Lifchitz. Theory of Elasticity. Pergamon Press, London, 1959.

8 Y. Remion, J.M. Nourrit, D. Gillard. Dynamic animation of spline like objects. In *Proceedings of WSCG'99*, pages 426-432, 1999.

9 Y. Remion, J.M. Nourrit, D. Gillard. A dynamic Animation Engine for Spline Like Objects. *Journal of Visualisation and Computer Animation*, 11:17-26, 2000.

10 S. P. Timoshenko and J. N. Goodier. Theory of Elasticity, Third Edition. McGraw-Hill Publishing Company, 1987.

Editors' Note: see Appendix, p. 204 for colored figures of this paper

Deformed Distance Fields for Simulation of Non-Penetrating Flexible Bodies

Susan Fisher   Ming C. Lin

Department of Computer Science
University of North Carolina at Chapel Hill
U. S. A.

Abstract

We present a novel penetration depth estimation algorithm based on the use of deformed distance fields for simulation of non-penetrating flexible bodies. We assume that the continuum of non-rigid models are discretized using standard techniques, such as finite element methods. As the objects deform, the distance fields are deformed accordingly to estimate penetration depth, allowing enforcement of non-penetration constraints between two colliding elastic bodies. Our approach can automatically handle self-penetration and inter-penetration in a uniform manner. We demonstrate its effectiveness on moderately complex animated scenes.

1 Introduction

Due to recent advancements in physically-based modeling, simulation techniques have been increasingly used to improve the quality and efficiency of producing computer animation for major film productions, medical simulation and computer games. These techniques produce animation directly from input objects, simulating natural motions and shape deformations based on mathematical models that specify the physical behavior of characters and complex structures.

Modeling deformation is a key component of physically-based animation, since many real-world objects are not rigid. Some examples include realistic motion generation of articulated characters with passive objects (such as clothing, footwear and other accessories), deformation of soft tissues and organs and interaction among soft or elastic objects. Automatic, predictable and robust simulation of realistic deformation is one of the many challenges in computer animation and medical simulation [8].

One of the most difficult issues in generating realistic motion of non-rigid objects is to simulate contact between between them. When two flexible objects collide, they exert reaction forces on each other resulting in the deformation of both objects. Similarly when one flexible body self collides, multiple portions of the object may deform. The reaction force is called the *contact force*, and where the two surfaces touch is often called the *contact surface*. Simulating such events is non-trivial. It is known as the *contact problem* in computational mechanics, and has been actively investigated for decades [5]. The difficulty of this problem for modeling deformation of non-rigid bodies arises from unclear boundary conditions; neither the contact force nor the position of the contact surface is known a priori.

Ideally, no two objects should share the same space. This is the *non-penetration constraint*. The non-penetration constraint can be imposed using techniques such as constrained optimization techniques or penalty-based methods. Due to dual unknowns in the contact problem for deformable models mentioned above, penalty-based methods are often preferred. When using a penalty based method, a penetration potential energy must first be defined that measures the amount of intersection between two models, or the degree of self-intersection of a deformable body. One of the more accurate measurements of the amount of intersection is the penetration depth, commonly defined as the minimum (translational) distance required to separate two intersecting rigid objects. No general and efficient algorithm for computing penetration depth between two non-convex objects is known. In fact, an $O(n^6)$ time bound can be obtained for computing the Minkowski sum of two *rigid*, non-convex polyhedra to find the minimum penetration depth in 3D [7]. Neither a complexity bound for this problem nor a formal definition of penetration depth for deformable models has yet been established.

1.1 Main Contribution

We present an efficient algorithm based on the use of deformed distance fields for simulating deformation between non-penetrating elastic bodies. The underlying geometric models are composed of polygonal meshes. Models consisting of implicit representations or parametric surfaces, such as NURBS, can be tessellated into polygonal meshes with bounded error.

We assume that each non-rigid body is modeled using finite element methods (FEM) [5] in our current implementation [11], but the algorithm itself is applicable to other discretization techniques, such as finite difference methods or spring-mass systems. We employ the Fast Marching Level Set Method [18, 19] to precompute the internal distance field of each *undeformed* model. When two flexible bodies come into contact and deform, the precomputed distance fields are likewise deformed to compute the estimated penetration depth between two deforming objects. This penetration measure can be incorporated into a penalty-based formulation to enforce the non-penetration constraint between two elastic bodies. This enables efficient computation of contact forces and helps to yield a versatile and robust contact resolution algorithm. We have successfully integrated our penetration depth estimation algorithm to compute collision response of two elastic bodies efficiently. Specifically, our penetration depth estimation algorithm has the following characteristics:

- Both **self-collisions** and **soft object contacts** are handled in a uniform manner.
- **No prior assumption** or knowledge about the locations of contacts is required.
- The algorithm can **trade off accuracy for speed or storage** if desired.

1.2 Organization

The rest of the paper is organized in the following manner. We briefly survey the state of the art in section 2. In section 3, we give an overview of our algorithm and the basic terminologies used in this paper. Section 4 describes the numerical method used to pre-compute the distance field and how it is updated *on the fly* as the objects deform. Section 5 presents our new penetration depth estimation method for deformable objects based on linear interpolation of precomputed distance fields and the resulting collision response. Section 6 describes the system implementation and demonstrates the effectiveness of our algorithm.

2 Related Work

2.1 Penetration Depth Computation

The notion of penetration depth between overlapping objects was introduced by Buckley and Leifer [2] and Cameron and Culley [3]. Several algorithms [7, 9, 15] have been proposed for computing a measure of penetration depth using various definitions. Agarwal, et al. proposed a randomized algorithm that computes penetration depth between two convex polyhedra in $O(m^{\frac{3}{4}+\epsilon}n^{\frac{3}{4}+\epsilon} + m^{1+\epsilon} + n^{1+\epsilon})$ expected time for any constant $\epsilon > 0$ [1], where m and n are the number of vertices of the two polyhedra. However, all existing methods assume that at least one of the input models is a convex polytope.

It is well known that if two polytopes intersect, then the difference of their reference vectors lies in their convolution or Minkowski sum [10]. The problem of penetration depth computation reduces to calculating the minimum distance between the boundary of the Minkowski sum of two polyhedra and a point inside it. However, the construction of the Minkowski sum can be quite expensive. In three-dimensional space, the size can be easily quadratic even for two convex polyhedra. An $O(n^6)$ time bound can be obtained for computing the Minkowski sum of two rigid, non-convex polyhedra to find the minimum penetration depth [7], where n is the number of vertices for each polyhedron. There seems to be little hope to compute the penetration depth at interactive rates based on some of these well-known theoretical algorithms.

Few methods have been proposed to compute the penetration depth for NURBS models or other *non-rigid* model representations. As it stands today, *interactive* computation of penetration depth between two general geometric models of high complexity remains an open research issue.

2.2 Distance Field

Computing the minimum geodesic distance from a point to a surface is a well known complex problem [16]. Osher and Sethian [18, 19], introduced a new perspective on this problem by using a partial differential method to perform curve evolution. Hoff, et al. introduced the use of graphics hardware to compute generalized Voronoi diagram and its corresponding discretized distance field [12]. Recently, this approach has been applied to perform general proximity queries in 2D [13]. Frisken, et al. also presented an adaptive technique to compute distance fields [4].

3 Preliminaries

In this section, we define basic notations and methodologies used in this paper, give a brief overview of the simulation framework used to test our algorithm, and give an outline of our approach for estimating penetration depth between deformable models.

3.1 Discretization Methods

Deformation induces movement of every particle within an object. It can be modeled as a mapping of the positions of all particles in the original object to those in the deformed body. Each point $\mathbf{p}$ is moved by the deformation function $\phi(\cdot)$:

$$\mathbf{p} \to \phi(t, \mathbf{p})$$

where $\mathbf{p}$ represents the original position, and $\phi(t, \mathbf{p})$ represents the position at time t. We limit the discussion to the static analysis here, hence t is omitted: $\mathbf{p} \to \phi(\mathbf{p})$.

Simulating deformation is in fact finding the $\phi(\cdot)$ that satisfies the laws of physics. Since there are an infinite number of particles, $\phi(\cdot)$ has infinite degrees of freedom. In order to model a material's behavior using computer simulation, some type of *discretization* method must be used. For simulation of deformable bodies, spring networks, the finite difference method (FDM), the boundary element method (BEM), and the finite element method (FEM) have all been used for discretization.

3.2 Tetrahedral Elements

In our prototype simulator, we have chosen FEM as the discretization method due to its generality and diversity. The FEM uses a piecewise approximation of the deformation function $\phi(\cdot)$. Each "piece" is called an element, which is defined by several node points. The elements constitute a mesh.

Our algorithm uses a FEM with 4-node tetrahedral elements and linear shape functions. Other non-linear shape functions can be used as well, but the update of the distance field computation as the objects deform will be affected (section 5).

The deformation function $\phi(\cdot)$ maps a point in a tetrahedral element at $\mathbf{p} = [x, y, z]^T$ to a new position $\phi(\mathbf{p})$. As shown in Fig. 1, by definition, $\phi(\cdot)$ moves four nodes of an element from their original positions

$$\mathbf{n_i} = [n_{ix}, n_{iy}, n_{iz}]^T, 1 \le i \le 4,$$

to the new positions

$$\tilde{\mathbf{n}}_\mathbf{i} = [\tilde{n}_{ix}, \tilde{n}_{iy}, \tilde{n}_{iz}]^T, 1 \le i \le 4.$$

The displacements of the four nodes due to deformation is

$$
\begin{aligned}
\mathbf{U_i} &= [U_{ix}, U_{iy}, U_{iz}]^T \\
&= [\tilde{n}_{ix} - n_{ix}, \tilde{n}_{iy} - n_{iy}, \tilde{n}_{iz} - n_{iz}]^T, 1 \le i \le 4.
\end{aligned}
$$

3.3 Simulation Framework

Given the basics of FEM, we reformulate the problem of simulating deformable objects as a constrained minimization problem using Constitutive Law [5]. Details of the simulator are given in [11]. Here we give a brief overview of the simulator used to test our algorithm for computing estimated penetration depth between flexible models:

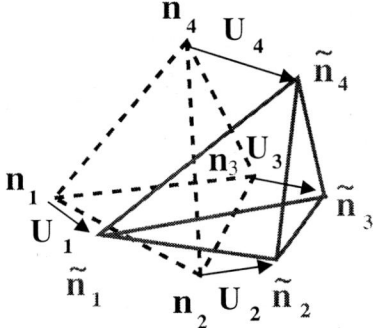

Figure 1: $\phi(\cdot)$ maps four nodes of a tetrahedral element, $n_1, ..., n_4$ to their new position at $\tilde{n}_1, ..., \tilde{n}_4$. $U_1, ..., U_4$ are the corresponding displacement vectors.

1. Generate an internal distance field for each input object using the Fast Marching Level Set Method (sec. 4).

2. Construct a tetrahedral element mesh for each object.

3. Apply finite element analysis:

   (a) Estimate the penetration depth based on the deformed distance fields (sec. 5) for penetration avoidance.

   (b) Minimize the total energy due to deformation, taking into account all material properties and external forces, using our numerical method [11].

4. Incrementally update portions of the distance fields, given the new positions and orientations of the deformed bodies.

3.4 Algorithm Overview

As two objects come into contact and deform, the algorithm uses

1. A *hierarchical sweep-and-prune* [14] when the NURB representations of the models are given;

2. A lazy evaluation of possible intersections using bounding volume hierarchies of axis-aligned bounding boxes [20].

The collision detection module identifies the "regions of potential contacts", as well as the intersecting tetrahedral elements. The intersecting tetrahedral elements are then used to compute the estimated penetration depth based on the pre-assigned distance values at the nodes of each element (sec. 5). This is a fast output-sensitive computation requiring $O(K)$ time, where K is the number of pairs of intersecting tetrahedral elements, and is normally small compared to the number of elements within each model.

Since the pre-assigned distance values at each node of the tetrahedral elements may no longer be valid after the deformation, we need to either recompute or adaptively update these distance values. Since recomputation of the entire internal distance field for each deformed model can be rather expensive, we perform a partial recomputation of distance field only at and near the regions of potential contacts indicated by the collision detection module and FEM simulation. We also ensure the continuity and differentiability of the distance field at the boundary of these regions. The values of updated distance fields are then used for the next simulation step.

This process continues iteratively to estimate the penetration depth between elastic bodies quickly and efficiently during the simulation.

4   Internal Distance Fields

The Fast Marching Level Set Method was first designed to track the evolution of fronts through a 3D space. In our application, the surface of an arbitrary 3D object is treated as a front. The surface is propagated *inwards*, opposite of the direction of the surface normal. As the surface evolves with uniform speed, distance values from the surface are assigned to points on a discretized grid.

The input to the Fast Marching Level Set Method consists of a polygonal mesh. Models consisting of implicit representations or parametric surfaces, such as NURBS, can be tessellated into polygonal meshes with bounded error. The user may also specify the resolution of the 3D grid, trading accuracy for speed. The output of the method is a discretized distance field for the volume encompassed by the 3D surface. In practice, interpolation methods are used when sampling the distance field for penetration depth computations.

Several key terms are used in the presentation of this algorithm. A gridpoint may be marked with one of three labels: ALIVE, NARROW_BAND, or FAR_AWAY. An ALIVE point represents a grid point that has already been assigned a distance value. A NARROW_BAND point represents a point on the evolving front. A FAR_AWAY point represents a point without an assigned distance value.

4.1   Initialization

To compute distance values for an arbitrary object requires initializing the location of the surface within a 3D grid. For each triangle of the polygonal mesh, an axis-aligned bounding box is created. Distance values for each grid point in the bounding box are then defined. When the initialized value is greater than or equal to zero, the grid point lies outside of the object or on the surface. These grid points are marked ALIVE. When the distance value is negative, it lies inside the object, and the grid point is marked NARROW_BAND.

The set of NARROW_BAND points represents those within a neighborhood of the zero level set. Restricting work to only this neighborhood of the zero level set yields a considerable reduction in computational cost. This method of computation is known as the *narrow band approach*, and is discussed in detail in [19].

4.2   Marching

Once the 3D grid has been initialized, the marching phase of the algorithm may commence. At each step, the grid point with the minimum distance value is extracted from the set of NARROW_BAND grid points. The data structure underlying this phase of the algorithm is discussed in section 4.3. Upon selection of the minimum valued NARROW_BAND grid point, it is marked ALIVE, and any FAR_AWAY neighbors are moved to the set of NARROW_BAND points. The distance value for each neighboring

NARROW_BAND point is then updated by solving for T in the following equation, selecting the largest possible solution to the quadratic equation:

$$\frac{1}{F_{ijk}} = \sqrt{M + N + O}$$

where

$$M = (\max(D^{-x}T + \frac{\Delta x}{2}D^{-x-x}T, D^{+x}T + \frac{\Delta x}{2}D^{+x+x}T, 0))^2$$

where the finite differences are given by

$$D^{+x} = \frac{T_{i+1} - T}{\Delta x}$$

$$D^{-x} = \frac{T - T_{i-1}}{\Delta x}$$

$$D^{+x+x} = \frac{T_{i+2} - 2T_{i+1} + T}{2\Delta x}$$

$$D^{-x-x} = \frac{T - 2T_{i-1} + T_{i-2}}{2\Delta x}$$

Similarly,

$$N = (\max(D^{-y}T + \frac{\Delta y}{2}D^{-y-y}T, D^{+y}T + \frac{\Delta y}{2}D^{+y+y}T, 0))^2$$

$$O = (\max(D^{-z}T + \frac{\Delta z}{2}D^{-z-z}T, D^{+z}T + \frac{\Delta z}{2}D^{+z+z}T, 0))^2$$

The term F_{ijk} represents the speed of the propagating front. Because we wish to find the distance from each point to the surface, this value is uniform (constant) in our application. The equations use a second order scheme whenever possible to produce higher accuracy. That is, both T_{i+2} and T_{i+1} must be ALIVE in order to compute D^{+x+x}, D^{+y+y} or D^{+z+z}, where $T_{i+2} > T_{i+1}$. The choice of when to use the second order scheme simply depends on whether two known (ALIVE), monotonically increasing values exist as neighbors of the test point. If not, then the first order scheme is used.

This process of selecting a minimum NARROW_BAND point, marking it ALIVE, and updating neighbors continues until no NARROW_BAND points remain. This algorithm to compute an internal distance field for each object can be summarized as follows:

```
GridPoint G;
InitializeGrid();
heap = BuildHeap();   //NARROW_BAND POINTS
while (heap.isEmpty() != TRUE)
{
        G = heap.extractMin();
        G.status = ALIVE;
        markNeighbors(G);
        updateNeighbors(G);
}
```

4.3 Data Structures

With each step of the algorithm, the minimum valued NARROW_BAND grid point must be extracted. The need for an efficient extraction operation, as well as an efficient insertion operation makes the use of a heap ideal. However, once the minimum valued grid point NARROW_BAND grid point has been identified, the algorithm updates each neighboring point. Thus, in addition to the need for an efficient sorted data structure, we must also retain spatial information.

Our solution is simply to use both a minimum heap structure and a 3D array. Each heap node contains a pointer to the 3D array grid point that it references. Similarly, each NARROW_BAND grid point in the 3D array points to a node in the heap. ALIVE and FAR_AWAY points have NULL pointers as only NARROW_BAND points are included in the heap.

4.4 Partial Update of Distance Field

When an object deforms, the simulator use the collision detection module to quickly identify the neighborhood where partial update of distance field needs to be performed. This information also finds the instances where boundary nodes penetrate other elements.

4.4.1 Collision Detection

For collision detection, we use the *hierarchical sweep-and-prune* described in [14], when the original, corresponding NURB representations of the models are available. Each surface patch is subdivided into smaller patches and represented hierarchically. Each leaf node corresponds to a spline patch whose surface area is less than an input parameter Δ used in generating the polygonal meshes of the patch. The resulting tree has a shallow depth and each node can have multiple children. An axis-aligned bounding box is computed for the control polytope of each patch and dynamically updated. At each level of hierarchy, the sweep-and-prune [6] is used to check for overlap of the projections of the bounding boxes onto $x-, y-, z-$ axes. Only when the boxes overlap in all three dimensions, a potential contact is returned. Coherence is exploited to keep the runtime linear to the number of bounding boxes at each level. The resulting hierarchical sweep-and-prune can be efficiently employed to check for potential overlaps of the hierarchies.

If the NURB representations of the models are not available, we lazily construct the bounding volume hierarchies (BVHs) based on axis-aligned bounding boxes for each model *on the fly* and check for collision between them using these binary BVHs. For more details, we refer the readers to [20].

4.4.2 Lazy Evaluation

Given the regions of potential contacts returned (as one or more bounding boxes) by the collision detection module, we perform partial update of the internal distance field by only recomputing the distance values at each grid point within these regions. With such methods as FEM and finite difference methods, this information is easy to obtain. These methods treat objects volumetrically, and therefore they retain information on how far the effects of deformation have propagated throughout the object.

Given the bounding box, a second 3D grid is created that overlays the first. The algorithm to compute this partial grid is the same algorithm previously described; the savings in computation time comes from the reduction of the number of grid points being computed. Once the marching completes, we combine two sets of computed distance values (one from the precomputation and one from the partial update), while preserving the continuity and differentiability of the solutions that are crucial for computing collision response robustly [11].

In practice, these two separated sets of distance values are almost always continuous. We verify continuity by examining the gradient across the border of the two sets. In rare cases where the distance values are discontinuous, other options are available.

One option is to linear interpolate the two data sets to obtain a continuous solution. This option is only viable when the degree of discontinuity is low. In cases where the resulting data set is highly discontinuous, the entire object is recomputed. In our test applications, this situation never occurred. This is due to the accuracy of the bounding boxes for partial update generated by our collision detection and FEM algorithm.

Without partial updates, the distance field can become less and less accurate due to large deformations as the simulation proceeds. Eventually the accumulated errors in the resulting distance fields can cause visually disturbing artifacts in simulations.

5 Penetration Depth Estimation

When using the penalty based method, we need to first define a penetration potential energy $W_{penet}(\cdot)$ that measures the amount of intersection between two polyhedra, or the degree of self-intersection of a single polyhedron. This definition requires an efficient method to compute it, and its first and second derivatives, for computing the collision response robustly [11].

5.1 Defining the Extent of Intersection

There are several known methods to define the extent of intersection. The node-to-node method is the simplest way to compute $W_{penet}(\cdot)$. This method computes $W_{penet}(\cdot)$ as a function of the distances between sampled points on the boundary of each objects. The drawback of this method is that once a node penetrates boundary polygons, the repulsive force flips its direction, and induces further penetration. Such penetration often occurs in intermediate steps of the aggressive numerical methods. Furthermore, once a node is inside a tetrahedral element, it is no longer clear which boundary polygon the node has actually penetrated.

The most complicated yet accurate method is to use the intersection volume. Using this method, $W_{penet}(\cdot)$ is defined based on the volume of intersection between two penetrating polyhedra. Since polyhedra deform as simulation steps proceed, it is difficult to create and reuse previous data from the original model. Furthermore, it is susceptible to accuracy problems and degenerate contact configurations. As a result, efficient computation of the intersection volume is rather difficult to achieve.

We have chosen a method that provides a balance between the two extremes by computing an *approximate* penetration depth between deformable objects. With our method, $W_{penet}(\cdot)$ is defined as a function of distances between boundary nodes and boundary polygons that the nodes penetrate. We define

$$W_{penet}(\cdot) = k * d^2 \tag{1}$$

where d is the minimum distance from a boundary node to the intruded boundary and k is a penalty constant.

5.2 Estimating Penetration Depth

Suppose a boundary node $\mathbf{m}$ is within an element with nodes $\mathbf{n_1, n_2, n_3}$ and $\mathbf{n_4}$ as shown in Figure 2 (Appendix). Using a linear shape function, $\mathbf{m}$ can be written in terms of linear interpolation of $\mathbf{n_1}, \ldots, \mathbf{n_4}$:

$$\mathbf{m} = u_1\,\mathbf{n_1} + u_2\,\mathbf{n_2} + u_3\,\mathbf{n_3} + (1 - u_1 - u_2 - u_3)\,\mathbf{n_4} \tag{2}$$

Our algorithm estimates the computation of the penetration depth d by replacing it with $\tilde{d}$ at $\mathbf{m}$ using the linear interpolation of pre-assigned distance values:

$$\tilde{d} = u_1\,d_1 + u_2\,d_2 + u_3\,d_3 + (1 - u_1 - u_2 - u_3)\,d_4 \tag{3}$$

where d_1, d_2, d_3 and d_4 are distance values at the four nodes of each tetrahedral element. These distance values are sampled from the distance field generated by the fast marching level set method as described in section 4. u_1, u_2 and u_3 are the interpolation parameters derived from the shape functions of the elements by solving Eqn. 2:

$$[u_1, u_2, u_3]^T = G^{-1}\,[\mathbf{m} - \mathbf{n_4}] \tag{4}$$

where
$$G = [\mathbf{n_1} - \mathbf{n_4}, \mathbf{n_2} - \mathbf{n_4}, \mathbf{n_3} - \mathbf{n_4}]$$

Thus,
$$\tilde{d} = [d_1 - d_4, d_2 - d_4, d_3 - d_4]\,G^{-1}\,[\mathbf{m} - \mathbf{n_4}] + d_4 \tag{5}$$

Once an accurate value of distance is assigned to each node, no matter how the mesh is deformed, the value of $\tilde{d}$ is quickly computed at any point inside the object. Figure 3 (Appendix) shows an example where the distance field of a sphere is quickly re-computed as the sphere deforms.

This approximated distance field shares a few properties with the exact distance field. Some of these properties are essential for proper computation of penalty forces and their derivatives:

1. It vanishes on the boundary polygons.

2. It is twice differentiable inside the elements and C^0 continuous everywhere.

$W_{penet}(\cdot)$ is computed by using $\tilde{d}$ instead of d in Eqn. 1. This algorithm is insensitive to which object (or connected mesh) the nodes $\mathbf{m}$ and $\mathbf{n}$ belong to. Therefore, self-intersections and intersections between two objects are treated in a uniform manner. It is also robust enough to recover from penetrations of significant depth.

6 System Implementation and Results

We have implemented the algorithm described in this paper and have successfully integrated it into a moderately complex simulation with video clips shown at our project website:

http://www.cs.unc.edu/~geom/DDF/

We used Maya developed by Alias|Wavefront to generate the models used in our simulation sequences. We used a public domain mesh generation package, SolidMesh [17], to create tetrahedral elements used in our FEM simulation. Rendering of the simulation results was displayed using OpenGL on a 300MHZ R12000 SGI Infinite Reality.

6.1 System Demonstration

Figure 4 (Appendix) shows a large deformation simulated by our algorithm. Two sets of positional constraints were specified for internal nodes in the head part and the tail part. Given the positional constraints, the head of snake is forced to move toward its tail. The snake model has about 14,000 elements. Our algorithms enables the simulation to automatically generate the natural coiling deformation. It is not obvious from the images, but many small self-penetrations were resolved during the deformation.

Figure 5 (Appendix) are snapshots from a simulation sequence where a snake swallows a deformable red apple from a bowl of fruit. The snake and the apple models have a total of 23,000 elements. Eight major keyframes were used to set the positional constraints. The deformation of the apple and the snake was computed by the simulator using our algorithm to estimate penetration depths between deformable bodies.

6.2 Choice of Grid Resolution

The choice of the grid resolution has a significant effect the runtime performance and accuracy of the distance field computation using fast marching level-set methods. In fact, fast marching level-set methods runs in $O(kn^2)$ worst-case time using the "narrow band approach" [19], given the grid resolution of n x n x n and k is the number of cells in the narrow band. Table 1 gives an example of the computation time using different grid resolutions n x n x n on a sphere of 1000 triangles with the correct distance value of 1.0 at the center of the sphere for the entire distance field vs. updating 1/8 of the distance field.

Resolution	Value at Center	Dist. Field	1/8 D. Field
60x60x60	0.921986	57.4696 sec	2.02469 sec
55x55x55	0.916389	28.9428 sec	1.16319 sec
50x50x50	0.912209	17.4810 sec	0.71547 sec
40x40x40	0.898008	3.81680 sec	0.29566 sec
30x30x30	0.878681	0.52117 sec	0.08658 sec
20x20x20	0.875549	0.10853 sec	0.02734 sec

Table 1: The effect of grid resolutions on the accuracy and performance (in seconds) of a distance field & partial update computations

Note that the computed values for the internal distance field are much more accurate at the regions near the surface of the object. This is appropriate for our application where the penetration is normally not deep. The deviation between the correct distance value and the computed distance value at the center of the sphere indicates the maximum error possible due to the accumulation of numerical inaccuracies, as the level-set computation marching in toward the center.

6.3 Partial Update of Internal Distance Fields

Table 1 also illustrates the performance gain in computing partial updates of the distance field over the recalculation of the entire distance field. The last two columns of Table 1 give the computation time (in seconds) required for computing the entire distance field of the sphere vs. updating only 1/8 of its distance field. The speed up is quite substantial, especially for those with higher grid resolutions. The better performance gain on grids with higher resolution is due to faster cache access for smaller datasets.

The timing (in seconds) for partial update vs. complete recomputation of the distance fields for various models, including a torus, an apple and a deformed sphere is given in Table 2. Note that the torus model with more triangles and the same grid resolution takes less time to compute than a simpler apple model with far less polygons. This is due to the fact that the torus model actually only occupies a small portion of the grids allocated; while the apple occupies majority of the grid space allocated.

Model	Resolution	Tri's	Dist. Field	1/8 D. Field
Torus	50x50x50	2048	1.04334 sec	0.290281 sec
Apple	50x50x50	384	10.6384 sec	0.958958 sec
Sphere	50x50x50	972	5.21021 sec	0.516960 sec

Table 2: Timing (in seconds) on partial update of the distance field vs. the recomputation of the entire distance field

6.4 Discussion

Although our current implementation is based on the use of a FEM simulator [11], our algorithm can be applied to simulation methods using finite difference methods (FDM) and will require little modification. One can replace the linear interpolation step using shape functions of FEM (explained in section 5) with a linear interpolation suitable for FDM. For the spring-mass systems, each mass can be considered as a node of each finite element and the same formulation will apply.

There is some limitation to our approach. Our method computes the internal distance fields within each object. Therefore, it is not best suited for handling self-penetration of very thin objects, such as cloth or hair, which are often encountered in character animation.

7 Summary

In this paper, we present a novel geometric technique, which first precomputes internal distance fields for each object, *deforms* each field *on the fly*, and then later utilizes them for enforcing the non-penetration constraints based on a penalty method. By taking advantage of precomputed distance fields that deform as the finite element mesh deforms, our algorithm enables efficient computation of penalty forces and their derivatives, and yields a versatile and robust contact resolution algorithm.

This algorithm can be useful for many applications, such as simulation of passive deformable tissues in computer animation. It can also be incorporated into medical simulation used for multi-modal image registration, surgical planning and instructional medical illustration.

Acknowledgements

We wish to thank Gentaro Hirota for the use of his simulator and his assistance in testing our algorithm, and the anonymous reviewers for their feedback. This implementation also benefited from discussions with David Adalsteinsson. This research is supported in part by ARO DAAG55-98-1-0322, NSF DMI-9900157, NSF IIS-9821067, ONR N00014-01-1-0067 and Intel.

References

[1] P. Agarwal, L. J. Guibas, S. Har-Peled, A. Rabinovitch, and M. Sharir. Penetration depth of two convex polytopes in 3d. *Nordic J. Computing*, 7:227–240, 2000.

[2] C. E. Buckley and L. J. Leifer. A Proximity Metric For Continuum Path Planning. *Proc. of Int. Conf. on Artificial Intelligence*, 1096-1102, 1985.

[3] S. Cameron and R. K. Culley. Determining the minimum translational distance between two convex polyhedra. *Proceedings of International Conference on Robotics and Automation*, pages 591–596, 1986.

[4] S. Frisken, R. Perry, A. Rockwood, and T. Jones", Adaptively sampled distance fields: a general representation of shapes for computer graphics. *Proc. of ACM SIGGRAPH*, pages 249–254, 2000.

[5] P. G. Ciarlet and J. L. Lions, editors. *HANDBOOK OF NUMERICAL ANALYSIS*, volume I - VI. Elsevier Science B.V., 1994.

[6] J. Cohen, M. Lin, D. Manocha, and M. Ponamgi. I-collide: An interactive and exact collision detection system for large-scale environments. In *Proc. of ACM Interactive 3D Graphics Conference*, pages 189–196, 1995.

[7] D. Dobkin, J. Hershberger, D. Kirkpatrick, and S. Suri. Computing the intersection-depth of polyhedra. *Algorithmica*, 9:518–533, 1993.

[8] S. F. Gibson and B. Mirtich. A survey of deformable modeling in computer graphics. Technical Report Technical Report, Mitsubishi Electric Research Laboratory, 1997.

[9] E.G. Gilbert and C.J. Ong. New distances for the separation and penetration of objects. In *Proceedings of International Conference on Robotics and Automation*, pages 579–586, 1994.

[10] Leonidas J. Guibas and J. Stolfi. Ruler, compass and computer: the design and analysis of geometric algorithms. In R. A. Earnshaw, editor, *Theoretical Foundations of Computer Graphics and CAD*, volume 40 of *NATO ASI Series F*, pages 111–165. Springer-Verlag, 1988.

[11] G. Hirota, S. Fisher, and M. C. Lin. Simulation of nonpenetrating elastic bodies using distance field. Technical report, Department of Computer Science, University of North Carolina, 2000.

[12] K. Hoff, T. Culver, J. Keyser, M. Lin, and D. Manocha. Fast computation of generalized voronoi diagrams using graphics hardware. *Proceedings of ACM SIGGRAPH 1999*, pages 277–286, 1999.

[13] K. Hoff, A. Zaferakis, M. C. Lin, and D. Manocha. Fast and simple geometric proximity queries using graphics hardware. *Proc. of ACM Symposium on Interactive 3D Graphics*, 2001.

[14] M. Hughes, C. Dimattia, M. Lin, and D. Manocha. Efficient and accurate interference detection for polynomial deformation and soft object animation. In *Proceedings of Computer Animation*, pages 155–166, Geneva, Switzerland, 1996.

[15] K. Sridharan, H. E. Stephanou, K. C. Craig and S. S. Keerthi Distance measures on intersecting objects and their applications. In *Information Processing Letters*, Vol. 51, Aug. 1994, pp. 181-188.

[16] R. Kimmel, A. Amir, and A. M. Bruckstein. Finding shortest paths on surfaces using level sets propagation. *IEEE Transactions on Pattern Analysis and Machine Intelligence*, 17(1), 1995.

[17] D.L. Marcum and N.P. Weatherill. Unstructured grid generation using iterative point insertion and local reconnection. *AIAA Journal*, 33(9), September 1995.

[18] S. J. Osher and J. A. SEthian. Fronts propagating with curvature dependent speed: Algorithms based on hamilton-jacobi formulations. *J. of Comp. Phys.*, 1988.

[19] J. A. Sethian. *Level Set Methods and Fast Marching Methods: Evolving Interfaces in Computational Geometry, Fluid Mechanics, Computer Vision, and Materials Science*. Cambridge University Press, 1999.

[20] A. Wilson, E. Larsen, D. Manocha, and M. C. Lin. Partitioning and handling massive models for interactive collision detection. *Computer Graphics Forum (Proc. of Eurographics)*, 18(3):319–329, 1999.

Editors' Note: see Appendix, p. 205 for colored figures of this paper

Real-Time Simulation of Deformation and Fracture of Stiff Materials

Matthias Müller   Leonard McMillan   Julie Dorsey   Robert Jagnow

Laboratory for Computer Science, Massachusetts Institute of Technology

Abstract. Existing techniques for real-time simulation of object deformation are well suited for animating soft materials like human tissue or two-dimensional systems such as cloth. However, simulation of deformation in malleable materials and fracture in brittle materials has only been done offline because the underlying equations of motion are numerically stiff, requiring many small steps in explicit integration schemes. In contrast, the better-behaved implicit integration techniques are more expensive per time step, particularly for volumetric meshes. We present a stable hybrid method for simulating deformation and fracture of materials in real-time. In our system, the effects of impact forces are computed only at discrete collision events. At these impacts, we treat objects as if they are anchored and compute their static equilibrium response using the Finite Element technique. Static analysis is not time-step bound and its stability is independent of the stiffness of the equations. The resulting deformations, or possible fractures, are computed based on internal stress tensors. Between collisions, disconnected objects are treated as rigid bodies. The simulator is demonstrated as part of a system that provides the user with physically-based tools to interactively manipulate 3D models.

1 Introduction

Modeling and simulation of deformable objects has a long history in material sciences and engineering. In computer graphics, deformable objects have been studied for nearly two decades [6], but, with very different objectives. In graphics applications, the primary concern is usually the computational efficiency of generating plausible behaviors, rather than the accurate prediction of exact results. As long as the simulation looks realistic, simplifications are deemed acceptable.

Deformable models have been used across a wide range of computer graphics applications, including the animation of cloth, facial expressions, and general non-rigid models. In these cases, the simulation is typically performed off-line because simulation time is significantly slower than wall clock time.

Another application for deformable models is in real-time systems, such as surgical training and virtual sculpting, where users interactively modify deformable models. In real-time systems, the speed of the simulator and its stability are the two major concerns. One approach toward achieving both performance and robustness is to use simplified physical models, such as mass-spring models [6]. However, it is difficult to express important material properties with these approaches, such as the stress-strain relationship. Alternatively, the computational cost of continuum methods are considerably more expensive but they allow for the modeling of volume conservation and yield stress information that is useful for determining fracture positions and orientations. Continuum models have mainly been used in off-line simulators. Real-time performance has only been achieved in the simulation of soft materials such as human tissue or in the simulation of cloth represented by a 2D mesh.

In this paper, we describe techniques for simulating the deformation of malleable materials, such as soft metals and plastics, and the fracture of brittle materials, such as stone or glass. Our approach employs continuum methods and operates in real-time. We have integrated these techniques into a physically-based animation system for objects represented by volumetric tetrahedral meshes. Simulating the dynamics of such materials is computationally expensive because explicit integration of the equation of motion is stable only for small time steps. The range of possible time steps is bound by the largest natural frequency of the system. In contrast, implicit integration is stable independent of the size of the time step, but at every step, a linear system of equations has to be solved, which makes it computationally much more expensive per time step. Implicit integration as been used in real-time simulation, but only for 2D meshes, such as cloth [1].

We solve these problems by exploiting the fact that the transient behavior of stiff materials can be neglected in a real-time simulation without significant loss of realism. The natural frequencies of stiff materials tend to be higher than the frame rate of the simulator, and these vibration modes are quickly damped, at least visually, by the object's mass. This makes simulation of these high frequency vibrations dispensable. As long as an object is anchored, we only compute its static equilibrium response to forces. No time steps are involved in the process of finding the object's final steady state. By using this approach, we still have access to all the stress information needed to deform the model and/or simulate its fracture. However, static analysis cannot be used to compute the trajectories of disconnected pieces. Because we neglect internal vibrations, we treat disconnected pieces as rigid bodies between impacts. Their trajectories are computed using rigid body dynamics. When a collision occurs, we compute the effect of the impact force using a static analysis. The body is fractured according to its internal stresses, and new bodies are generated if the fracture process causes fragments to become disconnected.

1.1 Related Work

To improve the numerical stability of the simulation of stiff materials Terzopoulos *et al.*[11] proposed a hybrid model that breaks a deformable object into a rigid and a deformable component. The rigid reference body captures the rigid-body motion, while a discretized displacement function gives the location of mesh nodes relative to their position within the rigid body. This method is intended to improve the numerical condition of the underlying equations of motion, however, it does not significantly decrease the computational cost of the simulation. Our approach is similar, but it is hybrid in time. We neglect the displacements from the rigid reference frame between collision events, which makes the simulation both stable and fast. However, when objects collide, we compute the displacements, stresses and fracture bases on a continuous model.

O'Brien *et al.* [7], described a technique for simulating brittle fracture of stiff materials. They discretized the continuum mechanics equations using the Finite Element method based on constant strain tetrahedra. Their use of an explicit integration scheme restricts the time step of the simulation to very small values that are not suitable for real-time animation. Another problem is the crack-tip propagation or growth rate. Because the cracks can only grow one tetrahedron per time step, many iterations are required to break an object in two or more pieces. Our approach is similar in that we use the same continuous model and the constant-strain tetrahedron approximation to compute displacements and stress tensors. However, we solve for static equilibrium configurations rather than integrating the general equation of motion, and we do this only at collision events. We use the orientation of stress tensors to compute fracture planes and cracks, thus making the rate and size of crack propagation independent of the tetrahedral mesh's granularity.

Real-time performance in simulating deformation based on continuous models has been achieved for soft materials such as human tissue for use in virtual surgical training systems. Zhuang [13] uses the Finite Element method to simulate global deformation of human tissue in real-time. However, his explicit integration scheme is appropriate only for soft materials and not suitable for cloth — which is stiff in certain directions — or other stiff materials like plastic or stone.

Baraff *et al.*[1] describe a technique for simulating cloth using an implicit integration scheme. The implicit integration method can take large time steps without loss of stability. However, for every time step, a system of linear equations has to be solved. Cloth is represented as a 2D mesh of triangles. The method is not as well suited for 3D meshes of tetrahedra. First, the number of vertices is substantially larger in a volumetric model, and second, the linear system is not as "banded" as in the 2D case, which makes implicit integration computationally expensive for 3D objects.

Recently, Smith *et al.*[9] have proposed a novel approach for simulating brittle fracture of stiff materials in real-time. They represent objects as a set of point masses connected by distance-preserving linear constraints. The forces exerted by these constraints during impact are computed using Lagrange multipliers. In contrast to our approach, these rigid constraints do not allow for computing object deformations caused by collision forces, nor do they yield strain orientation information that we need for our fast crack propagation procedure.

1.2 Overview

In the next section, we describe the continuous model that we use. We discretize it using the Finite Element method based on constant strain tetrahedra. First we provide an overview of standard techniques to compute static elastic and plastic responses. Then we introduce our new hybrid algorithm to simulate the dynamics of freely moving objects. Then we show how to accelerate the core procedures of the Finite Element method. Last, we present a collection of our results.

2 Modeling Deformation

Our virtual animation system provides tools for manipulating objects. These objects are represented by 3-dimensional tetrahedral meshes. A tool generates a local force field. The shape of that force field depends on the type of tool as well as on the direction and intensity of its application. The task of the physical simulator is to compute the deformation of the object and the fracturing process based on the applied force field.

A variety of models have been used to simulate the behavior of deformable objects. Mass-spring models are simple and fast to compute. However, models that treat objects as a continuum yield a range of important additional information, not to mention results that are more accurate. The deformations of objects in a continuous model are described by a set of partial differential equations. For realistic objects, these equations cannot be solved analytically. The Finite Element method is a standard technique to solve partial differential equations [2]. Here, the object is subdivided into elements of finite size. Over an element, the continuous deformation field is interpolated from deformation values at the nodes. By connecting elements, the deformation field is interpolated over the entire object in piecewise continuous fashion. Instead of solving for a continuous vector field, deformations at discrete points or nodes in the objects have to be computed, and the differential equations at these nodes are treated as set of simultaneous algebraic equations.

2.1 Continuous Model

In one dimension, Hooke's law of elasticity can be stated as follows:

$$\sigma = \frac{\Delta F_n}{\Delta A} = E\frac{\Delta l}{l} = E\varepsilon. \tag{1}$$

The scalar stress σ measures the force ΔF_n applied perpendicular to the surface ΔA. This force causes a deformation (strain) ε of the object measured by the change in length perpendicular to ΔA with respect to the original length of the object. The scalar elasticity Modulus E relates the strain ε to the stress σ.

In three dimensions, forces, orientations of surfaces, and node displacements can be represented as 3-dimensional vectors, and the quantities that relate them, namely σ and ε can be expressed as 3 by 3 matrices. The derivation of these tensors can be found in continuum mechanics textbooks [3]. In this paper, we focus primarily on how these quantities can be computed efficiently. The following equations are very similar to those presented by O'Brien et al. [7], although we have chosen to use matrix notation for reasons of compactness and ease of manipulation. Matrix notation also exposes various symmetries that we will later take advantage of to speed up the computation of forces.

Let $\mathbf{u} = [u_1, u_2, u_3]^T$ be the spatial coordinates of an undeformed object point. The deformation of the object can be described by a function $\mathbf{p}(\mathbf{u}) = [p_1, p_2, p_3]^T$, which maps locations in the undeformed coordinate frame to locations in world coordinates. This function must be differentiable within connected pieces of the object. In three dimensions, there are several ways to measure deformation. One approach is to use Green's strain tensor, which is invariant with respect to rigid body transformations applied to $\mathbf{p}$, and vanishes when the material is not deformed. It is accurate for arbitrary deformations. However, the fact that it is non-linear causes some difficulties that we will treat later. Green's 3 by 3 symmetric tensor reads:

$$\varepsilon = \mathbf{J}_u(\mathbf{p})\mathbf{J}_u^T(\mathbf{p}) - \mathbf{I}, \tag{2}$$

where $\mathbf{J}_u(\mathbf{p})$ is the Jacobian of the vector function $\mathbf{p}$ with respect to the vector $\mathbf{u}$.

Hooke's law relates stress, σ, to the strain, ε. For isotropic materials, this relation can be expressed using only two constants μ and λ, which are the Lamé constants of the material:

$$\sigma = 2\mu\varepsilon + \lambda \text{Trace}(\varepsilon)\mathbf{I} \tag{3}$$

Both the strain and stress tensors are symmetric and functions of the material coordinates $\mathbf{u}$. They are used to compute the elastic potential density, η, as

$$\eta = \frac{1}{2}\text{Trace}(\sigma\varepsilon). \tag{4}$$

The total elastic potential is obtained by integrating η over the volume of the body. According to the principles of energy conservation, the internal work (elastic potential) has to be equal to the external work done by the external forces. Thus, given an external force field, the deformation function $\mathbf{p}$ can be computed as the solution to a partial differential equation.

2.2 Finite Element Formulation

The Finite Element method approximates the deformation function $\mathbf{p}$ as piecewise smooth between discrete elements. The elements can be of arbitrary shape as long as they share nodes and faces with adjacent elements and cover the region of interest. We use tetrahedral meshes because they are simple, flexible and computationally inexpensive. Within a tetrahedron, a linear approximation of $\mathbf{p}$ is used. Such linear deformations yields constant strain and stress tensors within each element. Therefore, these quantities can be moved outside of any integration over an element's volume. Like O'Brien *et al.* [7], we assume constant strain tetrahedra and use barycentric coordinates for interpolating within them. We will restate these formulas and later show how to compute them efficiently as well as show how to compute the static equilibrium using a non-linear strain tensor.

Let $\mathbf{m}_1, \mathbf{m}_2, \mathbf{m}_3, \mathbf{m}_4$ be the coordinates of the four nodes of a tetrahedron in the undeformed material coordinate frame, and let $\mathbf{x}_1, \mathbf{x}_2, \mathbf{x}_3, \mathbf{x}_4$ be their deformed world coordinates. First we need the linear continuous deformation function $\mathbf{p}(\mathbf{u})$ for this tetrahedron, which maps $\mathbf{m}_i$ to its corresponding $\mathbf{x}_i$. Let $\mathbf{b} = [b_1, b_2, b_3, b_4]^T$ be barycentric coordinates defined in terms of the element's nodal positions in the undeformed coordinate frame.

$$\begin{bmatrix} \mathbf{u} \\ 1 \end{bmatrix} = \begin{bmatrix} \mathbf{m}_1 & \mathbf{m}_2 & \mathbf{m}_3 & \mathbf{m}_4 \\ 1 & 1 & 1 & 1 \end{bmatrix} \mathbf{b}. \tag{5}$$

We use these barycentric coordinates $\mathbf{b}$ to identify the interpolated point, $\mathbf{u}$, with its corresponding position in world coordinates, $\mathbf{p}$:

$$\begin{bmatrix} \mathbf{p} \\ 1 \end{bmatrix} = \begin{bmatrix} \mathbf{x}_1 & \mathbf{x}_2 & \mathbf{x}_3 & \mathbf{x}_4 \\ 1 & 1 & 1 & 1 \end{bmatrix} \mathbf{b}. \tag{6}$$

These relations can be combined to define a direct mapping

$$\mathbf{p}(\mathbf{u}) = \begin{bmatrix} \mathbf{x}_1 & \mathbf{x}_2 & \mathbf{x}_3 & \mathbf{x}_4 \\ 1 & 1 & 1 & 1 \end{bmatrix} \beta \begin{bmatrix} \mathbf{u} \\ 1 \end{bmatrix}, \tag{7}$$

where

$$\beta = \begin{bmatrix} \mathbf{m}_1 & \mathbf{m}_2 & \mathbf{m}_3 & \mathbf{m}_4 \\ 1 & 1 & 1 & 1 \end{bmatrix}^{-1}. \tag{8}$$

This defines our linear deformation function $\mathbf{p}$, allowing the computation of the strain tensor, ε, the stress tensor, σ and the potential density η defined in Eq. 2, Eq. 3 and Eq. 4. These terms turn out to be constant within each element.

The elastic force on the ith node, $\mathbf{f}_i$, is defined as the partial derivative with respect to $\mathbf{x}_i$ of the elastic potential density, η, integrated over an element's volume. Using Eq. 4 and Eq. 7 we get

$$\mathbf{f}_i = \frac{v}{2} \beta \mathbf{G} \sigma \mathbf{G}^T \beta^T \mathbf{x}_i, \tag{9}$$

where v is the element's volume in the undeformed coordinate frame and where

$$\mathbf{G} = \begin{bmatrix} 1 & 0 & 0 \\ 0 & 1 & 0 \\ 0 & 0 & 1 \\ 0 & 0 & 0 \end{bmatrix}. \tag{10}$$

In Section 3 we discuss how to compute these force vectors efficiently by exploring symmetry and other properties of the strain and stress tensors.

In order to compute the static equilibrium, we also need to compute the Jacobian of the internal forces and stresses with respect to the nodal positions x_i. First, we rewrite Eq. 9:

$$[\mathbf{f}_1, \mathbf{f}_2, \mathbf{f}_3, \mathbf{f}_4]^T = F'_e(\mathbf{x}_1, .., \mathbf{x}_4). \tag{11}$$

Only the deformed coordinates, $\mathbf{x}_i$, of F'_e vary since the undeformed coordinates $\mathbf{m}_i$ are constant during the animation. The index e represents element number e in the mesh. For technical reasons, we expand F'_e to the unprimed function F_e which has the positions of all N nodes in the mesh as input and produces force vectors for all nodes. It ignores positions of nodes that do not belong to element e and produces zero forces for these nodes. Now, the global function F can be computed as a sum of all the F_e's, as forces coming from adjacent tetrahedra can be added at the nodes

$$[\mathbf{f}_1, .., \mathbf{f}_N]^T = F(\mathbf{x}_1, .., \mathbf{x}_N) = \sum_{e=1}^{E} F_e(\mathbf{x}_1, .., \mathbf{x}_N), \tag{12}$$

or simply, $\mathbf{f} = F(\mathbf{x})$, where $\mathbf{f} = [\mathbf{f}_1, .., \mathbf{f}_N]^T$ and $\mathbf{x} = [\mathbf{x}_1, .., \mathbf{x}_N]^T$.

2.3 Static Analysis

In a static analysis, we solve for the positions of all nodes ($\mathbf{x}$) such that the internal forces $F(\mathbf{x})$ are in balance with the externally applied forces $\mathbf{f}_{\text{ext}}$

$$F(\mathbf{x}_{\text{eq}}) = \mathbf{f}_{\text{ext}}. \tag{13}$$

To compute the coordinates $\mathbf{x}_{\text{eq}}$, we have to solve a nonlinear system of $3N$ equations. The non-linearity of F is due to the fact that we are using a non-linear strain tensor in Eq. 2. The most common method to solve systems of non-linear algebraic equations is the Newton-Raphson iteration [8]. First we replace $F(\mathbf{x})$ by its first-order Taylor series approximation at $\mathbf{x}_k$:

$$F(\mathbf{x}_k + \Delta\mathbf{x}) = F(\mathbf{x}_k) + J(\mathbf{x}_k)\,\Delta\mathbf{x} + O(\|\Delta\mathbf{x}\|^2) \tag{14}$$

where $J \in \mathbb{R}^{3N \times 3N}$ is the Jacobian of F and $J_{ij} = \frac{\partial F_i}{\partial x_j}$. We can now rewrite Eq. 13 as

$$F(\mathbf{x}_{\text{eq}}) = F(\mathbf{x}_k + \Delta\mathbf{x}) \approx F(\mathbf{x}_k) + J(\mathbf{x}_k)\,\Delta\mathbf{x} = \mathbf{f}_{\text{ext}} \tag{15}$$

or

$$J(\mathbf{x}_k)\,\Delta\mathbf{x} = \mathbf{f}_{\text{ext}} - F(\mathbf{x}_k). \tag{16}$$

Given an estimate of $\mathbf{x}_k$ for $\mathbf{x}_{\text{eq}}$, we first evaluate J at position $\mathbf{x}_k$ and solve this linear system for $\Delta\mathbf{x}$ using the iterative Conjugate Gradients method [8]. Then, $\mathbf{x}_{k+1} = \mathbf{x}_k + \Delta\mathbf{x}$ is the next guess for $\mathbf{x}_{\text{eq}}$.

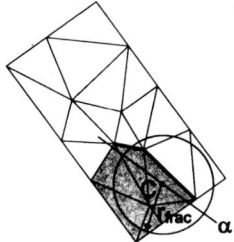

Fig. 1. Tetrahedra within radius r_{frac} from the tetrahedron under tensile stress are marked depending on their position with respect to the fracture plane α

2.4   Simulating Plastic Behavior

So far, our analysis has dealt with only perfectly elastic objects. Such objects remain deformed as long as forces are applied. When the forces are removed, such objects resume their original shape. There is another interesting class of materials that exhibit plastic deformations, such as malleable metals or clay. A perfectly plastic material absorbs the elastic energy. That is, it keeps its deformed shape when the forces are removed.

To simulate the plastic behavior of malleable materials, we use a technique similar to Terzopoulos and Fleischer in [10]. Whenever the deformed coordinates **x** deviate too much from the original shape of the object **m**, we copy the deformed world coordinates to the undeformed coordinates, thereby absorbing the elastic potential energy. Figure 4 (see Appendix) shows a clay teddy bear. The deformations caused by impacts are absorbed and accumulate over time.

2.5   Fracture Modeling

In order to simulate fracture at interactive rates we devised a simplified physically-based method to separate tetrahedra. In the process of computing the forces for the static analysis, the stress tensors for all tetrahedra in the mesh have to be evaluated. The stress tensor σ is a symmetric 3 by 3 matrix and has thus 3 real eigenvalues. These eigenvalues correspond to the principal stresses, and their eigenvectors to the principal stress directions [2]. A positive eigenvalue indicates tension while a negative value represents compression.

The maximum tensile stress criterion assumes that fracture of a material occurs when the maximum tensile stress exceeds a specific stress threshold, which is a material parameter. For all tetrahedra, we evaluate the largest eigenvalue d_{max} of σ. If d_{max} is greater than the fracture threshold of the material, we split the tetrahedral mesh along a plane α perpendicular to the eigenvector of d_{max}. Most isotropic materials break in this way, since this is how the greatest deformation energy is released [5]. Depending on the size of d_{max} and the material type, we determine a radius r_{frac} of impact. All tetrahedra within distance r_{frac} from the greatest stress tetrahedron, where the crack originates in our model, are marked with a plus or a minus depending on whether their center of mass lie on the positive or negative side of the fracture plane α. Then, tetrahedra with opposite signs are disconnected (see Figure 1). We also use the orientation and position of α to split large tetrahedra before the mesh is separated.

O'Brien [7] models fracture by splitting single tetrahedra per time step. A dynamic crack growth simulation over multiple time steps is more accurate than our technique.

However, realistic results can only be achieved with very small time steps because cracks within brittle materials propagate at very high speeds (at approximately the speed of sound within the material) [5]. The crack growth rate of our technique is independent of both, the time step and the granularity of the tetrahedral mesh. Both properties are crucial if the time step size of the simulator does not permit the computation of a more accurate crack propagation. Moreover, the fact that cracks in homogeneous isotropic materials tend to be locally planar [5] justifies our simplified approach.

2.6 Dynamics

Static analysis can only be performed for supported objects. We therefore anchor our models to a ground plane before forces are applied — just as objects have to be fixed to a workbench before they can be machined. For simulating free floating objects, an anchoring method that captures their motion and dynamics is needed. The standard technique for simulating the dynamics of deformable objects is to integrate Newton's equations of motion using numerical methods like Euler's integration scheme. The equations of motion used in conjunction with the Finite Element method have the following form:

$$M\ddot{\mathbf{x}} + C\dot{\mathbf{x}} + F(\mathbf{x}) = \mathbf{f}_{\text{ext}}, \tag{17}$$

where the coordinates $\mathbf{x}$ are functions of time, $\dot{\mathbf{x}}$ and $\ddot{\mathbf{x}}$ their time derivatives, M is the mass matrix and C the damping matrix [4]. At equilibrium, when $\mathbf{x} = \mathbf{x}_{\text{eq}}$, $\ddot{\mathbf{x}} = \mathbf{0}$ and $\dot{\mathbf{x}} = \mathbf{0}$, Eq. 17 becomes Eq. 13. The dynamic equation defines a coupled system of $3N$ ordinary differential equations.

2.7 Hybrid Dynamics

It is possible to simulate a few hundred elements in real-time using implicit integration of Eq. 17 and the fast Jacobian-computation discussed in Section 3. However, for simulating even larger models efficiently, we have devised a hybrid dynamics approach. The key idea is to separate rigid body dynamics from internal effects such as vibration and fracturing. We evaluate elastic forces only during collision events while treating the body as rigid otherwise. This is a reasonable simplification for stiff materials. As discussed previously, the natural frequencies of stiff materials tend to be much higher than rendering frame rates, and these vibrations are quickly damped. Therefore, this approximation has little impact on the visualization. Malleable materials that absorb the deformation energy of collisions can also be modeled using this simplification if we assume that all deformations occur at the instant of contact.

We treat free-floating objects as rigid bodies and compute their dynamic behavior using rigid body dynamics based on explicit Euler integration [12]. Each rigid body has four state variables, its position $\mathbf{x}_{\text{cm}}$, its center of mass velocity $\mathbf{v}_{\text{cm}}$, its rotational orientation A, and, its angular velocity ω. In general, these states can be initialized according to specific user inputs or according to simulation objectives. In the case where a new rigid body can also be generated due to a fracture, the state of all elements in the child components are initialized based on the previous state of the parent object. Each child's state variables are initialized as follows:

$$\begin{aligned}
\mathbf{v}_{\text{cm}}^0 &= \mathbf{v}_{\text{cm}}^p + \omega^p \times (\mathbf{x}_{\text{cm}} - \mathbf{x}_{\text{cm}}^p) \\
A^0 &= \text{Identity} \\
\omega^0 &= \omega^p
\end{aligned} \tag{18}$$

where the superscript p indicates a state value of the parent body.

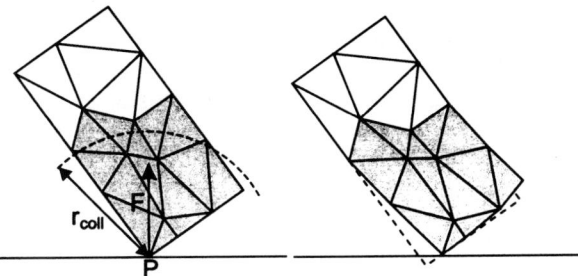

Fig. 2. Only tetrahedra within radius r_{coll} from collision point P are deformed. All other tetrahedra are fixed and support the object for a static analysis

2.8 Collision Response

Whenever a collision occurs, the effect of the impact force **F** on the body is evaluated. Here, our method deviates from a pure rigid body simulation. As a first step, we compute the deformation caused by the collision force using Eq. 13. In rigid body dynamics, the change in impulse $\Delta \mathbf{j}$ is computed rather than a collision force. We evaluate the force as $\mathbf{F} = \Delta \mathbf{j}/\Delta t$, where Δt is a simulation parameter representing the duration of the impact. For a static analysis, the body must be anchored. We fix the positions of all tetrahedra that are further away from collision point P than a distance r_{coll} (see Figure 2). The radius r_{coll} is a user-specified simulation parameter that is typically defined as fraction of the size of the rigid body. Anchored tetrahedra model the effect of the body's inertia.

Once the deformed coordinates are determined, the stress tensors and fracture planes can be computed as described in Section 2.5. After the fracture process, the old body is deleted and one or more child bodies are generated, depending on whether the body gets disconnected. These new bodies inherit dynamic properties from their parent body via Eq. 18.

2.9 Collision Detection

Performing real-time collision detection between deformable rigid bodies proves challenging for a variety of reasons. Vertex positions within a single rigid body are constantly changed as the body is deformed by collision forces. This dynamic characteristic of the data limits possibilities for precomputing efficient data structures. It also creates a potential for intra-object collisions. Furthermore, the rigid bodies in our system are rarely convex, which limits the use of common closest-feature tracking algorithms. Finally, as new bodies are generated by the fracture algorithm, the faces of the new rigid body are in close proximity to the faces of the parent body. Thus, even though the bodies are not in contact with one another, boundary hierarchy algorithms will likely have to traverse the data to each of its leaf nodes and check each pair of neighboring faces for intersection. Bounding hierarchies are efficient when the rigid bodies are separated, but cumbersome during the fracture process, when bodies tend to be closely aligned along irregularly shaped interfaces.

To determine regions of possible collision, we divide our model space into a regular three-dimensional grid, and then walk through all of the rigid bodies, marking each grid cell with the rigid bodies that lie inside. For cells containing multiple rigid bodies, we look for intersections between the vertices of one body and the tetrahedral subvolumes of the other bodies. In practice, the cost of this method does not vary substantially as the positions of the bodies are changed.

The algorithm has two primary shortcomings. First, by only checking for vertex-tetrahedra intersections, it is possible to miss some collision events, such as edge-edge collisions. Furthermore, it ignores intra-object collisions, which occasionally result from substantial model deformation.

3 Implementation

For real-time simulation, fast computation of the core procedures of the Finite Element method is crucial. We have achieved a ten-fold speedup by taking advantages of special properties of the strain and stress tensors.

3.1 Forces

Most of the computing time is spent within the computation of the nodal forces $\mathbf{f}_i$ based on their actual coordinates $\mathbf{x}_i$ in Eq. 9. A direct implementation requires $4 \times 4 \times 3 \times 3 \times 2 = 288$ multiplications. We reduce this number dramatically by first splitting the sum into two parts, the evaluation of 4×4 weights

$$\mathbf{W} = \beta \mathbf{G} \sigma \mathbf{G}^{\mathbf{T}} \beta^{\mathbf{T}} \tag{19}$$

with $\mathbf{G}$ as defined in Eq. 10, and the computation of the force components:

$$\mathbf{f}_i = \frac{\mathrm{vol}}{2} \mathbf{W} \mathbf{x}_i \tag{20}$$

Fist we note that the $\mathbf{f}_i$ are independent of the undeformed position and the orientation of the tetrahedron, which means that we can make $[\mathbf{m}_1, \ldots, \mathbf{m}_4]$ lower triangular via a rotation (as determined by a QR decomposition). This causes β_{00}, β_{01} and β_{10} to be zero. Then we precompute all products $\beta_{ij}\beta_{kl}$. By taking advantage of the symmetry in Eq. 19 and the zero entries, only 45 values need to be computed and stored. This computation can be performed before simulating, or whenever a new tetrahedron is generated.

Second, because the stress tensor is symmetric, we have $w_{ij} = w_{ji}$. The fact that β_{00}, β_{01} and β_{10} are zero cancels out most of the addends in Eq. 19. By unrolling all the loops, and making use of the above observations, we achieved a speedup of 10.

3.2 The Jacobian

For static analysis as well as for implicit integration in a dynamic analysis, the Jacobian J of F is needed. The $3N$ by $3N$ matrix J can be computed by adding the local 12 by 12 matrices J_e of each element. Also, if during the simulation tetrahedra are deleted or generated by the fracturing process, their matrices can be subtracted and added dynamically to the global matrix J. The components of J_e are

$$f'_{ij} = \frac{\partial f_{ij}}{\partial x_{rs}}, \tag{21}$$

where f_{ij} is the jth component of the force vector at the ith node of tetrahedron e and x_{rs} is the sth component of the deformed coordinate of node r ($i, r \in 1 \ldots 4$ and $j, s \in 1 \ldots 3$).

The derivatives of the weights with respect to x_{rs} are

$$\mathbf{W}' = \beta \mathbf{G} \sigma' \mathbf{G}^T \beta^T, \tag{22}$$

where σ' is the the derivative of the stress tensor with respect to x_{rs}. For derivatives of the forces we get

$$f'_{ij} = \frac{\mathrm{vol}}{2}(\mathbf{W}'\mathbf{x}_i + \mathbf{W}\mathbf{x}'_i) \tag{23}$$

Since both σ' and $\mathbf{W}'$ are symmetric, the acceleration methods discussed in the previous section can also be applied to computation of the entries of J, and likewise results in a ten fold speedup.

4 Results

The following examples demonstrate that with our hybrid simulation technique, malleable and brittle objects can be animated in real-time without significant loss of realism. All animations are computed with rates in the range of 5 to 10 frames per second on an SGI Octane 2 (R12000, dual 400 MHz). The integration of the rigid body equations takes between 10 to 20 milliseconds per time step in all the examples. The time to compute deformation and fracture depends on the number of tetrahedra in the object and for our models (1000 - 4000 tetrahedra) varies between 10 and 80 milliseconds. The real-time system can also dynamically texture exposed surfaces without substantially impacting the frame rate. A video demonstration in AVI format can be downloaded from our webpage at graphics.lcs.mit.edu/simulation.

4.1 Vase

The frames from the animation sequences shown in Figure 3 (see Appendix) demonstrate brittle fracture of a china vase composed of 1440 tetrahedra striking the ground. Because of the material properties of the object, the vase fractures with only minimal deformation. Cracks grow instantaneously and separate the body into multiple new objects. The velocities and angular momenta of these objects are derived from the state of the original object as described in Section 2.7. Pictures (a) and (b) of Figure 6 show internal tensile stresses in shades of red.

4.2 Clay Teddy

Figure 4 shows a teddy bear modeled with 3747 tetrahedra. It is made of soft clay that deforms at the instant of impact. The deformations are computed as the static response to collision forces, which are absorbed by the material. After several hits (a), the bear's shape (c) deviates substantially from the undeformed model (b).

4.3 Cinder Blocks

Our third example demonstrates a real-time collision detection sequence in which one cinder block is dropped onto another (see Figure 5. Each block is modeled with 824 tetrahedra. Our system renders solid textures to the exposed surfaces of the blocks, dynamically generating new textures as additional faces are exposed by the fracture process. Figure 6(c) shows the internal stresses at the moment of impact.

124

5 Conclusions

We have described a fast method for simulating the deformation and fracture of malleable and brittle objects in real time. By employing a hybrid simulation strategy that alternates between a rigid body dynamics simulation and a continuum model at the point of impacts, we are able to compute robust solutions to otherwise stiff system equations. Our continuum model finds the static equilibrium of the system after all the initial transient behavior has settled out. The added information provided by this solution allows us to compute plausible deformations and fracturing of an interesting class of plastic and brittle materials.

One limitation of our system is that it only considers deformation and fracture behaviors at the instant of contact. We have also found that the problem of real-time collision detection for object in a near-contact state along a significant boundary, such along a fracture line, is at least as time-consuming as the system simulations. Furthermore, appropriate collision responses are extremely important in judging the realism of an animation.

We are excited by the performance of our current system and we are investigating a range of applications that might benefit from simulation approach. We are planning to use our system in a real-time sculpting environment, within which we are hoping to incorporate more dynamic simulation capabilities.

References

1. D. Baraff and A. Witkin. Large steps in cloth simulation. In *Computer Graphics Proceedings*, Annual Conference Series, pages 43–54. ACM SIGGRAPH, August 1998.
2. K. J. Bathe. *Finite Element Procedures in Engineering Analysis*. Prentice-Hall, New Jersey, 1982.
3. T. J. Chung. *Applied Continuum Mechanics*. Cambridge Univ. Press, NY, 1996.
4. R. D. Cook. *Concepts and Applications of Finite Element Analysis*. John Wiley & Sons, NY, 1981.
5. E. E. Gdoutos. *Fracture Mechanics*. Kluwer Academic Publishers, Netherlands, 1993.
6. S. F. Gibson and B. Mitrich. *A survey of deformable models in computer graphics*. Technical Report TR-97-19, Mitsubishi Electric Research Laboratories, Cambridge, MA, 1997.
7. J. F. O'Brien and J. K. Hodgins. Graphical modeling and animation of brittle fracture. In *Computer Graphics Proceedings*, Annual Conference Series, pages 287–296. ACM SIGGRAPH, August 1999.
8. C. Pozrikidis. *Numerical Computation in Science and Engineering*. Oxford Univ. Press, NY, 1998.
9. J. Smith, A. Witkin, and D. Baraff. Fast and controllable simulation of the shattering of brittle objects. *Computer Graphics Interface*, pages 27–34, May 2000.
10. D. Terzopoulos and K. Fleischer. Modeling inelastic deformation: Viscoelasticity, plasticity, fracture. In *Computer Graphics Proceedings*, Annual Conference Series, pages 269–278. ACM SIGGRAPH, August 1988.
11. D. Terzopoulos and A. Witkin. Physically based models with rigid and deformable components. *IEEE Computer Graphics & Applications*, pages 41–51, November 1988.
12. A. Witkin and D. Baraff. Physically based modeling: Principles and practice. *SIGGRAPH Course notes*, August 1997.
13. Y. Zhuang. *Real-time Simulation of Physically Realistic Global Deformation*. Ph. D. thesis of Univ. of California, CA, 2000.

Editors' Note: see Appendix, p. 206 for colored figures of this paper

5

Hair Animation

A Simple Physics Model to Animate Human Hair Modeled in 2D Strips in Real Time

Chuan Koon Koh and Zhiyong Huang

Department of Computer Science, School of Computing
National University of Singapore, Singapore 117543
Email: {kohchuan | huangzy}@comp.nus.edu.sg

Abstract.
This paper presents a simple Physics model to animate human hair modeled in 2D strips in real time. A major difficulty in animating human hair results from the large number of individual hair strands in a hairstyle. To address this problem, we have presented a framework of human hair modeling based on grouping hair strands into strips. Each hair strip is modeled by one patch of parametric surface. Polygon tessellation and the alpha-mapping using hair textures are then applied. To continue that work, we present a simple Physics model. In particular, a simple dynamic model is adapted and applied to the control point meshes. A set of dynamics equations are defined and solved. The parametric representation of hair strips can handle deformation of any complexity and still appear smooth. Moreover, because the number of control points is much smaller than that of the tessellated triangle vertices, the computation is fast and achieves real time animation. The animation of hair is controlled using event-triggered procedural animation primitives that implement wind, gravity as well as head movement. Inter hair strip collision avoidance is achieved by introducing springs between any two neighboring hair strips. Collision detection and avoidance of hair with other objects is implemented using ellipsoids and reaction constraints.

Keywords: Hair animation, Physically-based modeling

1. Introduction

Hair modeling and animation are very challenging tasks in human animation due to the presence of a large number of hair, the complex interaction of light and shadow amongst them, and the small scale of a hair strand's width compared to an image pixel. Furthermore, the dynamics of hair motion requires some Physics model together with collision detection and response of hair.

Various methods have been employed to model and animate human hair [Anjy92, Chen99, Dald93, Kong99, Neyr98, Wata92]. These approaches concentrate mainly on modeling hair accurately, and often require specialized rendering algorithms. As such, hardware acceleration is unlikely to be available for the above approaches, making them more suitable for off-line graphics systems.

We have presented a strip-based framework that is suitable for real-time applications [Koh00]. The main idea is to model and animate hair in 2D strips. Each hair strip, modeled by one patch of parametric surfaces in particular NURBS, represents a group of hair strands. A variety of shapes may be defined for each strip. For the rendering, we apply alpha-mapping on the tessellated polygons to achieve a realistic visual effect.

However, in [Koh00], animation is achieved by keyframing of the control points of hair strips. It is very difficult to create motion sequences with naturally-looking and Physically-plausible movement. In this paper, we present a simple Physics model to the strip-based hair model. In particular, a simple dynamic model is adapted and applied to the control point meshes. A set of dynamics equations are defined and solved for the control points. The parametric representation of hair strips can handle deformation of any complexity and the results still appear smooth. Moreover, because the number of control points is much smaller than that of the tessellated triangle vertices, the computation is fast and achieves real time animation. The animation of hair is controlled using event-triggered procedural animation primitives that implement wind, gravity as well as head motion. Inter hair strip collision avoidance is achieved by introducing springs between any two neighboring hair strips. Collision avoidance of hair and other objects are implemented using ellipsoids and reaction constraints.

2. Related Work

There are four basic problems to solve in order to produce realistic human hair: hair modeling and creation, hair motion, collision detection and response, and hair rendering [Dald93].

Since all motions are governed by Physical laws, almost all hair animation work is based on different physics models [Terz88]. Two well-known approaches include a method using one-dimensional projective differential equations and pseudo-force fields [Anjy92] and a method using mass spring model [Rose91].

An integrated system for modeling, animating and rendering hair is described in [Dald93]. It uses an interactive module called HairStyler [Thal93] to model the hair segments that represents the hairstyle. Hair motion is simulated using simple differential equations of one-dimensional angular moments as described in [Anjy92]. Collision detection is performed efficiently with a cylindrical representation of the head and body [Kuri93]. Detected collisions between hair strands and the body will respond according to the reaction constraint method [Plat88].

3. A Brief Summary of the Strip-Based Hair Model

To make this paper self-contained, we first brief summarize the strip-hair model [Koh00]. We model hair in 2D strips. The motivation is to reduce the large number of geometric objects when each hair strand is individually represented. A hair strip is a group of hair strands in the shape of thin flat patch (Fig. 1d), which are modeled geometrically by NURBS surfaces. Each surface patch represents one hair strip with different shape and size for different hairstyles. Thus, all the hair strands are represented in layers of strips overlaying each other on top of the scalp. A real-world human head has around 100,000 hair strands. For simplicity, a 3D hair model typically uses less, perhaps around 20,000 strands. A hairstyle will then need around 800,000 line segments if each hair strand uses 40 segments. By modeling hair in strips, each strip will represent tens of hair strands. For a typical hair model shown in Fig. 1, a hair strip is represented by a bi-cubic NURBS patch having 10 control points. The entire hairstyle uses less than 100 hair strips, i.e. less than 1,000 control points.

For rendering, we tessellate the NURBS representation into polygon mesh. The Oslo algorithm is implemented using the multiple knot insertion for the tessellation [Cohe80, Meye91]. If more than a few knots are being inserted at once, the Oslo algorithm is more efficient than the Böhm algorithm [Böhm80]. Finally, texture maps of hair images can be applied on either one or both sides of each surface patch. The alpha map defines transparency and creates an illusion of complex geometry to the otherwise "rectangular" surfaces and adds to the final realism (Fig. 1a, b, c, and e).

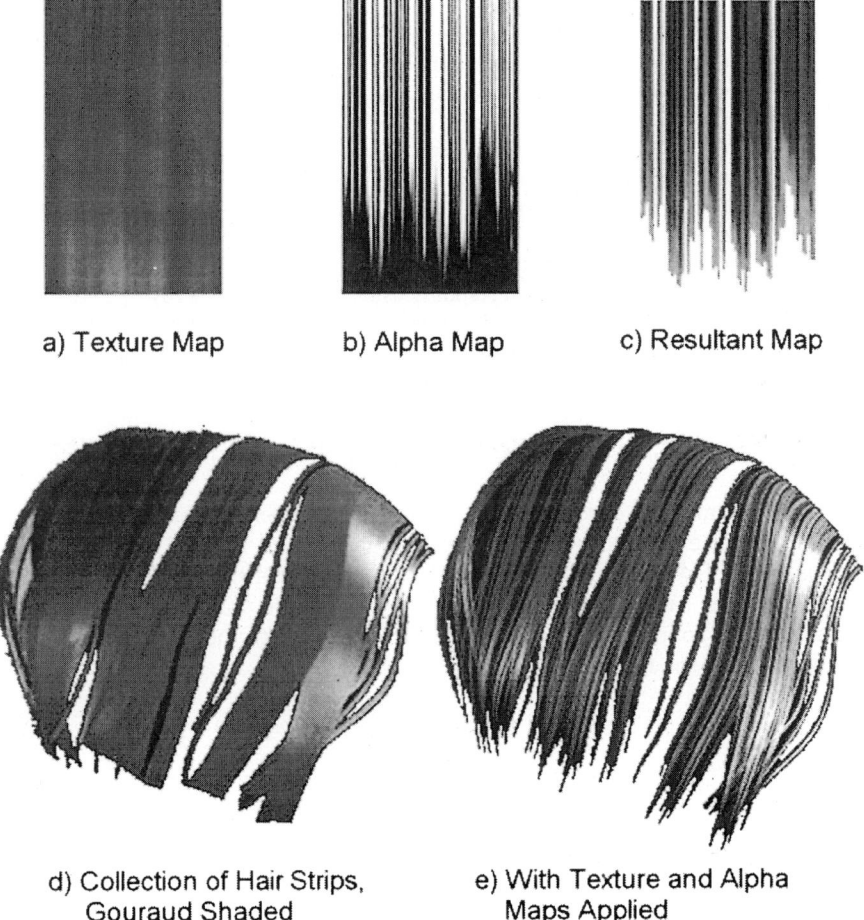

a) Texture Map   b) Alpha Map   c) Resultant Map

d) Collection of Hair Strips,   e) With Texture and Alpha
Gouraud Shaded   Maps Applied

Fig. 1. The Strop-Based Hair Model

4. Hair Animation

In this section, we start to describe our work on hair animation. First we overview the animation process using a pseudo code that indicating the equations to be used. Then, we describe the simple Physics model using equations. Finally, we discuss the collision detection and avoidance in the animation.

4.1 Overview of the Animation Framework

The pseudo code of our animation process is listed as follows:

```
Wait for Event to trigger (Wind, Head motion etc)
At each time step dt
   Perform tessellation to the desired level of detail
   For each hair strand
      For each control point Pᵢ, from top to bottom
         Compute force F₁ due to head movement and gravity
         Compute force F₂ due to wind
         Compute force F₃ due to springs                        (11)
         Compute F_total = F₁ + F₂ + F₃                         (6)
         Break F_total into two components, F_θ total and F_φ total  (5)
         Compute M_θ external and M_φ external                  (4)
         Compute M_θ spring and M_φ spring                      (3)
         Compute M_θ and M_φ                                    (2)
         Compute new position                                   (7)
         Collision detection and response using ellipsoids      (10)
```

The details of equations and symbols used are described in the following subsections.

4.2 The Physics Model for the Strip-Based Hair Model

In this subsection, we describe a simple dynamic model adapted and applied to the control point meshes. A set of dynamics equations are defined and solved for the control points. By working on the control points rather than the mesh points after the tessellation, we can cut the computational cost of the simulation by an order of magnitude. Of course, by working with an approximate model, we are trading the accuracy for the speed [Fig. 2].

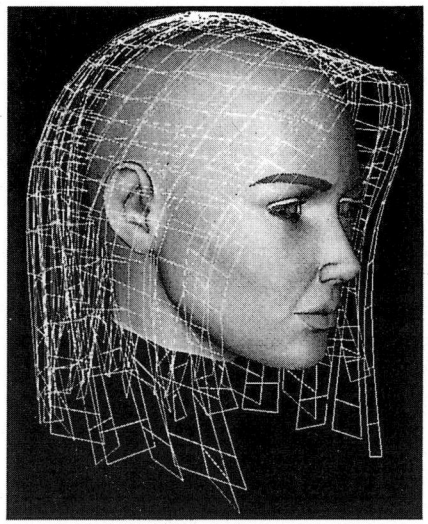

a) Hairstyle using hair strips

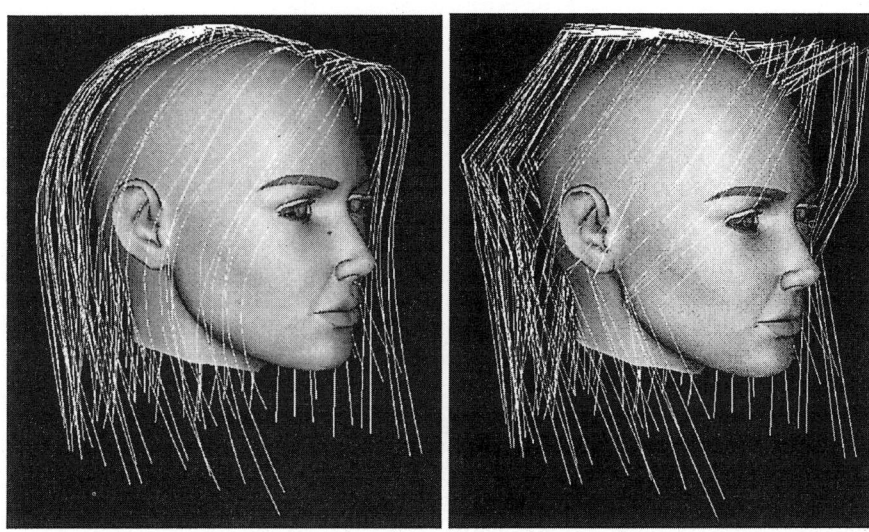

b) Only consider vertical rows   c) Only consider control points

Fig 2. An approximate hair model

The simple Physics model is similar to the model proposed by Anjyo [Anjy92] and later extended by Kurihara [Kuri93]. We brief the major equations by using the illustration of Fig. 3.

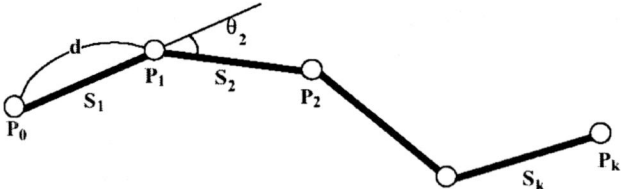

Fig. 3. Illustration of a Single Strand of Hair

Consider a hair strand modeled by a series of connected line segments. Taking the polar coordinate system as shown in Fig. 4, the variables $q_i(t)$ and $f_i(t)$ with time parameter t are governed by the ordinary differential equations:

$$I_i \frac{d^2\theta_i}{dt^2} + \gamma_i \frac{d\theta_i}{dt} = M_\theta,$$

$$I_i \frac{d^2\phi_i}{dt^2} + \gamma_i \frac{d\phi_i}{dt} = M_\phi, \tag{1}$$

where I_i is the moment of inertia of the segment s_i. γ_i is the damping coefficient. M_θ and M_ϕ are the torques according to θ and ϕ components respectively.

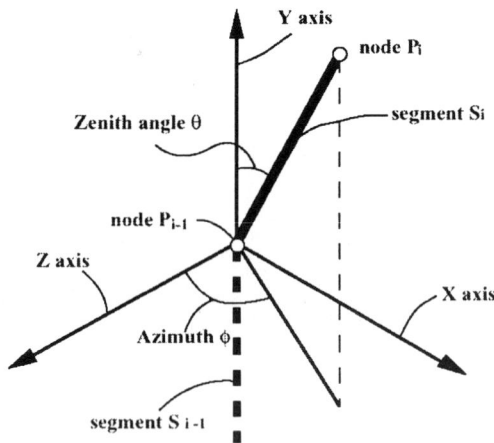

Fig. 4. Polar co-ordinate system for a hair segment

The torque M_θ and M_ϕ applied to the segment s_i are derived from the hinge effect $M_{\theta\ spring}$ and $M_{\phi\ spring}$ between two segments, and external moment $M_{\theta\ external}$ and $M_{\phi\ external}$ from external force, such as gravity, inertial force and wind:

$$M_\theta = M_{\theta\text{ spring}} + M_{\theta\text{ external}},$$
$$M_\phi = M_{\phi\text{ spring}} + M_{\phi\text{ external}}, \qquad (2)$$

$M_{\theta\text{ spring}}$ and $M_{\phi\text{ spring}}$ are defined as

$$M_{\theta\text{ spring}} = -k_\theta(\theta - \theta_0),$$
$$M_{\phi\text{ spring}} = -k_\phi(\phi - \phi_0), \qquad (3)$$

$$M_{\theta\text{ external}} = u\,F_\theta,$$
$$M_{\phi\text{ external}} = v\,F_\phi, \qquad (4)$$

where u is $(1/2)d$, v is the half length of the segment that is the projection of s_i onto the ϕ plane. F_θ and F_ϕ are the "θ, ϕ -components" of force F respectively.

$$F_{\text{total}} = F_{\theta\text{ total}} + F_{\phi\text{ total}}, \qquad (5)$$

The above θ component F_θ of the applied force F is the scalar value defined by $F_\theta = (F, V_\theta)$, where V_θ is the unit vector on the θ plane that is perpendicular to the segment s_i. Similarly, the ϕ component F_ϕ is defined by $F_\phi = (F, V_\phi)$, where V_ϕ is the unit vector on the ϕ plane that is perpendicular to the projected segment of s_i onto the ϕ plane.

The external force F is defined as

$$F = \rho d\,(g + a) + d\,f, \qquad (6)$$

where g is the acceleration due to gravity, a is the acceleration due to the movement of the head itself, and f is the density of the applied force, such as wind.

In the numerical simulation, equation (1) is discretized as

$$\theta_i^{n+1} - 2\theta_i^{n-1} + \gamma_i\Delta t\,(\theta_i^{n} - \theta_i^{n-1}) = (\Delta t)^2\,M_\theta,$$
$$\phi_i^{n+1} - 2\phi_i^{n-1} + \gamma_i\Delta t\,(\phi_i^{n} - \phi_i^{n-1}) = (\Delta t)^2\,M_\phi, \qquad (7)$$

The calculation starts with the segment s_1, and the new angle of s_i is successively determined using (7).

4.3 Collision Detection and Avoidance

In order to properly achieve hair animation, the model must include a collision detection and treatment process. Our model takes into account the two types of collisions involved:

a) Collision avoidance between hair strips and external objects

The goal is to have a quick and robust method to avoid hair strip penetration with the other objects. A set of ellipsoids is used to approximate the bounds for all the external objects (such as head and shoulders). For each ellipsoid, e_o is the origin of the ellipsoid and S is a matrix that transforms a unit sphere from the modelling space to the ellipsoid in the world space with a size, position, and orientation. Detecting the strip-object intersection can be done in the modelling space using spheres. The intersection results can be transformed back to the world space using the inverse matrix of S. Using this method, we can quickly test whether along the animation path the hair strip collides with the bounds of the external objects.

If a hair strip intersects the external objects, the reaction constraint method [Plat88] is applied to keep it outside of the body. Let F_{input} be the applied force to a point P of the hair strip inside an ellipsoid. Then the unconstrained component of F_{input} is

$$F_{unconstrained} = F_{input} - (F_{input} \cdot N) N, \tag{8}$$

where N is the normal vector at the point T, the nearest point on the surface of the ellipsoid to the point P. The constrained force to avoid the collision is

$$F_{constrained} = - (k PT + c V \cdot N) N, \tag{9}$$

where V is the velocity of point P, k is the strength of the constraint, and c is the damping coefficient.

The output force applied to the point P is a summation of $F_{unconstrained}$ and $F_{constrained}$.

$$F_{output} = F_{input} - (F_{input} \cdot N) N - (k PT + c V \cdot N) N, \tag{10}$$

b) Collision avoidance between hair strips

There are two main reasons for this: 1) to avoid visual artifacts from self-intersection and the use of the over-compressed or over-stretched hair strips, and 2) to model the volume effect of the hair. This is done by using springs within each hair strip and between each neighboring hair strips.

For each connected spring s of a control point z,

$$F_z = \Sigma(-k_s * x_s), \tag{11}$$

where k_s is the spring constant (controls stiffness), and x_s is the displacement from the initial rest length. Thus, a repulsion force from the spring is introduced when two strips are closer than a proximity factor. The proximity factor can be adjusted depending on hair density and shape. Similarly, an attractive spring force prevents neighboring hair strips from moving too far away from each other.

5. Results

Our implementation uses Java3D version 1.2.1 on Windows 2000. The hardware platform is a PC with an AMD 900 Duron processor, 256MB RAM, and a Riva TNT graphics chipset. Depending on the complexity of the scene, we can achieve an average of 10 to 20 frames per second using a hairstyle consisting of 100 hair strips.

Four snapshots are shown in Fig. 5. Practically, we have achieved interactive hair animation with collision detection and avoidance. The visual quality is good. Using the latest family of consumer 3D graphics card with the hardware implementation of parametric keyframing, we can have a higher frame rate.

a)

b)

c)

d)

Fig. 5. a) and b) Wind blowing sideways; c) and d) Wind blowing from behind

6. Conclusion

We have proposed and implemented a simple Physics model applied on the control points of the 2D strip-based hair model. Because of the simplicity of the model and much smaller number of control points used in the dynamic simulation, we have achieved the real time animation with the naturally-looking and Physically-plausible results.

By using a 2D strip-based hair model, the volumetric aspect of hair is not directly modeled. However, this is partially compensated by using high quality hair textures with alpha transparency. We feel that the loss in visual quality is a reasonable trade-off for the high frame rate, which can be important in real-time applications such as 3D games and interactive walkthrough of virtual environments.

We are still working on increasing the performance by introducing flocking behavior to the animation of hair strips to further improve the frame rate.

138

7. Acknowledgement

The first author was under the scholarship of PSA Corporation, Singapore. This work was partly supported by the Academic Research Grant (R-252-000-051-112) of National University of Singapore.

Reference

[Anjy92] K. Anjyo, Y. Usami, and T. Kurihura. *A Simple Method For Extracting The Natural Beauty Of Hair*, SIGGRAPH (92), pp. 111-120 (1992).

[Böhm80] W. Böhm. *Insert New Knots into B-spline Curves*, Journal of Computer Aided Design, 12 (4), pp. 199-201 (1980).

[Chen99] L. H. Chen, S. Saeyor, H. Dohi, and M. Ishizuka. *A System of 3D Hair Style Synthesis Based on the Wisp Model*, The Visual Computer, 15 (4), pp. 159-170 (1999).

[Cohe80] E. Cohen, T. Lyche, and R. Risenfeld. *Discrete B-Splines and Subdivision Technique in Computer-Aided Geometric Design and Computer Graphics*, CGIP, 14 (2), pp. 87-111 (1980).

[Dald93] A. Daldegan, T. Kurihara, N. Magnenat Thalmann, and D. Thalmann. *An Integrated System for Modeling, Animating and Rendering Hair*, Proc. Eurographics (93), Computer Graphics Forum, Vol.12, No3, pp.211-221 (1993).

[Koh00] C. K. Koh and Z. Huang, *Real-time Animation of Human Hair Modeled in Strips*, In: Computer Animation and Simulation, Springer-Verlag, pp.101-110 (2000).

[Kong99] W. Kong and M. Nakajima. *Visible Volume Buffer for Efficient Hair Expression and Shadow Generation*, Computer Animation (99), IEEE Computer Society, pp. 58-65 (May 1999).

[Kuri93] T. Kurihara, K. Anjyo, and D. Thalmann. *Hair Animation with Collision Detection*, Models and Techniques in Computer Animation (93), Springer-Verlag, Tokyo, pp. 128-138 (1993).

[Meye91] A. Meyer. *A Linear Time Oslo Algorithm*, TOG (10), pp. 312-318 (1991).

[Neyr98] F. Neyret. *Modeling, Animating, and Rendering Complex Scenes Using Volumetric Textures*, IEEE Transactions on Visualization and Computer Graphics, 4 (1), pp. 55-70 (January-March 1998).

[Plat88] J. C. Platt and A. H. Barr. *Constraint Methods for Flexible Models*, SIGGRAPH (88), pp. 279-288 (1988).

[Rose91] R. E. Rosenblum, W E. Carlson, and I. E. Tripp. *Simulating the Structure and Dynamics of Human Hair: Modeling, Rendering and Animation*. The Journal of Visualization and Computer Animation, 2 (4), pp. 141-148 (1991).

[Tann98] C. C. Tanner, C. J. Migdal, and M. T. Jones. *The Clipmap: A Virtual Mipmap*, SIGGRAPH (98), pp. 151-158 (1998).

[Terz88] D. Terzopoulos and K. Fleischer, *Deformable Models*, The Visual Computer, 4 (6), pp. 306-33 (1998).

[Thal93] N. Magnenat Thalmann and A. Daldegan. *Creating Virtual Fur and Hair Styles for Synthetic Actors*. In Communicating with Virtual Worlds, Springer-Verlag, Tokyo, pp. 358-370 (1993).

[Wata92] Y. Watanabe and Y. Suenaga. *A Trigonal Prism-Based Method For Hair Image Generation*, IEEE CGA, 12 (1), pp. 47-53 (1992).

A Layered Wisp Model for Simulating Interactions inside Long Hair

Eric Plante

Taarna Studios Inc.
Current affiliation: discreet. Eric.Plante@discreet.com

Marie-Paule Cani

iMAGIS-GRAVIR/IMAG, joint lab of CNRS, INPG, INRIA, UJF. Marie-Paule.Cani@imag.fr

Pierre Poulin

Université de Montréal. poulin@iro.umontreal.ca

Abstract. This paper presents a method for animating long hair while modelling both interactions between the hair and the character's body and between different hair wisps. Our method relies on a layered model paradigm. Hair is structured into a number of volumetric wisps whose motion and deformation are computed using a layered model: A first layer, the skeleton curve, computes the large scale motion of a wisp. This skeleton is coated by a second layer, the deformable wisp envelope, linked to the skeleton through highly viscous springs. A third layer is used for rendering the individual hair strands within each wisp. During motion, anisotropic interactions are computed between hair wisps, in addition to interactions with character body: two quasi-parallel wisps are allowed to interpenetrate while a viscous collision is computed between colliding wisps of different orientation. This results in a visually-realistic animation, that captures both continuities and discontinuities that can be observed in thick, long hair.

Keywords: hair, collision detection and response, layered models, physically-based animation, natural phenomena.

1 Introduction

Since the first appearance of synthetic humans in computer graphics, hair has been a major obstacle in producing realistic characters. In particular, the motion of hair is rather difficult to animate, due to the large number of primitives involved (about 100,000 hair strands), and to the complexity of its interactions with the 3D scene and with itself.

Most techniques to animate hair are based on dynamics. One of the first attempts was presented by Rosenblum *et al.* [14]. The movement of each individual hair strand is approximated using a chain of point-masses linked by stiff springs and hinges. The enormous amount of calculation required for their examples limited the number of s-trands to about 1000, which might explain why subsequent research has not followed this approach.

Instead, several researchers [7, 2, 16] have been inspired by an approach introduced by Anjyo *et al.* [3]. The initial position of each strand is determined by a cantilever beam simulation, and its movement is simulated with a set of rigid sticks, only from root to tip. Penetrations of sticks into the character body are detected and avoided during this process. However, since a given stick has no influence on the sticks closer to the root, the motion of a hair strand cannot be adequately modified during a collision. Most researchers simply avoid the problem by animating only short hair that do not reach the shoulders.

Watanabe and Suenaga [19] were the first ones to take advantage of the coherence in the movement of hair by animating wisps of hair. They were followed by Kim [11] and by Koh [12], who respectively modelled wisps using thin-shell volumes and semi-transparent polygon strips. None of these methods use physically-based animation of wisps. They mainly focus on improving the aspect of hair, and easing the modelling of hair-styles.

For approaches based on dynamics, coherence in hair motion has been exploited by animating only a few strand guides, and interpolating the motion of the strands in between [7]. However, this approach only detects collisions between the guides and the character, causing interpolated strands to possibly penetrate surfaces. This happens when initially neighboring guides end up on opposite sides of the head. A solution for modelling hair strands that avoid obstacles is to attach them to the streamlines of a fluid flow [9]. However, this technique generates neighboring hair that always have the same orientation, and thus fail to capture the case when two wisps of different orientations collide. Both the interpolation and the fluid flow approaches can lead to animations that appear too continuous, restricting these methods to fairly straight and clean hair.

The very nature of the previous approaches has caused researchers to ignore phenomena which have a great influence on the movement of hair, namely hair self-interactions in the form of inelastic collisions and friction between hair strands. With these methods, the kinetic energy is not sufficiently dissipated, and the hair does not tend to come back to its rest density after compression. This explains why computer generated hair always seems too "light" and lacks "volume". In later works from Hadap *et al.* [10], the problem of volume is addressed thanks to their fluid continuum approach, yet the strong discontinuities typical of long hair in movement are still absent.

2 Overview

Similarly to previous techniques, our hair motion is derived from physically-based animation. In doing so, our goal is not one of exact physical correctness, but instead, of increased visual realism obtained within a reasonable amount of computation time. We believe that modelling the complex interactions that occur both within the hair and between the hair and obstacles is a key step towards this goal.

It is generally accepted that the movement of hair strands should be approximated by calculations at a coarser level. Perhaps the inherent difficulties of previous techniques can be explained by the underlying assumption that this coarser level is still a single hair strand. They animate a few strands from which they deduce the positions of others. The approach we present in this paper breaks away from animating individual strands. Instead, we cluster groups of strands into wisps, modelled as anisotropic viscous volumes.

Since the wisp provides the coarser level of computation required to attain reasonable calculation times, all wisps can be animated, and thus the aforementioned disadvantages of interpolation are avoided. Our approach allows for more precise and efficient collision detection with the character's body, and can model the discontinuities easily observed in thick, long hair. Most importantly, complex hair interactions are simulated easily and relatively efficiently, by modelling their effects on both the shape and the motion of wisps.

The next section presents our model for hair wisps. Section 4 explains how wisps are used for processing interactions. Implementation details and results are given in Section 5. We finally conclude and discuss future directions.

3 A Layered Model for Hair Wisps

Interactions seem to be a dominent factor in hair motion, since each hair strand is always in contact with others. However, simulating collisions and friction between 100,000 hair strands would be prohibitively expensive. This paper is based on the idea of structuring hair into a number of deformable wisps. Each wisp, modelled as a viscous volume, simulates the motion of neighboring hair strands of similar orientations, subject to friction with one another. Wisps are also used for processing other interactions inside hair at a coarser level. This section details the layered model we use for a wisp.

3.1 Modelling a Hair Wisp

Defining layered models [6] is a very good way of modelling complex objects to animate. Such models decrease the complexity of the phenomena to model by structuring the object into a small set of distinct layers that may interact together. The different aspects of the model, embedded into different layers, may be simulated and controlled at totally different scales. This paradigm has been used, for instance, for modelling animated characters [6, 15], and for simulating a variety of complex deformable bodies [17, 5]. Most often, one of the layers is used for capturing high scale motion, another one models deformations, and a third defines the geometry to render. We are using the same kind of paradigm for animating hair wisps.

In our model, a wisp is structured into:

1. A *skeleton curve* that defines its large-scale motion and deformations.
2. A deformable *envelope* that coats the skeleton, and defines the deformation of the wisp sections around it.
3. A certain number of *hair strands* that are distributed inside the wisp envelope and that are only used at the rendering stage of the process.

The remainder of this section details these layers.

3.2 Wisp Skeleton

In our model, the general (global) movement and deformation of a wisp is modelled by its skeleton, which defines a curve in space. We animate this curve using point dynamics, thus neglecting the dynamic twisting of hair wisps. This approximation is acceptable since wisps of hair offer a relatively strong resistance to torsion.

The first segment of the wisp skeleton is not part of the simulation: It is set to penetrate inside the character's head, and thus provides a reference point that always stays outside the head.

Instead of using a chain of rigid links for the remaining part of the skeleton, as in most previous approaches [3, 7, 2, 16], we use a chain of point-masses linked by linear damped springs, thus modelling wisps of varying lengths. This allows to simulate wavy and curly hair, whose wisps can stretch, as well as almost straight hair. However, we should keep in mind that using a rigid sticks animation, although less general with respect to the kind of hair that can be modelled, would have optimized the computations for straight, and therefore completely inextensible wisps.

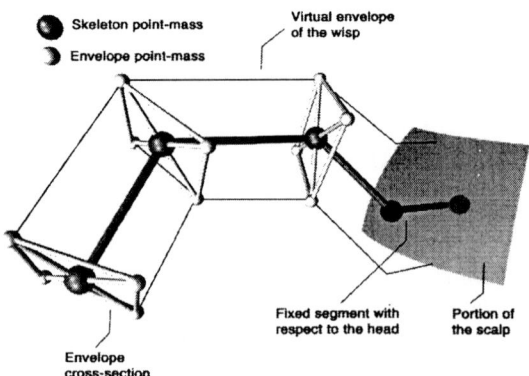

Fig. 1. The elements defining the skeleton and the envelope of a wisp, and their configuration.

In addition to the spring forces along the wisp axis, forces are introduced to simulate a certain resistance to bending, depending of the wisp's thickness. This is achieved with a damped spring for which the force increases linearly with the bending angle. The general configuration of the elements of a skeleton is illustrated in Figure 1.

3.3 Wisp Envelope

The second layer in our model is aimed at modelling radial wisp deformations around the skeleton. Thanks to this layer, the tip of a single swinging wisp will adequately squash and stretch during motion, due to the action of gravity and of air friction forces. Wisp sections will also be adequately compressed during interactions with other wisps or with the character's model.

Since different wisp deformations will occur along the skeleton, we discretize the wisp envelope into a given number of *cross-sections*, each of them being associated with one of the skeleton point-masses. The cross-section lies in the plane bisecting the two skeleton segments adjacent to that point-mass, similarly to what was done for defining the skin envelope control cross-section by Shen and Thalmann [15] (see Figure 1).

A coherent set of 2D frames for the cross sections along a wisp skeleton is needed to position the points modelling the wisp envelope. While designing the wisp skeleton model, we chose to rely on point dynamics only, so such local frames are not provided by the skeleton structure. However, a simple method can be used for recursively generating these frames since we are not modelling twisting effetcs: we attach the first local frame, associated with the first point of the wisp skeleton, to the head. Then, we successively define the other local frames using the quaternion that minimally rotates a given cross section plane onto the next one. This solution completely avoids twisting effects when a wisp moves, which is, as stated earlier, a desirable effect.

The wisp envelope models *radial deformations* only. We model each cross-section using a number of *envelope point-masses*, whose motion is restricted to a given half line of the cross-section plane originating at the skeleton point-mass. Each envelope point-mass thus controls the deformation of the envelope at a constant position over its surface. The envelope point-masses are much lighter than the associated skeleton point-mass, since they represent a small number of strands located near the envelope.

They are linked to the associated skeleton point-mass by non-linear damped springs that model the way the wisp resists to compression, and, to a lower extend, resists to stretching (the latter is due to high friction forces between the hair strands within a wisp). The choice of non-linear springs allows to model the fact that a wisp becomes progressively stiffer during a compression. Envelope point-masses of the same cross section are also linked together by soft, highly damped springs. This ensures a certain conservation of volume, encouraging the wisp to stretch in one radial direction if it is compressed in the other. Figure 1 illustrates the structures of a wisp.

3.4 Hair Strands

A third layer is used for rendering the individual hair strands within each wisp. The idea is to draw hair strand curves at fixed postions with respect with the wisp envelope. The strands will thus move and deform according to the wisp's current local deformations, while ensuring temporal coherence.

The large number of hair strands prevents us from storing much related data for each strand. We rely instead on the pseudo-random number generator for defining the hair stand position inside a wisp while ensuring the required frame-to-frame coherence. Because the number of random values required for modelling the hair is always the same, we can reset the seed of the random number generator at the beginning of every frame, thus providing the necessary coherence. Details on hair strand generation are given in Section 5.

4 Anisotropic Interactions

The idea of clustering hair strands into a number of wisps greatly simplifies interaction processing. In addition to modelling the effect of friction forces between neighboring hair strands of similar orientations, wisps provide an adequate level of detail for approximating other self-interactions inside the hair, and for computing interactions between hair and the character body (or any other obstacle). Since direct modification of velocities and positions has proven useful for processing the interactions of very light material such as cloth [4, 8, 18], we use similar solutions for hair.

4.1 Interactions between Wisps

Interaction detection relies on a standard 3D grid data structure for quickly determining a shorter list of wisp segments susceptible to intersect at a given time step. A mailbox parameter [1], which indicates the last time step when a given pair of such segments has been tested, ensures that each pair is tested only once. Collision detection between two wisp segments is achieved first by comparing their bounding boxes. If they intersect, a collision is detected when at least one of the skeleton or envelope point-masses of a wisp segment penetrates inside the volume of the other one. This volume is defined by its two cross sections.[1] Wisps self-collisions are handled exactly the same way than collisions between two different wisps of hair.

Wisps are highly anisotropic, since they are just a virtual representation for a group of hair strands. While two perpendicular colliding wisps should be compressed in order to avoid intersection, interpenetration has to be allowed between neighboring wisps

---

[1]Because our wisps segments are mostly as wide as they are long, this simple and efficient intersection scheme has appeared sufficient.

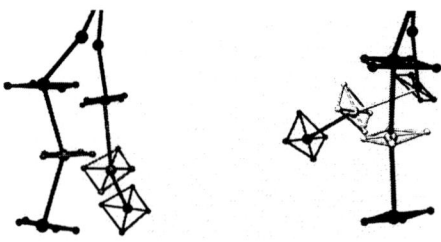

Fig. 2. On the left, the two wisps will interpenetrate, producing viscous friction, while on the right, whey will collide.

of similar orientations and velocities. Another major feature of hair self-interactions is that they are highly dissipative, since the extreme lightness of hair strands causes friction forces to play a very important role. The way we respond to wisp interactions is described next.

Viscous friction between quasi-parallel wisps. If the orientations of the two wisp segments lie in the same plane, and if their relative velocity is also roughly in this plane, wisps are allowed to interpenetrate (see Figure 2). Since the hair strands of the wisps should not go through each other during interpenetration, we eliminate the residual relative velocity lying outside the plane. This is done with a velocity modification.

Suppose a point-mass at position $\mathbf{p_p}$, moving at velocity $\mathbf{v_p}$, has penetrated in a wisp segment whose velocity is $\mathbf{v_s}$ at this same position $\mathbf{p_p}$. Let $\sigma_\mathbf{p}$ and $\sigma_\mathbf{s}$ be the directions of the two wisp skeletons near $\mathbf{p_p}$. The direction $\sigma_\mathbf{p} \times \sigma_\mathbf{s}$ is normal to the plane containing both wisps, and the relative velocity to eliminate is $(\mathbf{v_p} - \mathbf{v_s}) \cdot (\sigma_\mathbf{p} \times \sigma_\mathbf{s})$. We do this by applying to the point-mass the velocity modification:

$$\Delta \mathbf{v_p} = -\left(\frac{(\mathbf{v_p} - \mathbf{v_s}) \cdot (\sigma_\mathbf{p} \times \sigma_\mathbf{s})}{2} \right) (\sigma_\mathbf{p} \times \sigma_\mathbf{s})$$

Since similar modifications will be applied to point-masses of the other wisp at the same time step, this operation sets the velocities of the two wisps outside the plane that contains them, to the average of their initial values.

In addition, the relative velocity of the two wisps in the plane that contains them is submitted to a viscous drag, approximating the friction of the strands against each other. This drag is again implemented through a direct velocity modification, proportional to the hair strand density at position $\mathbf{p_p}$ and to the time step.

Collision between wisps of different orientations. If viscous friction conditions are not met, a very dissipative collision is modelled. We simply eliminate the relative velocities of the point-masses located in the contact area. Similarly to the viscous friction case, we use velocity modifications to set the velocities to the average of their initial values.

4.2   Collisions with the Character

The 3D grid data structure used for optimizing collision detection between wisps is also used to reference the polygons of the character for quickly detecting if a point-mass is close to the character.

Sliding Contact. If a point-mass moves closer to the character's surface than a user-specified threshold, then the part of the relative velocity approching the point-mass to the surface is eliminated. A viscous drag is added between the tangential velocity of the wisp point-mass with respect to the surface and the velocity of the polygon, in order to model viscous friction.

Penetration Reaction. If the character moves fast, the sliding contact mechanism may not be sufficient for preventing some wisp point-masses from penetrating inside the model. Detecting these points is simplified by the specific order in which we process each wisp: A wisp is traversed from root to tip, each skeleton point-mass being processed before its associated envelope point-masses. Since the point-mass at the top of the wisp skeleton is guaranteed to be outside the character, any intersection between a polygon of the character and a radial or axial spring of the wisp model means that the point-mass at the extremity of the current spring has moved into the character.

If collision occurs for a skeleton point-mass, it is moved out from the surface at a distance slightly under the sliding contact threshold. If penetration occurs for an envelope point-mass, it is moved out to the surface of the character along the half line it is constrained to lie on. The sliding contact mechanism is then engaged with the nearest polygon, resulting in a completely inelastic collision.

5 Implementation and Results

5.1 Algorithm for the Animation

As stressed in Section 3, we would like to take into account the effect of local thickness variations of the wisp envelope on subsequent wisp skeleton motion. So rather than decoupling the animation of the two sub-models, we animate all the point-masses within the same loop, enabling an envelope point-mass and a skeleton point-mass to interact through the radial damped spring that connects them.

Due to our interaction processing mechanism, constraints yielding velocity and position modifications have to be allowed. We thus use the following algorithm for the animation:

1. Compute the set of applied forces; these forces include gravity, air resistance, and forces generated by springs;
2. Detect interactions between pairs of wisps, and between wisps and the character's model;
3. Process velocities, using the current velocity values and applied forces; then apply the velocity modifications;
4. Process positions, using the current position and the new velocity; then apply the position modifications.

At each step, all point-masses are processed before going to the next step. A given wisp of hair is processed from root to tip, the envelope point-masses being processed after their associated skeleton point-mass. For envelope points, only forces, velocity modifications and position modifications projected onto the permitted axis, defined in the newly computed cross-section plane, are allowed.

146

Fig. 3. Our model (left) captures both continuities and discontinuities that can be observed in real long hair motion.

5.2 Individual Hair Strand Generation

In practice, we use only four envelope mass-points for modelling the cross-sections of wisps. A cross-section defines a 2D coordinate system whose origin is the skeleton point-mass, and the four envelope point-masses determine the orthogonal axes and s-caling factors. A set of 2D points, one per hair strand in the wisp, are generated in a circle according to a given distribution. This set is translated and scaled in 3D for each cross-section in the wisp. The 3D points resulting from a 2D point from this set are then linked to form the control points of a Catmull-Rom piecewise cubic curve defining a hair strand. The first and last control points are duplicated so the curve goes through all the control points. In order to prevent any pattern from appearing in the strands of a wisp, a user-specified jittering is applied to each control point, moving it towards its skeleton point-mass. Jittering is also applied to reduce the total length of the strand. Any strand therefore always remains within the wisp envelope.

Wavy hair can be obtained by specifying the number of hair-strand waves as well as their amplitude when the wisp's radius is at rest. Then, if a wisp segment stretches due to gravity for example, the amplitude is scaled down. The waves frequency is scaled too so that the number of waves in the segment is maintained.

5.3 Results

Our results are shown at www-imagis.imag.fr/Membres/Marie-Paule.Cani/hair.html Figure 5.3 (right) shows a frame of a motion tracking session. It illustrates the complex nature of hair motion, where wisps are easily observed. The data acquired from this session was then applied on a synthetic character with three different hair lengths (short, medium, and long). The short hair style is composed of 199 wisps with 4.0 segments per wisp. The medium hair style is composed of 73 wisps with 9.9 segment per wisp in average. The long hair style, of 56 wisps with 7.7 segments. In the three hair styles, from which a frame is displayed in Figure 4, wisps are usually fairly wide. On average, a wisp segment intersects 17.5 other segments in the short hair style, 21.0 in the medium hair style, and 12.8 in the long hair style.

All three simulations, available from our web site, were computed at 1000 Hz using standard explicit integration, but collision detection was computed at 120 Hz, and wisps self-interactions at 24 Hz. Even with this choice, 92 to 95% of the total computation time was spent on detecting wisps self-interactions (64 to 70% of this percentage) and

Fig. 4. Results with various hair lengths.

wisps collisions with the character (30 to 36%). The total animation times[2] (264 frames) were 3.2 hours for the short hair style and 2.9 hours for the medium and the long hair styles.

These statistics confirm that the complete treatment of wisp interactions is the most significant portion of the total computation time in our simulation of hair motion. Avoiding the simulation at 1000 Hz thanks to implicit integration would probably improve performances, but not improve them as much, since the collision processing cost would remain.

6 Conclusion

Most previous models for hair animation have focussed on animating straight light hair, and resulted into very continuous shapes since almost no interactions were modeled. We have presented an alternative approach that precisely models the deformations and discontinuities due to the multiple interactions that occur in long, possibly wavy, hair.

The main feature of our model is to cluster hair into a number of deformable volumes representing hair wisps. We use a layered model including a skeleton and a deformable envelope for animating each of these wisps. The skeleton captures the global motion and the axial elongation of a wisp, while the envelope models the local radial deformations of its cross-sections. At each animation step, the two layers exchange informations since the envelope, which is positioned around the current position of the skeleton, is used to process interactions.

The method currently handles both straight and wavy hair. Similarly, curly hair could be modelled using a static twisting of the hair strands drawn inside each wisp.

We have seen that our model neglects the effects of dynamic twisting of hair wisps. A more general hair model would be obtained by replacing the standard point-masses used in the wisp skeleton model by a set of oriented particles [13], defining local coordinates systems in which the wisp cross-sections would be defined. This would allow to model a wisp that twists along its axis, which is currently impossible with our model. Moreover, the specific "shape-memory" forces in oriented-particle systems would allow the modelling of different hair styles. However, this solution would increase the computational time.

---

[2] All statistics were acquired on an SGI O2 with one R12000 processor at 270 MHz.

Acknowledgments

We would like to thank Arash Habibi of Université Louis Pasteur, for his help in the early stages of this work. This research has been made possible through an NSERC Industry Partnership Grant with Taarna Studios, inc. It also benefited from a grant from the "Centre Jacques Cartier".

References

1. J. Amanatides and A. Woo. A fast voxel traversal algorithm for ray tracing. In *Eurographics '87*, pages 3–10, August 1987.
2. M. Ando and S. Morishima. Expression and motion control of hair using fast collision detection methods. In *Image Analysis Applications and Computer Graphics. Third International Computer Science Conference. ICSC '95 proceedings*, pages 463–470, 1995.
3. K. Anjyo, Y. Usami, and T. Kurihara. A simple method for extracting the natural beauty of hair. In *Computer Graphics (SIGGRAPH '92 Proceedings)*, volume 26, pages 111–120, July 1992.
4. D. Baraff and A. Witkin. Large steps in cloth simulation. In *SIGGRAPH 98 Conference Proceedings*, Annual Conference Series, pages 43–54. ACM SIGGRAPH, July 1998.
5. M.-P. Cani-Gascuel, A. Verrout, and C. Puech. Animation and collisions between complex deformable bodies. In *Graphics Interface '91*, pages 263–270, June 1991.
6. J.E. Chadwick, D.R. Haumann, and R.E. Parent. Layered construction for deformable animated characters. In *Computer Graphics (SIGGRAPH '89 Proceedings)*, volume 23, pages 243–252, July 1989.
7. A. Daldegan, N. Magnenat-Thalmann, T. Kurihara, and D. Thalmann. An integrated system for modeling, animating and rendering hair. In *Eurographics '93*, volume 12, pages 211–221, 1993.
8. M. Desbrun, P. Schroeder, and A. Barr. Interactive animation of structured deformable objects. In *Graphics Interface '99*, pages 1–8, June 1999.
9. S. Hadap and N. Magnenat-Thalmann. Interactive hair styler based on fluid flow. In *Computer Animation and Simulation '00*, pages 87–100, August 2000.
10. S Hadap and N. Magnenat-Thalmann. Modeling dynamic hair as a continuum. 2001. to appear in Eurographics 2001.
11. T-Y. Kim and U. Neumann. A thin shell volume for modelling human hair. In *Computer Animation '00*, pages 121 – 128, May 2000.
12. C. Koh and Z. Huang. Real-time animation of human hair modeled in strips. In *Computer Animation and Simulation '00*, pages 101–112, August 2000.
13. J.-C. Lombardo and C. Puech. Oriented particles: A tool for shape memory objects modelling. In *Graphics Interface '95*, pages 255–262, 1995.
14. R.E. Rosenblum, W.E. Carlson, and E. Tripp. Simulating the structure and dynamics of human hair: Modelling, rendering and animation. *The Journal of Visualization and Computer Animation*, 2(4):141–148, 1991.
15. J. Shen and D. Thalmann. Interactive shape design using metaballs and splines. In *Implicit Surfaces '95*, pages 187–196, April 1995.
16. Z.-C. Shih and H.-D. Guo. The modeling and animation of human hair. *The Journal of Information Science and Engineering*, 11(3):465–488, 1995.
17. D. Terzopoulos and A. Witkin. Physically based models with rigid and deformable components. *IEEE Computer Graphics and Applications*, 8(6):41–51, November 1988.
18. P. Volino and N. Magnenat-Thalmann. Accurate collision response on polygonal meshes. In *Computer Animation '00*, pages 179–188, May 2000.
19. Y. Watanabe and Y. Suenaga. A trigonal prism-based method for hair image generation. *IEEE Computer Graphics and Applications*, 12(1):47–53, January 1992.

6

High Level Motion Planning

Efficient Multi-Agent Path Planning

Okan Arikan
University of California at Berkeley

Stephen Chenney
University of Wisconsin at Madison

D.A. Forsyth
University of California at Berkeley

Abstract.   Animating goal-driven agents in an environment with obstacles is a time consuming process, particularly when the number of agents is large. In this paper, we introduce an efficient algorithm that creates path plans for objects that move between user defined goal points and avoids collisions. In addition, the system allows "culling" of some of the computation for invisible agents: agents are accurately simulated only if they are visible to the user while the invisible objects are approximated probabilistically. The approximations ensure that the agent's behaviors match those that would occur had they been fully simulated, and result in significant speedups over running the accurate simulation for all agents.

Keywords: path planning, virtual agents, proxy simulations, simulation level of detail

1   Introduction

Simulations of thousands of interacting agents are in demand for entertainment applications (gaming [7] and film [16]), training simulations, and scientific visualization [2]. The *path planning* problem is to determine where each agent should move on each frame of the animation. Path planning algorithms are responsible for maintaining many essential aspects of plausible agent behavior, including collision avoidance and goal satisfaction. Path planning also consumes a significant part of the computation time for many simulations, particularly in highly dynamic environments where most of the agents are moving at the same time with varying goals. This work cannot easily be avoided, because of its high impact on visual quality and the outcome of the simulation (for instance, agents must show evidence of delays due to obstacle avoidance).

Path planning is typically performed on one agent at a time, and broken into at least two tasks. The first is concerned with global path planning, and identifies the ideal path from the agent's current position to its target location. Global path planning typically ignores local transient obstacles, such as other moving objects. The second, local task is concerned with moving the agent along the planned path at a reasonable speed and taking into account the obstacles ignored by the global path plan.

A key observation is that the local task is of less importance if the agent concerned is not in view. For instance, if the local simulation is primarily concerned with avoiding agent-agent collisions, and the viewer cannot see such collisions, then there is little point in incurring the computational cost to avoid them. The situation is analogous to geometry culling in the rendering sense, where invisible geometry is not considered by the renderer.

Local out-of-view interactions do, however, influence the overall simulation even if they occur out of view. For instance, an agent moving through a crowd would take longer to get somewhere than an agent moving alone. The difference in speed is due entirely to local interactions between agents. For this reason it is not sufficient to just ignore out-of-view motion. We can, however, approximate it. The viewer does not actually see the interactions, so the simulation is acceptable as long as their cumulative effect is still perceived by the viewer (for instance, agents still take longer to get places in crowds).

In this paper we present an efficient path planning methodology designed for large numbers of agents moving simultaneously around fixed obstacles and around each other. Our approach consists of a simulator that is designed for agents that the viewer can see, and a modified simulator, the *proxy simulator*, that operates on out-of-view agents. The proxy simulator achieves quantitatively similar simulation outcomes at a tiny fraction of the cost of complete, accurate path planning without significantly impacting the viewer's experience of the environment.

Section 2 looks briefly at related work on both path planning and efficient simulation. We then describe the accurate path planner (section 4) and the proxy planner (section 5).

2   Related Work

Early work on global path planning for a single agent phrased the problem as constrained optimization by defining a cost function favoring shorter paths and adding constraints to avoid the obstacles. Gradient descent methods may be applied to find the minimum cost path [5], but are subject to local minima problems and do not necessarily reach the goal state. Barraquand, Latombe, Overmars and Kavraki [1, 13, 9, 15] proposed temporary random navigation as a way to recover from the local minima. Unfortunately, most randomized or optimization driven path planning algorithms can be expensive in particular environments, and may even fail to reach the goal state.

Previous algorithms for multi-agent path planning have also been framed as optimization problems. Constraint forces are used to prevent the objects from running into each other [12]. Clearly these approaches are at least as expensive and prone to local minima as the single agent case. See [10] for an overview of probabilistic path planning.

The idea of landmarks survives in many computer games, where A^* search is almost universally used to find paths among the landmarks. The performance and quality of path planning on landmark based systems depends on the placement of the landmarks which is usually done by the level designer. Although A^* and its variants guarantee to give the optimal path, they can be too slow for large environments, particularly those of the size we address in this paper.

2D computational geometry algorithms for path planning use a polygonal description of the environment and operate on the visibility graph of the vertices of the obstacles (see [11] for a review). For our work, we adopt this type of planning as it does not involve discretizing the environment with landmarks and does not suffer from local minima issues.

Finally, the authors [4] have described *simulation proxies*: simulations that are intended to operate on out-of-view objects to significantly reduce the overall cost of large simulations. This paper focuses on a specific aspect of that work: the design of a proxy simulator for large scale path planning. An overview of cheap simulation methods is provided in [4].

3   System Overview

Our system is targeted to the path planning problems found in real time computer strategy games or similar applications. Typically, a virtual battle is modeled by simulating the behaviors of individual objects that move on a 2D terrain or attack other objects on the user's orders. In such games path planning and collision avoidance between objects constitutes the bulk of the computational workload of the simulator, due to both the large numbers of objects and the typically high complexity of path planning and collision detection algorithms. In most battle games the user is prevented from seeing the entire battlefield at any one time, so an approximate, or *proxy*, simulator can replace accurate path planning and collision avoidance for invisible objects. We describe such a proxy simulation that allows us to simulate very large numbers of objects moving on a plane.

The path planning problem in this situation has the following properties:

- The world is 2D and consists of free space and *fixed* obstacles defined by closed simple polygons.
- The agents in the world have a fixed size and are ordered by a user to move at constant speed to a target destination position. Agents without orders stay in the same place, and are said to be *stopped*. For our experiments, the user is replaced by a process that selects objects and gives them orders at random.
- Objects should move along the shortest path to their target. They may deviate from this path to avoid collisions with fixed, stopped and other dynamic obstacles.
- The viewer can only see a limited region of the world.

A simulator in this world moves the agents from frame to frame according to the above rules. The aim of our work is to perform this simulation as cheaply as possible, subject to the constraint that *the viewer experiences reasonable behavior at all times*. In this case reasonable behavior means that objects take times to reach their destinations that are consistent with the motion of all the other objects in the world, the restrictions on their motion, and their orders. We are not concerned that the moment-to-moment motion is correct *outside* the visible region of the world. This idea is explored further in section 5.

4   Full Path Planning

The path planning and collision avoidance problem is solved for an individual agent when it receives orders to move from its current location to a new destination point. The path is constructed in three stages — one stage for each type of obstacle to avoid.

1. When the order is first received, a path plan is constructed around all the fixed obstacles in the world. This stage makes extensive use of precomputed data structures, as described below. Precomputation is appropriate here because the fixed obstacles do not change through the simulation.
2. The agent next plans around agents that are stopped in its projected path. This step is also performed when the order is given, but does not rely on precomputation because it is not known ahead of time where objects will be stopped. After this phase the object is free to begin moving.
3. On a frame-by-frame basis the agent checks for collisions with other moving agents, or agents that have stopped since the order was given. If a collision is detected, the path plan is revised according to the guidelines below.

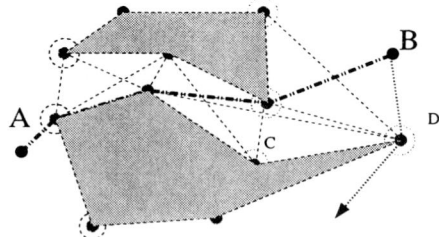

Fig. 1. Shaded polygons represent obstacles on a 2D terrain. The filled circles are the obstacle vertices and form nodes in the visibility graph. Dashed lines are the edges of the visibility graph for these obstacles. The horizon vertices for points A and B are circled in dashes and dots respectively. Note that a shortest path between any two points must first reach a vertex of the horizon of the starting point, traverse zero or more edges in the visibility graph and go from a vertex in the horizon of the destination point to the final destination point. The shortest path between A and B is shown in the figure. Note that horizon vertex C can not be on a shortest path to or from B as B can see both edges incident on these vertices. But since B can not see the both edges of D, it can be on a shortest path and one such path is also drawn.

When an object stops, i.e. reaches the end of its path plan, it is removed from the simulation until it is given another motion order so that stopped objects do not consume any dynamics time.

Objects can also construct partial path plans that are only valid up to an intermediate point along the path to their final destinations. This gives the path planner the option to terminate early before constructing the whole path. If an object reaches the end of its partial plan, another path is generated from the latest position of the current plan toward the final destination. The length of the sub-plan to be constructed is controlled by a parameter — the *plan ahead time*.

4.1 Fixed obstacles

In our simulator, fixed obstacles such as water and rocks are represented as simple polygons on the plane. We precompute a visibility graph over obstacle vertices: there is an edge between two obstacle vertices if a object can go between them without intersecting any fixed obstacle. Note that this assumes that all objects are the same size, but this is not a hard limitation as it can be circumvented by local revisions to the path plans.

The shortest paths between any two pairs of vertices in this graph are precomputed by running Dijkstra's algorithm for every vertex until shortest paths are found to every other vertex (figure 1). The shortest paths and their lengths between obstacle vertices can be stored compactly in a symmetric table where the entry (i,j) points to the next obstacle vertex to go on the shortest path from vertex i to vertex j. The algorithm for finding the edges of the visibility graph has complexity $O(n)$ [14] where n is the number of edges in the graph. The shortest paths between every pair of vertices on this graph can be computed in $O(n^3)$ and stored in a table of size $O(n^2)$. Recall that this is a precomputation, so the complexity does not affect the run-time performance. Our unoptimized implementation performs this computation in 5-10 minutes on a mid-performance PC for maps of typical game complexities.

Having computed the visibility graph and shortest paths, the plane is partitioned into *horizon regions*. Each horizon region contains points with the same *horizon*, or set of visible obstacle vertices (figure 1). In this context, two points are visible if an object can go between them on a straight line without intersecting a fixed obstacle. Asymptotically, the number of vertices forming the horizon of a horizon region can be on the order of the total number of obstacle vertices in the environment. The number of horizon regions in the environment can grow exponentially in the number of obstacle vertices making the storage $O(n^n)$.

Despite the worst case complexity of each horizon region, and the potentially exponential number of regions, in our test maps the number of horizon vertices was on the order of 4-8 and the typical number of horizons was on the order of hundreds. These maps were typical of the complexity one would expect from a computer game environment. Moreover, if an obstacle vertex has its two incident edges visible from within the horizon region, then that vertex does not have to be included in the horizon as it can never be the part of a shortest path beginning or ending at that horizon, decreasing the size of horizons (figure 1). Horizons exhibit a great deal of spatial coherence, i.e. nearby regions usually have the same horizon, and can be efficiently stored with spatial data structures.

The resulting precomputed visibility graph, shortest paths on the visibility graph and the horizon decomposition of the environment are then used at runtime to compute the shortest paths. Each order consists of the start point, p_{start} (the agent's current location) and a destination point, p_{end}. To generate the path, we first obtain the set of horizon vertices for p_{start}, H_{start} and the set of horizon vertices for p_{end}, H_{end}. These sets are available from the precomputed horizon regions. We then find the pair (v_{start}, v_{end}), $v_{start} \in H_{start}$, $v_{end} \in H_{end}$ such that the path $p_{start} \rightarrow v_{start} \rightarrow v_{end} \rightarrow p_{end}$ has the shortest distance. The shortest path between v_{start} and v_{end} is available from the pre-computation for any v_{start}, v_{end}.

The optimal path can be represented as the pair (v_{start}, v_{end}). The actual path is a line segment joining the p_{start} to v_{start}, then the stored shortest path from v_{start} to v_{end}, followed by the line segment joining v_{end} to p_{end} (figure 1). Note that v_{start} and v_{end} may be the same vertex. Moreover, if p_{end} is visible from p_{start} then the shortest path is simply the line segment joining the two vertices (a case detected by raycasting).

The worst case complexity for finding the closest pair of horizon vertices is $O(h^2)$ where h is the number of obstacle vertices. However, as indicated above, horizons tend to be of a small size, so the enumeration is very fast. In our path planning system, planning paths around fixed obstacles was cheap in terms of real time computation even on the most complicated maps. In terms of asymptotic cost, there exist $O(n)$ space and $O(log(n))$ query algorithms to compute the shortest path between two points in a polygonal environment where n is the number of obstacle vertices [6, 8]. However, the constant factors for the asymptotically optimal algorithms are large and such algorithms perform worse that our system.

4.2 Stopped objects

The cost of inserting objects into the horizon data structure when they stop moving (and removing them when they restart) is prohibitive. Instead, we plan paths around stopped objects on the fly. Once the global path plan that avoids fixed obstacles is available, it is checked against other objects for any collision. If a stopped object is on the intended path, then the plan has to be modified to go around the obstruction. Such stopped objects can be partitioned into object groups where the distance between any two objects in distinct groups is large enough to let an object through. Thus, if an object group obstructs the path, the only alternative is to traverse all the objects in the group.

156

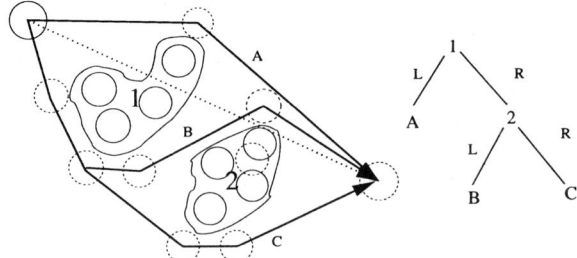

Fig. 2. There are static objects, groups 1 and 2, on a moving object's intended path (shown as a dashed line). The possible paths are enumerated by considering traversing the left and right sides of the obstructing group (1) and continuing the process recursively. Note that traversing the one side of the obstructing group (1) may reveal other obstructions (2). The plans discovered this way can be represented as a binary tree whose leaves are the candidate paths.

All the paths around the obstruction can be enumerated recursively by considering the left and right shoulders of the obstructing group (figure 2). Note that this enumeration procedure must still take the fixed obstacles into account. The enumeration procedure can stop when all the possible evasive patterns are discovered and evaluated for optimality or a long enough path segment is discovered (controlled by the plan ahead time parameter). In the first case, while we are guaranteed an optimal path, the cost of obtaining the path is considerable. In the second case, the partial path may not be optimal, but the cost of planning the partial path is much lower, allowing us to generate partial plans for more objects on any single frame.

During this enumeration step, the paths must be checked against fixed obstacles in order to avoid paths that go through them. If no path that doesn't go through fixed obstacles is found, then we must abandon the original path plan as it can not take us through the obstruction. This can happen if a bridge is blocked by other objects so the objects that need to pass the bridge must use an alternative route, found by searching the visibility graph for a path that doesn't contain the obstructed original path. As this step is usually time consuming, we can also precompute and store the second and third shortest paths along with the best paths between every two horizon vertices and only resort to a search if all three paths are blocked.

Note that a stopped object can start moving after an evasive path is computed around it. Thus, the computed path may not be optimal under the new situation. In our simulator we have achieved acceptable results without re-planning for such a case.

4.3 Moving objects

The intended path for a given object can be further obstructed by other moving objects. The simulator discovers such collisions by checking the new position of a moving object at every time step. If two dynamic objects will collide, we stop one of the parties, chosen at random, and wait for the other one to move and clear the path. If waiting for either one of the interacting parties does not solve the problem, we temporarily stop one of the objects and force the other one to plan around it using the previous section's algorithm for planning around stopped objects. If one of the objects is already stopped (as can happen in an agent stops after the path was initially planned) then we must also replan for the agent that is still moving.

In an environment with lots of dynamic objects, we are likely to encounter many potential agent collisions at run time, so this step causes lots of path replanning in order to find paths around other objects. This is the primary contributor to the computation time. However, if the agents are not visible, we are not concerned which precisely which local path they take to avoid each other. We care only that they appear to have taken some detour and hence been delayed by the presence of other agents, but have no interest in precisely which detour. In the next section we describe a modified algorithm that avoids replanning for out-of-view collisions but still captures the effects that such replanning would have on the agent's behavior.

5 Proxy Simulation

All that ultimately matters in a virtual environment is that the viewer have a reasonable experience in the environment. The viewer can typically only experience what they can see, so we are free to do anything with the out-of-view motion in the environment provided that it does not impact significantly on what happens in view. Ultimately, anything that impacts the viewer's experience must enter the view, so it is these view entry events that we are primarily concerned with capturing with our out-of-view simulation. We might also need to capture other out of view events to ensure that we get a reasonable stream of view-entry events.

We refer to a simulator that generates view-entry events as a *proxy simulator*. For highly efficient simulation, we will allow the proxy simulator to approximate the out-of-view motion, but in such a way that the viewer does not experience the difference. In a computer game environment, this means that we must be sure that a player who knows about the proxy should not have an advantage over a player who does not. Thus, the approximate simulation should meet the following requirements for every individually identifiable object:

- Objects in any part of the battlefield should not pass through fixed obstacles (otherwise the informed player could "teleport" objects across walls and rivers).
- Inter-object interactions must be accounted for. For example, an object should not be able to pass through a bridge whose entrance has been blocked by other static objects.
- Objects should have speeds consistent with their environments. For instance, the average speed of an object should not be very big if it has interacted with lots of other dynamic objects recently. This means that objects should (a) arrive at their destinations at times consistent with a full simulation and (b) have encounters along their paths that are also consistent. For example, objects should encounter ambushes at consistent times.

5.1 Tracking Agent Locations

In order to determine when an agent should re-enter the view, we will keep track of its approximate location. This allows us to determine which objects should be visible if the viewer moves, and also allows us to detect and account for the interactions between out-of-view agents and their environment. We subdivide the battlefield to smaller rectangles that act as our cells. The viewer has a rectangular overhead view of the battlefield, so can only see the cells that intersect with this rectangular region. Only the objects that are in these cells may be visible. Furthermore, only agents in the same cell at the same time can interact with each other.

The proxy model for path planning and collision avoidance is a discrete event simulator that is used to manage the membership information of every object for every cell. More specifically, the proxy is used to ensure that each cell contains a list of objects that are stamped with the times they will enter and exit the cell. At every frame, dynamics state for objects entering any of the visible cells is obtained from the proxy simulator and the proxy simulation is turned off for those objects. Similarly, objects leaving the visible cells are switched to the proxy simulation.

The behavior of a discrete event simulator is defined by the events it uses and the processing it performs on them. We begin by describing three events, and introduce another later. We also defer the discussion of how the times for these events are predicted.

Stop: An object in the proxy simulator has reached its destination. When this event happens, the proxy simulator switches the object from dynamic to static and removes it from all the cells that it has been associated with. Note that the stop event may have formed a blockade that prevents other dynamic events from moving. Thus, when a stop event is processed, we look for dynamic objects that collide with the stopping object and recompute their events if necessary.

Replan: Since objects may also have partial path plans, the validity of a path plan may expire before the object reaches its final destination. In this case the proxy must generate a new plan from the last point in the current plan to the final target of the object.

Entry: This event is scheduled for agents in the proxy simulator that will enter one of the visible cells. When this event happens, the proxy simulator deletes the agent from any cells it is in. A complete dynamic state must also be assigned to the agent. This is done by randomly assigning state based on the time the agent entered the cell and its expected behavior within the cell, as described below.

5.2 Setting Event Times

The proxy simulator needs to be able to predict when an agent will reach the end of its plan, so that stop or replan events can be scheduled, or when the agent reaches a visible cell, so that enter events can be scheduled. This is done through the use of hierarchical data structures that determine which objects might interact with each other, and a probabilistic model to estimate the impact of the interactions on the event times.

The process of giving orders and planning around fixed and stopped objects is not changed by the proxy simulator. These operations are already fast, and they provide valuable information about where the object will go and how long it will take to get there. In particular, combined with the constant velocity of the object, we can use the basic plan to compute the soonest that an event can occur. The proxy avoids replanning around the collisions between dynamic agents, which are the dominant simulation cost for the accurate model. These interactions can only add delays to an agent's travel time, and it is these delays that we model probabilistically.

The proxy simulator gathers the path plans for the objects that it needs to simulate and inserts each object into the cells that its planned trajectory intersects. The proxy simulator also marks each object with the corresponding entry and exit time stamps for every cell that it is scheduled to visit. The time stamps are computed by considering the object's speed and the other objects with which it is expected to interact along the path.

These interactions are discovered using a quad tree decomposition of every cell that is used to eliminate objects whose paths don't cross. Whenever an object is inserted into a cell, the root of the quad tree for that cell is investigated for other objects. If another object also occupies the same quad tree node, then both objects are refined by inserting them into the children node. Note that the object already in the node can be directly pushed to a lower level in the tree as it can not collide with another object for if it did, it would be in a lower node.

The process is continued by traversing the nodes in the order until no other object exists in the node, meaning object will not collide, or the maximum depth of the tree is reached, meaning a possible collision. Note that since the path plans are piecewise linear, the insertion can be done by traversing each linear segment and inserting it into the nodes that it intersects in order. If we descend all the way to the leaf, we then check the objects in the leaf node for a collision. The maximum depth of the tree is a user specified parameter that can be tuned with cell and object sizes.

Detected interactions are approximated by delays to the original path plans of both interacting parties. This is reasonable since a dynamic object will either move and clear the path or one of the interacting parties will plan around the other one, usually resolving the collision without getting stuck.

The delays are sampled from a probability mixture distribution obtained by sampling the delays that result from object interactions in the full simulation and fitting the mixture with a EM algorithm [3]. The resulting distribution is usually good enough to capture accurate speed relationships for the dynamic objects.

Introducing a delay in an object's intended plan may invalidate some of the interactions that have been computed previously, in particular all those objects that previously expected to interact with the delayed object. Thus, all the future interactions must be rechecked after the introduction of a delay. Since objects can have very long path plans into the future, this step may involve re-computation of interactions for lots of other objects already in the proxy simulator. We overcome this problem by computing interactions only for a particular amount of time in the future and rechecking. The amount of time that we will compute an object's interactions is controlled by a *latest interaction time* parameter. This introduces one additional event:

Reinsert: This event is generated for every object when their latest interaction time is hit and causes the proxy to look for additional interactions along the agent's path.

The above procedure provides sufficient information to estimate event times for the simulator. It is run after an order is given and the basic path plan is computed. The interactions along the path are noted, delays for each interaction are sampled, and then added to the minimum travel time to obtain estimated times for the events.

The use of a distribution on delay times makes some assumptions about the nature of the delays encountered by an object. The primary assumption is that the delay depends linearly on the number of agent's encountered along a path. This seems to be a reasonable assumption in our particular situations. If it was not valid, the distribution could be parameterized by the number of interactions, although at some cost to the learning process and storage. Another implicit assumption is that delays do not depend on how long the simulation has been running or other time-dependent parameters, which is certainly reasonable in this case and is likely to be a valid for most environments.

In this framework, the viewer motion can be accommodated by sampling states for the objects in the cells that are becoming visible. Since we have the entry times and the delays that objects accumulate for every object in the cells, we can efficiently estimate their positions. Objects becoming invisible due to the viewer motion don't require special treatment and can be handled by computing necessary events and inserting them into the cells they will visit.

5.3 Discussion

The main source of error in the proxy simulator is the approximation of dynamic object interactions as delays. However, these delays are estimated based on data from the full model, so on average they cancel out. One infrequent case where the proxy is seriously awry is when two objects deadlock in trying to pass. This happens if two objects try to pass a narrow bridge in opposite directions and is due to the lack of a "back up" logic in our path planner. If the bridge is only one object wide, then each object will wait for the other object to clear the path as active replanning fails to plan around the other object. Such a situation could be detected by checking if the interacting parties succeed to find an evasive path plan. The deadlock could then be resolved with a smarter path planner that can back up objects to clear the path for others. However, in our current implementation we ignore the deadlock because it has little impact on the behavior of the simulation as a whole. Narrow gaps are typically rare and the probability of units trying pass in opposite directions at the same time is low.

Note that proxy simulator does not have to give exactly the same results with the accurate simulation. Individual objects can have different states and follow different paths with the accurate simulator as long as they do not contradict a user's expectations. For example, an object should not appear or disappear from the user's screen or get to its destination too soon or late. Our proxy simulator satisfies this requirement most of the time, however, it is possible to create difficult scenarios where the proxy simulator, as it is, will generate inconsistent states with the full simulator. The true success of the proxy simulator must be measured with a large set of human experiments, which we have only performed within our research group.

6 Results

We have tested our proxy simulator on different terrains with different number of uniquely identifiable objects. Figure 4 shows the amount of dynamics computation time required to simulate 1600 objects for a simulator using a proxy compared to the full simulation. Figure 3 shows the amount of dynamics time required for simulating 1 second of dynamics as a function of the number of objects with constant density on a Pentium III 800MHz computer. For all simulations, objects are distributed randomly on the terrain and pick random places to go. The object density on the terrain is kept constant by increasing the size of the terrain as the number of objects is increased.

Increasing the number of objects increases the number of possible interactions quadratically. Since the full simulator needs to re-plan in order to avoid collisions, it may have to deal with additional collisions that the revised plan may cause, suffering additional cost for every interaction that needs plan revision. On the other hand, the proxy simulation approximates these interactions with probabilistic delays and thus does not re-plan. Even though the proxy simulator still detects all the interactions between the dynamical objects, the cost of handling these interactions is considerably cheaper than the full simulation.

7 Conclusion

We have demonstrated a novel path planning algorithm for large numbers of agents operating in a virtual environment. Our algorithm is particularly efficient because we take advantage of out-of-view motion to reduce the cost of the simulation.

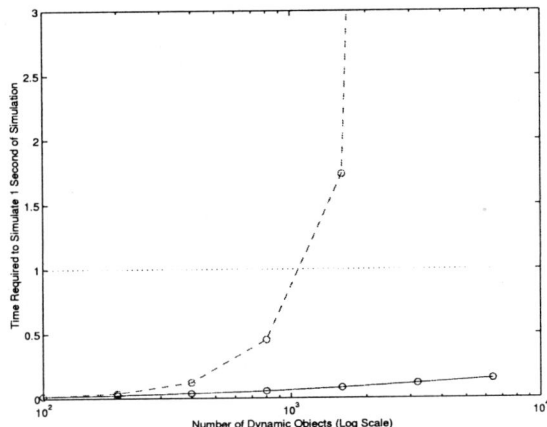

Fig. 3. The real time required to simulate 1 second of simulation time as a function of the log of the number of objects on a constant density terrain. The upper curve (dashes) represents the simulation without proxy and the lower curve (full) represents the simulation with proxy. The dotted horizontal line is the real-time cutoff. Since the object density is constant for all simulations, the user sees approximately the same number of objects in the view. Since the proxy simulator does very little work for the invisible objects and their interactions are handled using a discrete event simulator, the simulation cost increases much slower than the full simulation. The very fast increase in the full simulation cost comes from the fact that the path plan revisions needed to avoid collisions between dynamic objects tend to snowball, while the proxy approximates dynamic-dynamic object interactions with probabilistic models, thus avoiding local path plan revisions.

We can not guarantee the correctness of our proxy model all the time as it can be made to contradict with the accurate simulation with elaborate setups (e.g. objects passing through narrow bridge in opposite directions). However, proxy simulations may be the only way to simulate environments that are simply too big for the accurate simulation, or cut the state that has to be propagated in distributed virtual environments. Note asymptotic gains in the scalability of simulations are only possible through using proxies. Thus guaranteeing good behavior of proxy simulations is an important research topic.

Ultimately our aim is to provide tools that aid in the construction of proxy simulations. Such tools would accept an accurate simulation in some form and, possibly with user intervention, construct a proxy that saved computation but retained the important properties of the original simulation model.

References

1. J. Barraquand and J. Latombe. A monte-carlo algorithm for path planning with many degrees of freedom. In IEEE Int. Conf. Robot. & Autom., pages 1712–1717, 1990. 257, 1990.
2. Michael Batty, Bin Jiang, and Mark Thurstain-Goodwin. Working paper 4: Local movement: Agent-based models of pedestrian flows. Working Paper from the Center for Advanced Spatial Analysis, University College London, 1998.
3. Christopher M. Bishop. *Neural Networks for Pattern Recognition*. Oxford University Press, 1995.

162

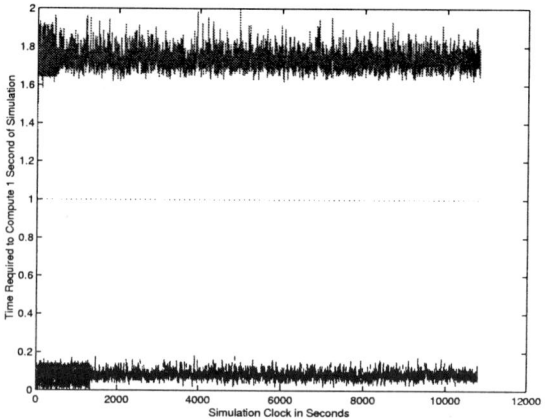

Fig. 4. The dynamics computation time required for one second of actual simulation on the vertical axis for 3 hours of simulation for the full simulation (at the top) versus the proxy simulation (at the bottom). The simulation is run with 1600 objects picking random places to go on a moderately dense map.

4. Stephen Chenney, Okan Arikan, and D.A.Forsyth. Proxy simulations for efficient dynamics. To appear in Eurographics 2001, Short Presentations.
5. B. Faverjon and P. Tournassoud. A local based approach for path planning of manipulators with a high number of degrees of freedom, int. conf. robotics & automation, 1987.
6. Guibas and Hershberger. Optimal shortest path queries in a simple polygon. In *COMP-GEOM: Annual ACM Symposium on Computational Geometry*, 1987.
7. Demis Hassabis. Level-of-detail ai. Lecture at the 2001 Game Developers Conference.
8. Joseph O'Rouke Jacob E. Goodman. *Discrete and Computational Geometry*. The CRC Press, Boca Raton, New York, 1997.
9. Lydia Kavraki, Petr Svestka, Jean-Claude Latombe, and Mark Overmars. Probabilistic roadmaps for path planning in high-dimensional configuration spaces. IEEE Transactions on Robotics and Automation, 1996.
10. Jean-Paul Laumond. *Robot Motion Planning and Control*. Lectures Notes in Control and Information Sciences. Springer Verlag, 1998.
11. J. Mitchell. Shortest paths and networks. In J. E. Goodman and J. O'Rourke, editors, Handbook of Discrete and Computational Geometry, CRC Press LLC, Boca Raton, FL, 1997.
12. L. Overgaard, H. Petersen, and J. Perram. Reactive motion planning: a multi-agent approach. Applied Artificial Intelligence, 10(1), 1996.
13. M. Overmars. A random approach to motion planning. Technical Report RUU-CS-92-32, Department of Computer Science, Utrecht University, The Netherlands, 1992.
14. S. N. Maheshwari Sanjiv Kapoor. Efficiently constructing the visibility graph of a simple polygon with obstacles. In *SIAM Journal on Computing*, volume 30(3), pages 847–871, August 2000.
15. Dimitris Metaxas Siome Goldenstein, Edward Large. Special issue on real-time virtual worlds: Non-linear dynamical system approach to behavior modeling. In *The Visual Computer*, volume 15, pages 341–348, 1999.
16. Marjolaine Tremblay and Hiromi Ono. Multiple creatures choreograhy on Star Wars: Episode I "The Phantom Menace". SIGGRAPH 99 Animation Sketch. In Conference Abstracts and Applications, page 205, August 1999.

Crowd simulation for interactive virtual environments and VR training systems

Branislav Ulicny and Daniel Thalmann

Computer Graphics Lab (LIG)
Swiss Federal Institute of Technology
EPFL, DI-LIG, CH 1015 Lausanne, Switzerland
http://ligwww.epfl.ch
Branislav.Ulicny@epfl.ch, Daniel.Thalmann@epfl.ch

Abstract. In this paper we present recent results concerning development of the crowd simulation for interactive virtual environments such as virtual reality training system for urban emergency situations. Our system aims to reproduce realistic scenarios involving large number of the virtual human agents with behaviors based on the behaviors of the real persons in such situations. We define architecture of multi-agent system allowing both scripted and autonomous behaviors of the agents as well as interactions among them, with the virtual environment and with the real human participants.

Keywords: crowd simulation, multi-agent systems, autonomous agents, VR training systems

1 Introduction

Crowds are ubiquitous feature of everyday life. People have long assembled collectively to observe, to celebrate, or to protest at various happenings. The collective assemblages or gatherings called crowds have been the object of scientific inquiry since the end of 19th century [10]. With computers it become possible not only to observe human crowds in the real world, but also to simulate various phenomena from the domain of collective behavior in the virtual environments. Collective behaviors have been studied and modelled with very different purposes. Besides single work concerned with generic crowd simulation [15], most approaches were application specific, focusing on different aspects of the crowd behavior. As a consequence they employ different modelling techniques ranging from those that do not distinguish individuals such as flow and network models, to those that represent each individual as being controlled by rules based on physical laws or behavioral models. Applications include animation production systems used in entertainment industry [4], crowd behavior models used in training of military personnel [20] or policemen [21], crowd motion simulations to support architectural design both for everyday use [3] and for emergency evacuation conditions [18, 19], simulations of physical aspects of crowd dynamics [7] and finally sociological and behavioral simulations [12].

The aim of this paper is to introduce recent results concerning development of crowd simulation for interactive virtual environments with application as a training system for urban emergency situations. Goal of the simulation is to reproduce realistic scenarios of such situations evolving in real-time involving large number of virtual human agents. In the next section we describe requirements and constrains for such system and then we define architecture of multi-agent system allowing both scripted and autonomous behaviors of the agents as well as their interactions with the virtual environment and immersed users. Next the behavior model is discussed in more details and finally before conclusion we present some early results of the simulation.

2 Requirements and constrains

Compared to the simulations of single virtual human, multi-agent systems pose different requirements and constrains for the design of the system in both conceptual and technical aspects. Main conceptual difference is the need for a variety of individual agents' visualizations and behaviors, for example variety of individual trajectories for the group traveling along the same path, variety of the animations for agents having same behavior or different reactions of individuals facing the same situations. Otherwise crowd composed of the same individuals with the same behaviors wouldn't be convincing even if each of such individuals would alone be very realistic. Main technical challenge is increased demand of computational resources which grows in some aspects linearly (for example in agent-environment interactions) but in many quadraticaly (for agent-agent interactions, such as collision avoidance) with the number of simulated agents.

Therefore designing multi-agent simulation is not straightforward task of combining simulations of many single agents, new approaches are required which allow both variety among single agents and in the case of real-time simulations are also computationaly less demanding. Further discussion concerning application specific requirements for crowd modelling can be found in [16].

3 System design

Our simulation consists of autonomous virtual human agents[1] existing in dynamic virtual 3D environment (see figure 1). In order to behave in believable way these agents must act in accordance with their surrounding environment, be able to react to its changes, to the other agents and also to the actions of real humans interacting with the virtual world.

Agents have 3D graphic body representations, which are able to perform certain low-level actions, such as playing of pre-recorded animation sequences (e.g. gestures, changes of postures, etc.) or walking to specified location with different gaits [2]. High-level behaviors are then composed of particular combinations of these low-level actions using hierarchical finite state machines. We give more detailed description of the behavior model in the section 4.

Figure 2 gives overview of the system architecture. System is designed with clear separation of the model part (where behavior is computed) from the visualization part (where behavior is displayed), thus allowing use of different virtual humans, objects and environments. In such way it's possible for example to scale up number of the simulated agents by lowering complexity of their 3D representations (e.g. by using levels of details or impostors [1]) without change of the underlying model just by plugging-in different visualization part, or on the other hand simulation can be run without any graphics only with textual output to log file which can later be used to render off-line high quality animations.

---

[1] We distinguish between visualization part of virtual human agent (further refered to as virtual human) and logic part (refered to as agent).

Fig. 1. Virtual environment

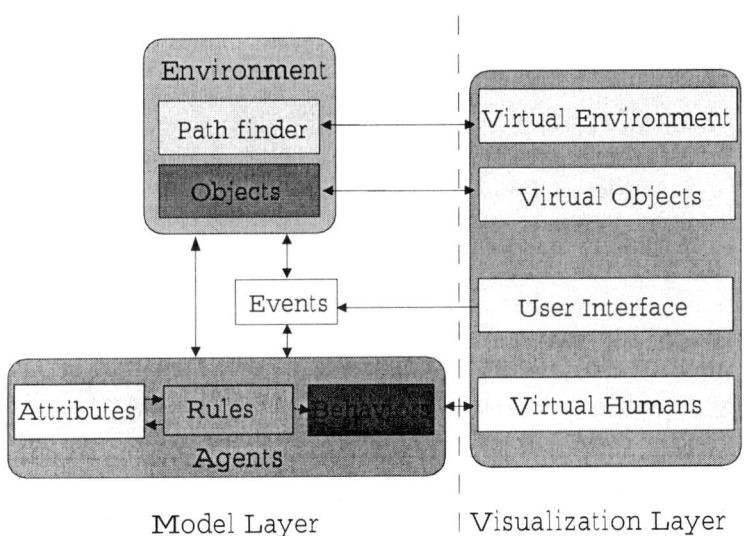

Fig. 2. System architecture

Model is composed of the set of agents, dynamic objects and static environment[2]. Agents contains set of internal attributes corresponding to various psychological or physiological states (e.g. fear, mobility, level of injuries, etc.), set of higher-level complex behaviors (e.g. wander, flee, etc.) and set of rules determining selection of these behaviors. Events provide way of agents' interaction with their environment, other agents or human participants of the simulation. Each agent is able to receive events from the environmental objects (e.g. agent hit by explosion), other agents (e.g. agent is requesting help) or user interface (e.g. order to stop walking). Combinations of different received events and different levels of agent's attributes can produce both changes of its internal attributes and change of the overt behavior. Further appearance of the agents can be linked to the values of some attributes (e.g. different textures can correspond to different levels injuries). For global path planning in static environment path finder module is used [6]. In case more agents are following the same global path, variety of the individual local trajectories is ensured by specifying path waypoints not by exact location, but by selecting random locations from some epsilon surrounding of the waypoint.

4 Behavior model

Our aim is to have behavior model that is simple enough to allow for real-time execution of many agents, yet still sufficiently complex to provide interesting behaviors. Considering requirements mentioned in the section 2 we proposed following model (see figure 3) based on the combination of rules [9, 17] and finite state machines (FSM) [5, 13, 14] for controlling agent's behavior using layered approach. First layer deals with the selection of higher-level complex behavior appropriate to agent's situation, second layer implements these behaviors using low-level actions provided by the virtual human [2].

At the higher level, rules select complex behaviors (such as flee) according to agent's state (constituted by attributes) and the state of the virtual environment (conveyed by events). In rules we specify for who (e.g. particular agent, or agents in particular group) and when the rule is applicable (e.g. at defined time, after receiving event or when some attribute reached specified value), and what is the consequence of rule firing (e.g. change of agent's high-level behavior or attribute). Example of such rule is:

```
FOR ALL
WHEN EVENT = in_danger_area AND ATTRIBUTE fear > 50%
THEN BEHAVIOR FLEE
```

At the lower level, complex behaviors are implemented by hierarchical finite state machines. Each behavior is realized by one FSM which drives selection of the low-level actions for the virtual human (like move to location, play short animation sequence), manages connections with the environment (like path queries, or event sending) and also can call other FSMs to delegate subtasks such as path following[3].

There are two types of complex behaviors. First we can specify scripted behavior which is more precise, but less autonomous and with less environment coupling by using explicit sequences of low-level actions. Or second we can let agents perform autonomously complex behaviors with the feedback from the environment. Examples

---

[2] We distinguish between static part of the environment like layout of the streets and buildings and dynamic part consisting of objects that can change their position or state during the scenario like fire or gas cloud.

[3] Hence hierarchical FSM.

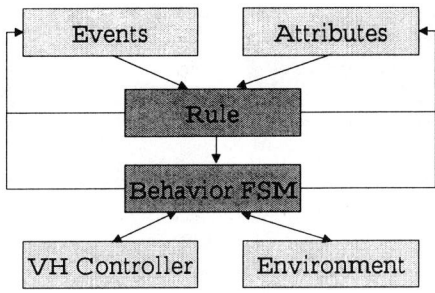

Fig. 3. Behavior model

of such autonomous behaviors are wandering, fleeing, neutralizing the threat, or help requesting and providing.

We can illustrate semantics of the autonomous behaviors on the example of two agents performing coupled behaviors - help requesting and providing. When first agent's health attribute is below certain level, rule triggers help requesting behavior FSM. Agent stops on the place and starts to play animation corresponding to asking for the help (such as waving of the hand) and sends event conveying his request to the other agents. Reception of this event leads to the activation of the rule for the second agent, which then starts performing help providing behavior FSM. He asks environment for the path leading to the first agent, executes path following FSM to perform movement to the injured agent and after arriving he starts playing help giving animation (such as giving first aid). Upon finishing animation first agent is notified and the level of his health attribute is increased. At the end both involved agents quit these behaviors and return to their previous behaviors.

Variety of the reactions to the same situation is achieved by different agents having different values of the attributes (at the beginning through different initializations, later because of their different histories) which consequently leads to different rules triggered. This behavior architecture also addresses variety of the animations issue (see section 2) by separating action selecting part (behavior FSM) from action executing part (virtual human controller). Behavior FSM is ordering controller to do type of the animation (e.g waving of hand) and controler then randomly chooses particular one from the set of such animations, so that even if more agents are executing the same behavior they don't necessarily act exactly the same.

5 Early results

To test feasibility of our approach we used early implementation of our system to reproduce simple scenario of urban emergency situation. Scenario is taking place in virtual city environment where people in the park area are confronted with the leak of dangerous gas (see figure 4). It includes simulation of pre-event, emergency event and post-event behaviors where behavioral rules guide transitions between agents' autonomous behaviors in concordance with the changes of the environment. There are three different groups of agents involved - ordinary people, firemen and medics. According to their

Fig. 4. Virtual world: a) before emergency, b) after gas leak happened

professions agents act differently facing the emergency situation. Ordinary people in proximity of the threat are panicking and trying to flee away, however as gas is affecting them, some are unable to move and are asking for help. In case they stay too long affected by gas their health decreases, eventually leading to death. Medics are localizing such persons and providing help to them. Finally firemen are approaching gas leak and acting towards neutralizing it.

Our system was able to recreate such scenario in real-time allowing user interaction with the virtual world. However major bottleneck proved to be visualization of complex virtual humans. We used three types of the visualization of the agents with different complexities. In the case of simple cube representation we were able to run simulations consisting of up to thousand of agents, for virtual humans with rigid bodies this number dropped to around hundred and finally with the most realistic deformable bodies interactive simulations with about twenty agents were possible[4].

6 Conclusions and future work

This paper presented our work on crowd simulation system for interactive virtual environments. We defined multi-agent architecture allowing virtual human agents to perform autonomous behaviors in the virtual world, where both individual agents and environment are modelled. Agents' behaviors are decided by behavioral rules and executed by hierarchical finite state machines. We used this system to create scenario of urban emergency situation. Possible application of our system could be any virtual environment system requiring real-time execution of complex autonomous behaviors of many agents such as various training systems, computer games or educational applications.

In comparision with the other crowd modelling approaches we focus on more complex behaviors in dynamic environment. In previous works crowds have been considered as already formed units with more or less uniform behavior placed in particular environments corresponding only to limited purpose of simulation e.g. pedestrian just fleeing from burning building [7, 18] or marching crowd during demonstration [20, 21]. In our system crowd is modelled as collection of individuals which reacts to the environment, other agents and real human participants of the simulation and can have very different behaviors both for one agent in different situations and for many agents in the same situation.

---

[4]On SGI Onyx2 workstation.

For the future work we plan to investigate following issues:

- Extension of agent-agent interaction possibilities for enabling of more complex group behaviors.
- Improvement of agent-object interaction and animation for example by using smart objects [8].
- Enhancement of the visual realism of multiple agents performing the same a nimation by using animation system allowing variation over single animation for example by example-based motion synthesis [11].

7 Acknowledgements

This work has been supported by the Swiss National Research Foundation and the Federal Office for Education and Science in the framework of the European project CROSSES.

References

1. Aubel, A., Boulic, R., Thalmann, D., "Real-time Display of Virtual Humans: Level of Details and Impostors", *IEEE Trans. Circuits and Systems for Video Technology*, Special Issue on 3D Video Technology, 10(2):207-217,2000.
2. Boulic, R., Becheiraz, P., Emering, L., and Thalmann, D., "Integration of Motion Control Techniques for Virtual Human and Avatar Real-Time Animation", Proc. VRST '97, pp. 111-118, ACM Press, 1997.
3. Bouvier, E., Guilloteau, P., "Crowd Simulation in Immersive Space Management", Proc. Eurographics Workshop on Virtual Environments and Scientific Visualization '96, pp. 104-110, Springer-Verlag, 1996.
4. Character Studio 3, data sheet,
   http://www2.discreet.com/docs/characterstudio3_1.pdf, 2001.
5. Cremer, J., Kearney, J., and Papelis, Y., "HCSM: Framework for Behavior and Scenario Control in Virtual Environments", *ACM Transactions on Modeling and Computer Simulation*, 5(3):242-267, 1995.
6. Farenc, N., Boulic, R., Thalmann, D., "An Informed Environment Dedicated to the Simulation of Virtual Humans in Urban Context", Proc. Eurographics'99, pp. 309-318, Blackwell, 1999.
7. Helbing, D., Farkas, I., and Vicsek, T., "Simulating dynamical features of escape panic", *Nature*, 407:487-490, 2000.
8. Kallmann, M., and Thalmann, D., "Modeling Objects for Interaction Tasks", Proc. Eurographics Workshop on Computer Animation and Simulation '98, pp. 73-86 Springer-Verlag, 1998.
9. Kalra, D., Barr, A.H., Modeling with Time and Events in Computer Animation, Proc. Eurographics'92, pp. 45-58, Blackwell, 1992.
10. LeBon, G., Psychologie des Foules, Paris:Alcan, 1895.
11. Lim, I.S., Thalmann, D., "A Vector-Space Representation of Motion Data for Example-Based Motion Synthesis", Proc. Avatars 2000, Lausanne, Switzerland, 2000.
12. McPhail, C., Powers, W.T., and Tucker, C.W., "Simulating individual and collective actions in temporary gatherings", Social Science Computer Review, 10(1):1-28, Spring, 1992.
13. Moreau, G., Donikian, S., "From Psychological and Real-Time Interaction Requirements to Behavioral Simulation", Proc. Eurographics Workshop on Computer Animation and Simulation'98, Springer-Verlag, 1998.
14. Motivate product information, Motion Factory,
    http://www.motion-factory.com.

15. Musse, S.R., Human Crowd Modelling with Various Levels of Behaviour Control, PhD thesis, EPFL, Lausanne, 2000.
16. Musse, S.R., Thalmann, D., "From One Virtual Actor to Virtual Crowds: Requirements and Constraints", Proc. Autonomous Agents'00, pp. 52-53, ACM Press, 2000.
17. Rosenbloom, P.S., Laird, J.E., Newell, A., The Soar papers: Research on Artificial Intelligence, MIT Press, 1993.
18. Still, G., K., Crowd Dynamics, PhD thesis, Warwick University, 2000.
19. Thompson, P.A., Marchant, E.W., "A Computer-model for the Evacuation of Large Building Population", *Fire Safety Journal*, 24(2): 131-148, 1995.
20. Varner, D., et al., "UMSC Small Unit Leader Non-Lethal Trainer", in Proc. ITEC'98, 1998.
21. Williams, J.R., A Simulation Environment to Support Training for Large Scale Command and Control Tasks, PhD thesis, University of Leeds, 1995.

The Orchestration of Behaviours using Resources and Priority Levels

F. Lamarche[1] and S. Donikian[2]

[flamarch, donikian] @irisa.fr

IRISA, Campus de Beaulieu, 35042 Rennes, FRANCE

Abstract.
Reproducing daily behaviours requires the ability to schedule behaviours depending on resources (body parts for example) and priority (intentions or physiological parameters) constraints. A simple way is to say that behaviours which are using the same resources are mutually exclusive. This approach is not sufficient to achieve realism purpose, as in real life, humans are able to combine them in a much microscopic way. All day long, humans mix different behaviours, as for example reading a newspaper while drinking a coffee and smoking a cigarette. If all behaviours using common resources were mutually exclusive, an agent could not reproduce this example, except if a specific behaviour is created. This solution becomes rapidly too complex and has motivated the work presented in this paper. It consists in an extension of HPTS, our behavioural model, by the introduction of resources and priority levels. In the contrary of some previous approaches, it is not necessary to specify exhaustively all behaviours that are mutually exclusive; this is done implicitly by attaching resources to nodes and a priority function to each state machine, and by using a scheduler.

Introduction

The goal of behavioural models is to simulate autonomous entities like organisms and living beings. The issue addressed in our work concerns the specification of a general formalism for behaviour modeling based on psychological studies and compatible with real-time constraints. Information needed to describe the behaviour of an entity depends on the nature of this entity. No theory exists for determining either necessary or sufficient structures needed to support particular capabilities and certainly not to support general intelligence. As direction and inspiration towards the development of such a theory, Newell[12] posits that one way to approach sufficiency is by modeling human cognition in computational layers or bands. Reproducing daily behaviours requires to schedule behaviours depending on resources (body parts for example) and priority (intentions or physiological parameters) constraints. A simple way is to say that behaviours which are using the same resources are mutually exclusive. This approach is not sufficient to achieve realism purpose, as in real life, humans are able to combine them in a much microscopic way. All day long, humans mix different behaviours, as for example reading a newspaper while drinking a coffee and smoking a cigarette. If all behaviours using common resources were mutually exclusive, an agent could not reproduce this example, except if a specific behaviour is created. This solution becomes rapidly too complex. We have proposed in the past the HPTS model which integrates

---

[1] University of Rennes I
[2] CNRS

several psychological requirements. In this paper, we propose to extend this model to be able to manage, in a generic way, resources, adaptation and priority levels. It becomes possible to describe behaviours independently and to adapt automatically their execution when they are running in parallel, with respect to their priorities.

In the next section, related works are presented, while section three focuses on the HPTS model. The integration of resources and priority levels and the overview of the scheduler are presented in section four. Finally section five focuses on an example to illustrate advantages of this new approach.

1 Related Works

Behavioural models have been developed to describe the human behaviour in specific tasks. The common characteristics of these models are: reactivity, parallelism and different abstract levels of behaviours. As humans are deliberative agents, purely reactive systems are not sufficient to describe their behaviour. It is necessary to integrate both cognitive and reactive aspects of behaviour. Cognitive models are rather motivated by the representation of the agent's knowledge (beliefs and intentions). Intentions enable an agent to reason about its internal state and that of others. The center of such a deliberative agent is its own representation of the world which includes a representation of his mental state and the one of other agents which he is currently interacting with[9]. To achieve such a purpose, Badler et al.[3] propose to combine Sense-Control-Action (SCA) loops with planners and PaT-Nets. SCA loops define the reflexive behaviour and are continuous systems which interconnect sensors and effectors through a network of nodes, exactly like in the sensor effector approach described above. PaT-Nets are essentially finite state automata that can be executed in parallel (for example the control of the four fingers and of the thumb for a grasping task). The planner queries the state of the database through a filtered perception to decide how to elaborate the plan and to select an action. More recently they have introduced Parameterized Action Representation (PAR) to give a description of an action, and these PARs are directly linked to PaT-Nets. It allows a user to control Autonomous Characters actions with instructions given in natural language[4]. In this system, like in others[13], the action is directly associated with each node, which does not allow an explicit management of concurrency.

A lot of models have also been proposed for human like minds in the agent community[11]. They are all based on the perception/treatment/action loop, but they mainly differ in the way the treatment unit is built. As in the Newell theory, A. Sloman[15] proposed an architecture of an intelligent agent in different layers (reflexes, automatic processes, resource-limited reflective management processes, meta-management processes), involving different routes through the system form perception to action. In his theory, automatic processes have dedicated portions of the brain and can operate in parallel whenever they need, while different management processes have to share a common working memory, and their parallelism is then restricted. F. Brazier et al. [5] proposed a model of a rational agent using notions such as beliefs, desires and intentions. In their task hierarchy, beliefs and desires influence each other reciprocally, and they both influence intentions and commitments. S. Ambroszkiewicz and J. Komar[2] distinguish six parts in an agent model: perception, desire, knowledge and belief, rational behaviour, reasoning process and intention, and they propose a formal model based on this decomposition.

V. Decugis and J. Ferber[6] address an interesting problem: how to combine reactivity and planning capabilities in a real-time application. They propose to extend the ASM (Action Selection Mechanism) proposed by Maes[10] into hierarchical ASMs.

At the bottom of the hierarchy, basic reflexes are found, such as reflex movements orientation and basic perceptive mechanisms, while higher levels integrate more complex behaviours. B. Rhodes [14] has proposed another extension of ASM, called Phish-Nets. This model permits to use parameterized actions and to specify relations between them (inhibiting and preceding). In such models, reactive planning is possible, but the main drawback is the need of an exhaustive specification of all possible interactions between actions.

According to Newell, our goal is to build a model which will allow some adaptative and flexible behaviour to any entity evolving in a complex environment and interacting with other entities. Interactive execution is also fundamental. This has lead us to state that paradigms required for programming a *realistic* behavioural model are: reactivity (which encompasses sporadic or asynchronous events and exceptions), modularity in the behaviour description (which allows parallelism and concurrency of sub-behaviours), data-flow (for the specification of the communication between different modules), hierarchical structuring of the behaviour (which means the possibility of pre-empting sub-behaviours). HPTS[8], as HCSM[1], is a model based on hierarchical concurrent state machines, and it offers a set of programming paradigms which permit to address hierarchical concurrent behaviours. HPTS offers also the ability to manage time informations (such as reaction time, state frequency, delay, minimal and maximal durations) and undeterministic choices[7].

2 HPTS

HPTS[8] which stands for Hierarchical Parallel Transition Systems, consists of a reactive system, which can be viewed as a multi-agent system in which agents are organized as a hierarchy of state machines. Each agent of the system can be viewed as a blackbox with an In/Out data-flow and a set of control parameters. The synchronization of the agent execution is operated by using state machines. To allow an agent to manage concurrent behaviours, sub-agents are organized inside sub-state machines. In the following, agents will be assimilated to state machines. Each state machine of the system is either an atomic state machine, or a composite state machine. Though the model may be coded directly with an imperative programming language like C++, we decided to build a language for the behaviour description. Figure 1 presents the syntax of the behavioural programming language which fully implements the HPTS formalism. As this paper focuses on the integration and management of resources and priority levels, the behavioural description language is not described in details. For a complete description of the model (except for resources and priorities) refers to [7]. Keywords are written in bold, whereas italic typeface represents a non-terminal rule. A * stands for a 0..n repetition while a + stands for a 1..n repetition and a statement enclosed in { } is optional. The description of a state machine is done in the following way: the body of the declaration contains a list of states and a list of transitions between these states. A state is defined by its name and its activity with regard to data-flows. A state accepts an optional duration parameter which stands for the minimum and maximum amount of time spent in the state. A state machine can be parameterized; the set of parameters will be used to characterize a state machine at its creation. Variables are local to a state machine. Only variables that has been declared as outputs can be viewed by the meta state machine. A transition is defined by an origin, an extremity, a transition expression, two optional parameters and a transition body. The transition expression consists of two parts: a *read-expr* which includes the conditions to be fulfilled in order to fire the transition, and a *write-expr* which is a list of the generated events and basic activity

```
SMACHINE Id ;
{
    // Parameters                                    {TRANSITION Id
    PARAMS type Id {, type Id}*;                    {PREFERENCE Value};
    // Variables                                     {
    VARIABLES { {type Id ;}* }                          ORIGIN Id ;
    OUT Id {, Id}* ; // Outputs                         EXTREMITY Id ;
    PRIORITY = numeric expression ;                    {DELAY float ;}
    INITIAL Id ; FINAL Id ;                            {WEIGHT float ;}
    STATES // States Declaration                        read-expr / write-expr
    {{                                                  {TIMEGATE} ;
        Id {[Id {, Id}]} {RANDOM}                       {{ /* transition body */ }}
        {USE resource list};                        }}*
        {{ /* state body */ }}                   }
    }+}
```

Figure 1. Syntax of the language.

primitives on the state machine. The body of a transition (C++ code) is executed after the action part. As for the body part of a state, it is possible to call extern functions or methods and to access to the value of outputs of sub-state machines. Afterwards, C++ code for our simulation platform is generated. It is totally encapsulated: all transitions systems are included in their own class directly inheriting from an abstract state machine class which provides pure virtual methods for running the state machines and debugging methods. An interpreter has also been implemented, which is very useful for the behaviour specification phase as it allows to modify state-machines during the execution phase.

3 Behaviour synchronization

In order to synchronize behaviours and to allow efficient mixing of behaviours in accordance with their relative importance, notions of resources, degrees of preference and priorities have been introduced. Resources allow to describe exclusions between behaviours while degrees of preference are used to describe different possible realizations or possibilities of adaptation of a behaviour. Using this information, a scheduler automatically synchronize the different behaviours according to their respective priorities.

3.1 Resources

For all state machines running in the HPTS hierarchy, a set of resources is defined. Those resources are considered as semaphores, thus they are used for mutual exclusion. A set of resources is associated to each node of a state machine; it contains all resources used by a node. Hence, resource allocations are adapted to the state machine granularity. This type of description allows to handle resource allocations automatically:

- Entering a node implies that its associated resources are taken.
- Exiting a node implies that its resources are released.

- A resource will be kept if two nodes connected by a transition use it.

As resources are semaphores, one constraint has to be respected while running parallel state machines: all nodes executed in parallel have to use different resources. Using this constraint it becomes possible to synchronize the execution of parallel state machines according to the resources they use, by only authorizing transitions in nodes which do not use allocated resources.

Given that several parallel state machines are using the same set of resources, the problem of dead lock has to be studied. A dead lock occurs when the dependency graph of resources is cyclic. Therefore, in order to ensure maximum security and to make synchronization easier to handle, it is necessary to provide a mechanism ensuring that no dead lock can arise. While compiling the different state machines, information about resource allocation dependencies are pre-compiled. Thus, at runtime, the scheduler is able to use this information in order to check upon the fact that executing two nodes in parallel can not lead to a deadlock. This mechanism is very useful because it allows describing behaviours without precise knowledge on other behaviours.

As HPTS is a hierarchical model, each state machine can create sons and wait for their ending; this type of synchronization creates dependencies between state machines. Consequently, it exists risks of dead lock if a state machine using same resources than one of its son is waiting until its ending. Thus, another constraint has been added: resources used by a state machine must be different than resources used by its descendants. Respecting this constraint ensures that all descendants can be executed and terminated before the ending of their ascendants. As structure of state machines is known before runtime, this constraint can be checked while compiling state machines. By now those resources are used to describe internal resources of the agent like its hands, eyes or legs. They allow synchronizing behaviour in accordance to body parts they use.

3.2 Degrees of preferences

The notion of degree of preference has been introduced in order to provide the ability to describe different possibilities of adaptation of a behaviour, depending on resources availability.

A degree of preference (p) is associated to each transition of a state machine. It is a real coefficient with value in interval $[-1; 1]$. This coefficient corresponds to the state machine proclivity to use this transition when the associated condition is true. Depending on its value, it has different meanings:

- $p > 0$: This transition favors the realization of the behaviour. By default, the transition having the greatest degree of preference should be chosen.
- $p < 0$: This transition does not favor the realization of the behaviour. Those transitions are used to describe a coherent way of stopping behaviour or adapting its execution while releasing some resources.
- $p = 0$: the behaviour is quite indifferent to this transition.

This coefficient allows to concentrate all information about a specific behaviour into one state machine. Due to state machine structure, the concentration ensures consistency during the realization of the behaviour. Let consider the state machine of figure 2; transitions are labeled with their associated conditions and degrees of preference. It describes a behaviour consisting in moving an object. While moving an object, eyes are necessary when taking the object and putting it somewhere; but while moving it, it is possible to focus on the object or to look at something else. Transition starting from state *MoveAndWatch* and ending by *MoveObject* has a degree of preference of -0.4

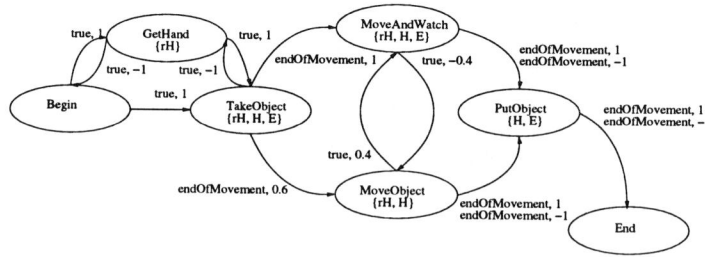

Figure 2. Moving object behaviour.

which specifies that, by default, this transition should not be used, except if another behaviour needs to take eyes resource. The reciprocal transition has a degree of preference of 0.4 according the same positive preference to return into state *MoveAndWatch*. Using degrees of preference, this behaviour is totally described. Then the scheduler will choose to force behaviour to transit in the state which does not use eyes or to stay in the state which uses the eyes if no other behaviour needs the eyes.

3.3 Priority

The notion of priority has been introduced to provide the ability to specify the importance of a behaviour relatively to others. A priority function is associated to each state machine running in HPTS hierarchy. This function returns a real value representing the importance of a behaviour in a given context. Depending on its sign, this function has different meanings:

- $priority > 0$: the behaviour must be achieved, and is adapted to the current context. This value can be interpreted as a coefficient of adequacy between context and behaviour.
- $priority < 0$: the behaviour is inhibited, the value can be interpreted as a coefficient of inadequacy between context and behaviour.

This function is user defined. Thus, it can be correlated to different parameters, such as for example:

- physiological parameters;
- a value related to a plan generated by a rational model, in that case, it is correlated to the importance of the goal this action contributes to satisfy:
- a stimuli related to the environment to handle reflex behaviours.

This priority function provides an easy way to control the behaviour realization.

3.4 Scheduling

Notions explained below are used to create a scheduler. It allows to schedule different parallel behaviours in such a way that behaviours having the greatest priority will be favored in their execution and will automatically adapt their execution, if it is possible, to the other ones which are running. State machines are executed at a fixed frequency. Thus, a scheduling is computed at each time step. At the beginning of the time step, the scheduler collects information from each state machine. This information is compounded of the current state of a state machine plus all accessible nodes (i.e. nodes ending a transition with a true condition and starting from current node) ; this results in the creation of a set of possible transitions.

Then the scheduler computes a weight for each transition of this set. Let note $prio$ the current priority of the considered state machine, p the degree of preference associated to the transition ending with the state e. The weight (W) associated to this transition is computed as follow:

$$W = prio * p \tag{1}$$

Let consider a weight W associated to a proposition, this weight has different meanings:

- $W > 0$: state machine is proned to transit in the state associated to the proposition. Two cases can arise:
  - $(prio > 0) \wedge (p > 0)$: transiting to this node favors the accomplishment of the behaviour.
  - $(prio < 0) \wedge (p < 0)$: the behaviour is inhibited; transitions that conduct to a coherent stop of the behaviour have to be favored.
- $W < 0$: state machine is not proned to transit in this node. Two cases can arise:
  - $(prio > 0) \wedge (p < 0)$: transiting in this state does not favor the realization of the behaviour. This case can be used for proposing a possibility of adaptation of the behaviour by releasing some resources. It can also be used to stop behaviour execution because a behaviour having a greater priority needs resources used by the considered behaviour.
  - $(prio < 0) \wedge (p > 0)$: the behaviour is inhibited, this case can be used to propose an other possibility of stopping behaviour by using less resources.
- $W = 0$: state machine is indifferent to transit in this node.

Once weights associated to each proposition of transition of the state machines are computed, the scheduler is searching for a combination of propositions between all state machines respecting resource constraints (no resource conflict and no possible deadlock) and maximizing the sum of associated weights. Therefore, behaviours having the greatest priorities will be favored in their execution while those having lowest priorities will release their resources, if possible and in a consistent way. Adaptation between concurrent behaviours becomes automatic when the concurrency concerns the sharing of common internal resources.

4   Example

Let us consider a complex behaviour consisting in drinking a coffee and smoking a cigarette while reading a newspaper. This kind of combination of multiple behaviours can not be directly handled by systems using mutual exclusion on behaviours which use themselves common resources. Moreover, a specific behaviour has to be created for systems using only semaphores synchronization without notions of priority and adaptation. In this section, we will study this example and show how the scheduler, helped with notions of resources, degrees of preference and priorities, is able to reproduce this behaviour just by describing independently the three sub-behaviours and their associated priority functions.

178

4.1 Behaviour description

All state machines use the following set of resources: Hl (left hand), Hr (right hand), rHl (reserve left hand), rHr (reserve right hand), M (mouth) and E (eyes). Resources rHl/rHr are used to handle releasing of resources Hl/Hr. The scheduler can only act on the next transition of a state machine. Hands are resources that often need more than one transition to be freed, for instance, putting down an object to free the hand resource. Then a state which only use resource Hr/Hl corresponds to a behaviour of freeing a hand resource.

The behaviour is compounded of three sub behaviours: read a newspaper, drink a coffee and smoke a cigarette. All state machines used to solve this problem are presented in figures 3, 4 and 5. In these state machines, resource H stands for Hr or Hl as it exists the same behaviour for each hand. Note that descriptions of state machines are totally independent one from each other.

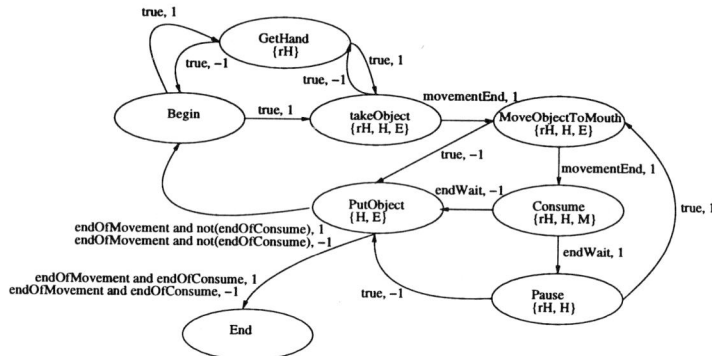

Figure 3. Common behaviour for drinking and smoking.

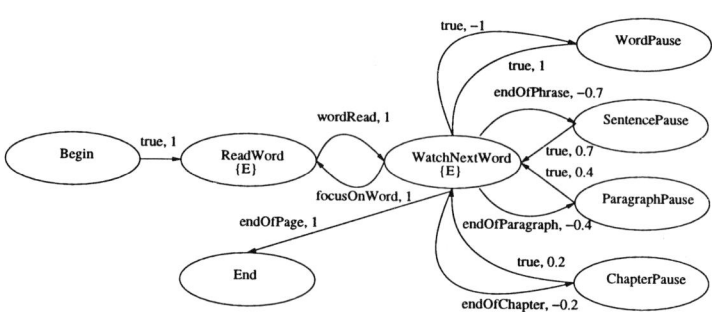

Figure 4. Reading behaviour.

Drinking and smoking: Those two behaviours are described through the same state machine consisting in grasping the object of interest, moving it to the mouth and keeping the object into the hand. The object is put on the table if another behaviour needs hand resource or if the current behaviour becomes inhibited.

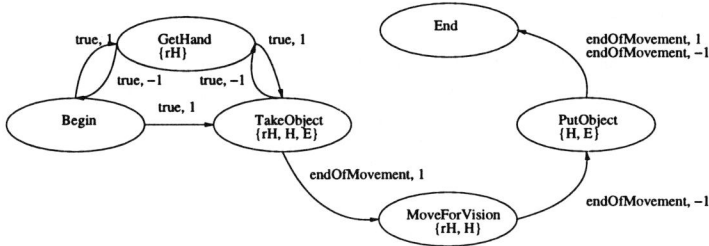

Figure 5. Behaviour handling hands while reading.

Reading the newspaper: This behaviour consists in two parallel sub-behaviours. One consists in reading the newspaper with different possibilities of pause depending on the text structure. Those different levels of interruption are described through degrees of preference. The second consists in manipulating the newspaper taking it into the hand and moving it near the eyes.

Note that thanks to resources, each behaviour is described independently from the others but propose different possibilities of adaptation. Each possibility of adaptation is described through degrees of preference which allow to specify the cost of such adaptation. Moreover, as a mechanism ensures that no deadlock can arise, conceiving a behaviour does not need to know other described behaviours.

Defining priorities: the importance of behaviours described below depends on different parameters. The difficulty arises with the fact of unifying priority functions that depend on different parameters.

Drinking and smoking: those two behaviours have variable priorities evolving with the time. Those priorities are directly correlated to the thirst/need of nicotine. Let note $p(t)$ the priority function where t represents the time. It has the following definition:

$$\begin{cases} p(t) = p(t - dt) + dp_1 \times dt \; if \; not(consuming) \\ p(t) = p(t - dt) - dp_2 \times dt \; if \; consuming \end{cases} \qquad (2)$$

where dp_1 (respectively dp_2) is the increase rate (respectively the decrease rate) of the thirst or the need of nicotine. Consuming stands for drinking or smoking depending on the behaviour. Then, when instantiating state machines corresponding to those behaviours, dp_2 becomes a parameter as well as the priority function which is linked to the thirst or the need of nicotine.

Reading: priority of reading behaviour is correlated to the interest of the reader for the text. In this example the function is defined as a constant. The behaviour having the greatest priority is the reading one while behaviour allowing to manipulate the sheet has a lower priority.

Note that once behaviours are described through state machines, they are controlled through their priority. This property allow to handle every type of executive behaviour without need of information about their internal structure in term of resources or possible adaptations.

4.2 Scheduling the example

In order to handle the reading behaviour, another behaviour has been added which consists in moving a sheet of paper with the right hand in front of the agent in order to read, and when the sheet is read, it is moved and the next sheet is taken. Moving the sheet of paper is handled by the behaviour described in figure 2. The priorities have been defined as follow:

- Moving sheet, followed by reading the sheet have a constant priority of 2.0.
- Manipulating the sheet while reading have a constant priority of 1.5 and can be realized with right or left hand.
- Drinking and smoking behaviours have a variable priority function. It is the function given in equation 2. Their increase rates are respectively set to 0.02/0.05 per second whereas their decrease rates are respectively set to 0.08/0.07 per second. Moreover, corresponding state machines stay in state *Consume* for a maximum time of one second, and stay in state *Pause* for a minimum of 10 seconds.

During execution phase, moving sheet behaviour is followed by manipulating and reading sheet behaviours, while drinking and smoking behaviours are continually running.

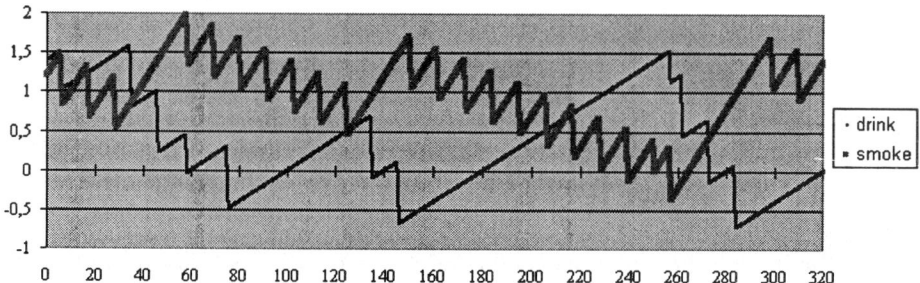

Figure 6. Evolution of drinking and smoking priorities during simulation. x axis corresponds to elapsed time in seconds, y axis corresponds to the priority value.

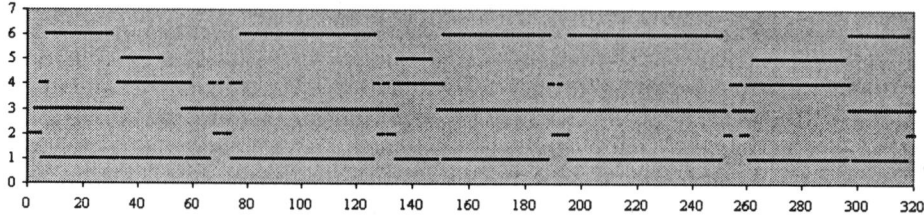

Figure 7. Activity of behaviours during simulation.

Figure 6 describes evolution of drinking and smoking priorities during the simulation. By default thirst and need of nicotine levels are increasing. Decrease is due to consumption linked to drinking and smoking behaviours. Note that thirst and need of nicotine never decrease at the same time, due to mutual exclusion on mouth noticed in node *Consume* of their corresponding state machines.

Figure 7 shows activity of each running behaviour. Activity is defined by states using resources Hr/Hl/E/M, which can be assimilated to active resources (i.e. resources enabling manipulation of body parts). In this figure, 1 stands for the activity of reading the sheet of paper, 2 the activity of moving the sheet of paper, 3 the activity of smoking with the left hand, 4 the activity of drinking with the right hand, 5 the activity of manipulating the sheet of paper with the left hand and 6 the activity of manipulating the sheet of paper with the right hand. Parallelization of actions shown in this figure and mutual exclusion of behaviours are automatically handled by the scheduler. It exploits all propositions of transitions of state machines describing behaviours. For example, at time $30 - 40$, interruption of smoking behaviour, whereas its priority is active, is due to request of left hand resource by behaviour consisting in manipulating the sheet, which has a greater priority. This organization of behaviours has been automatically generated by the scheduler such as the overall realization of the example (Cf. figure 8).

The overall example has been designed in one day, helped by a high level pilot allowing to control character animation through simple primitives. It shows the advances of the scheduling system which allows to describe independently all behaviours with their different possibilities of adaptation. During running phase, their adaptation to all other running behaviours is automatic. Moreover, consistency is ensured because the scheduler can only exploit for each state machine consistent propositions of transition.

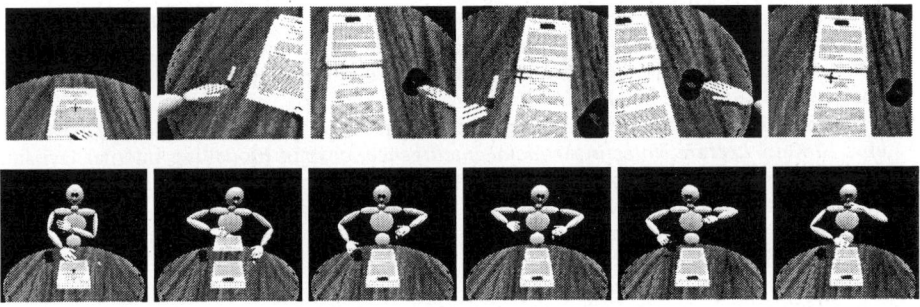

Figure 8. Behavioural Coordination Example.

5 Conclusion

We have presented in this paper a generic approach to integrate the management of resources and priority levels into HPTS, our formal model. This formal model has been implemented in a description language which is able to generate efficient C++ code for GASP, our Simulation Platform. The behavioral model allows us to describe, in a same way, different kinds of living beings, and to simulate them in the same virtual environment, while most of behavioral models are presently restricted to the animation of one model in a specific environment.

Another important point is that our behavioral model has been built to generate dynamic entities which are both autonomous and controllable, allowing us to use the same model in different contexts and moreover with different levels of control. Resources and priorities are described in an easy way, and behaviour incompatibilities are automatically detected. The scheduling algorithm enables us to combine together and to orchestrate several behaviours, depending on the human character intentions and desires. In the contrary of some previous approach, it is not necessary to specify exhaustively all behaviours that are mutually exclusive; this is done implicitly just by attaching resources to nodes and a priority function to each state machine, and by using a scheduler. Actually, our scheduler is able to handle a fixed number of resources declared at compilation time. An extension would be to allow resource declaration at runtime in order to handle external resources. Another extension will be to connect this work to a higher level of reasoning. Video sequences related to the example can be found at http://www.irisa.fr/prive/donikian/resources/.

References

1. O. Ahmad, J. Cremer, S. Hansen, J. Kearney, and P. Willemsen. Hierarchical, concurrent state machines for behavior modeling and scenario control. In *Conference on AI, Planning, and Simulation in High Autonomy Systems*, Gainesville, Florida, USA, 1994.
2. S. Ambroszkiewicz and J. Komar. *Formal Models of Agents*, volume 1760 of *Lecture Notes in Artificial Intelligence*, chapter A Model of BDI-Agent in Game-Theoretic Framework, pages 8–19. Springer, 2000.
3. N.I. Badler, B.D. Reich, and B.L. Webber. Towards personalities for animated agents with reactive and planning behaviors. *Lecture Notes in Artificial Intelligence, Creating Personalities for synthetic actors*, (1195):43–57, 1997.
4. R. Bindiganavale, W. Schuler, J. Allbeck, N.I. Badler, A.K. Joshi, and M. Palmer. Dynamically altering agent behaviors using natural language instructions. In C. Sierra, M. Gini, and J.S. Rosenschein, editors, *International Conference on Autonomous Agents*, pages 293–300, Barcelona, Spain, June 2000. ACM Press.
5. F. Brazier, B. Dunin-Keplicz, J. Treur, and R. Verbrugge. *Formal Models of Agents*, volume 1760 of *Lecture Notes in Artificial Intelligence*, chapter Modelling Internal Dynamic Behaviour of BDI Agents, pages 36–56. Springer, 2000.
6. V. Decugis and J. Ferber. Action selection in an autonomous agent with a hierarchical distributed reactive planning architecture. In *Autonomous Agents'98*, pages 354–361, Minneapolis, USA, 1998. ACM.
7. S. Donikian. HPTS: a behaviour modelling language for autonomous agents. In *Fifth International Conference on Autonomous Agents*, Montreal, Canada, May 2001. ACM Press.
8. S. Donikian and E. Rutten. Reactivity, concurrency, data-flow and hierarchical preemption for behavioural animation. In E.H. Blake R.C. Veltkamp, editor, *Programming Paradigms in Graphics'95*, Eurographics Collection. Springer-Verlag, 1995.
9. J. Funge, X. Tu, and D. Terzopoulos. Cognitive modeling: Knowledge, reasoning and planning for intelligent characters. In *SIGGRAPH'99*, pages 29–38, Los Angeles, August 1999.
10. P. Maes. Situated agents can have goals. *Robotics and Autonomous Systems*, 6:49–70, 1990.
11. J.J. Ch. Meyer and P.Y. Schobbens, editors. *Formal Models of Agents*, volume 1760 of *Lecture Notes in Artificial Intelligence*. Springer, 2000.
12. A. Newell. *Unified Theories of Cognition*. Harvard University Press, 1990.
13. H. Noser and D. Thalmann. Sensor based synthetic actors in a tennis game simulation. In *Computer Graphics International'97*, pages 189–198, Hasselt, Belgium, June 1997. IEEE Computer Society Press.
14. B. J. Rhodes. *PHISH-Nets : Planning Heuristically In Situated Hybrid Networks*. PhD thesis, Massachusetts Institute of Technology, 1996.
15. A. Sloman. What sort of control system is able to have a personality. In R. Trappl and P. Petta, editors, *Creating Personalities for Synthetic Actors*, volume 1195 of *Lecture Notes in Artificial Intelligence*, pages 166–208. Springer-Verlag, 1997.

Evolution and Cooperation of Virtual Entities with Classifier Systems

Cédric Sanza, Olivier Heguy and Yves Duthen

Image Synthesis and Behavioral Simulation group
IRIT laboratory - University Paul Sabatier
118 route de Narbonne
31062 Toulouse cedex, France
sanza@irit.fr

Abstract. This paper presents a behavioral system based on artificial life paradigms. The system, called αCS, is suited to be employed for the animation of virtual entities immersed in concurrent and changing environments. The αCS system is the extension of an original classifier system to collaborative abilities. The main modifications enable αCS to use cooperation and communication to build dynamically the behavior of virtual entities which goal is to achieve several tasks. Our classifier system is evaluated by the way of two applications. Firstly, we present the performances of αCS in an optimization problem consisting on following a moving target. Secondly, we investigate a complex 3D world where autonomous entities and avatars interact. Through the simulation of a virtual game, we show how the integration of our system in virtual entities enables to build evolving behaviors thanks to adaptation, communication and auto-organization.

1. Introduction

Immersion in virtual worlds where human clones and creatures are melted is a growing research field [1][7]. Required qualities for such environments are a realistic scene from one hand and a high level of interaction on the other hand. However, interaction between real and virtual actors is a complex problem. The behavior of a virtual entity has to be coherent and adaptive to ensure its evolution all along the simulation. In order to build such a behavioral system, we propose to use classifier systems [2,3].

A classifier system is a reinforcement system composed of three main parts : a set of binary rules called classifiers, a reward system and a genetic algorithm. A classifier has two parts and a strength that represents its efficiency. The two parts are the condition (sensor) and the action (effector).

Each cycle, a classifier system gets the environmental message that represents the state perceived by the system. Then, it selects a rule that matches the environmental message and triggers the action part of this rule. Finally, the reward system updates the strength of the rule thanks to a pre-defined fitness function. Periodically, the genetic algorithm creates new rules from the existing ones by using mutation and crossing-over.

Nowadays, there are many versions of LCS that enable different potentialities like prediction (XCS [11]) or anticipation (ACS [10]). All these systems are very powerful and present an important contribution to classifier systems. In our problem, the XCS or ACS are not applicable. Indeed, we want to integrate classifier systems in virtual entities that use cooperation and communication to solve multiple goals simultaneously. We have then extended a classical LCS to these characteristics with our model αCS.

The paper is organized as follows. In the first part, we describe αCS and the main ideas we have implemented. In the second part we present two applications of αCS ("Cat and Mouse" and "Virtual Soccer") and the encouraging results we obtain. In the last part, we conclude and give further applications of our model.

2. The Classifier System αCS

Based on the LCS, our model has been severely modified to take into account the constraints we have cited in the introduction. Inside αCS, these modifications concern the sensors, the effectors and the reward system. Outside αCS, the system is extended with a cooperation module and a communication layers (figure 1).

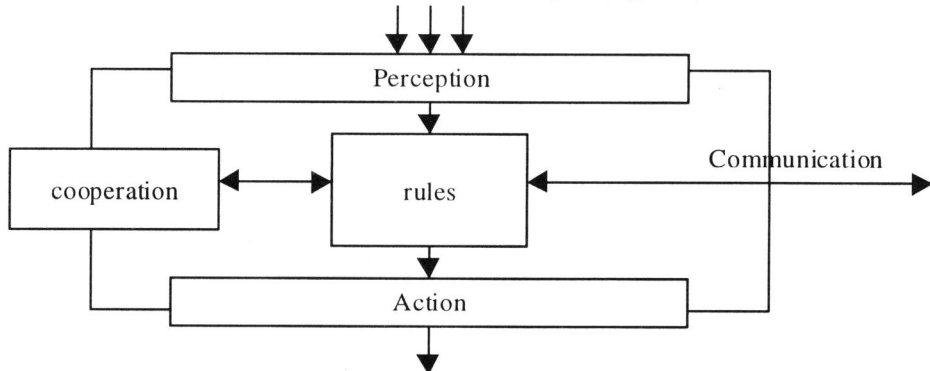

Fig.1. Interface between αCS and the environment

The heart of our system is a ruleset composed of length-fixed rules. Each rule has a strength and a binary structure. A rule uses the finite alphabet {0;1} to represent its condition part (sensors) and its action part (effector). In our approach, we consider the "1" bit as a True value and the "0" as a lack of information or a False value. The role of the "0" enables to represent uncertain information about the environment.

2.1. Architecture

Active Sensors. The environmental message that triggers the condition part of a rule is composed of bits that represent boolean sensors. We call them active sensors as they only represent the information that is perceived in the world. The selection of a rule is made though the comparison between the environmental and the condition part of each rule. In correlation with the definition of our sensors, the selection differs from the classical one. A rule is selected if all the bits "1" of its condition are active in the environmental message. This condition is traduced by the following property: each bit of the environmental message has to be inferior to the environmental message's one

This representation brings many advantages. Firstly, it enables to represent rules with sure conditions in noisy environments. For example, the rule 001100:000010101 means:

IF condition3 is sure AND condition4 is sure THEN effector000010101

Control of the Behavior. In simple environments, there is no need of hierarchy between the effectors. Indeed, each effector is represented by a unique binary sub-string that represents the condition part of a rule. In our virtual reality applications, we want to control the presence of selected effectors in the basis to favor some special actions. Indeed, there are often main behaviors and secondary behavior in animation of creatures and they would not be used at the same rate.

Our idea is based on the decomposition of the action part in "NbEff" sub-strings (NbEff is the number of effectors). Each sub-string "i" represents the weight of the effector "i" in the action part. For each rule, the selected action is the one which owns the highest binary sub-string. For example, the action part "000 010 101" correspond to the effector #3. If two sub-strings have the same weight, the winner is the first sub-string. The length of each sub-string is $1+\alpha$. The α parameter appears to be very influent on the repartition of the effectors in the basis. When α is high, finding two sub-strings with the same value is rare and all the effectors have the same probabilities. When α is low, an implicit hierarchy between the effectors emerges. For instance, with $\alpha=1$ and NbEff=2, we obtain the following probabilities:

- Effector 1: proba1 = 10/16
(action parts: 00 00 ; 01 00 ; 01 01 ; 10 00 ; 10 01 ; 10 10 ; 11 00 ; 11 01 ; 11 10 ; 11 11)

- Effector 2: proba2 = 6/16
(action parts: 00 01; 00 10 ; 00 11 ; 01 10 ; 01 11 ; 10 11)

Here, the probability of appearance of the effector1 will be higher than the second. With many effectors, α enables to optimize the behaviors by influencing the distribution of the actions in the basis.

The Reward System. The reward system works with a set of fitness functions (FFs [6]) that represent simple goals to achieve. At each time step, the reward R is computed as the weighted sum of the FFs. As shown in the figure 2, each environmental message is associated to a sub-network of the reward system. The weights enable to represent the degree of usefulness of the fitness in the reward.

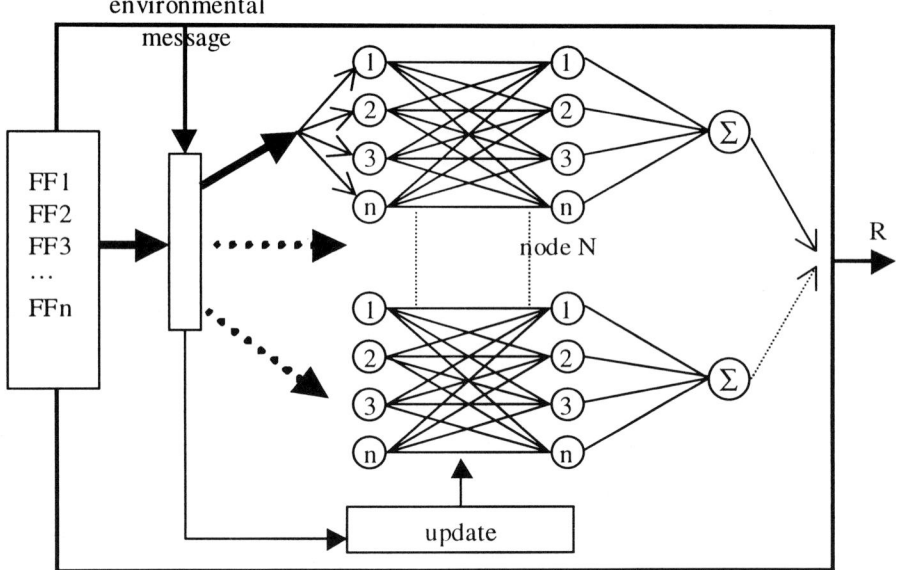

Fig. 2. The reward system works as a neural network. The environmental message triggers the sub-network that computes the nodes Nj. The weights wij are constant, the weights wii are updated thanks to the fitness FFi. The output of the network is the average of the nodes Nj

The weights wii are dynamically adjusted by the UpD function (figure 3) to give more power to a fitness whose results is very high or very low ((1) in figure 3). Then, an insignificant fitness will be ignored in the reward R ((2) in figure 3).

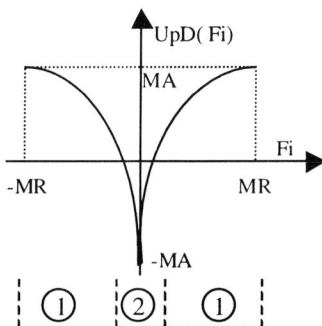

Fig. 3. The UpD function is used to update the weight wii corresponding to the fitness function FFi. MR and MA are respectively the maximum reward and the maximum add possible

We use the recent past of the classifier to compute the final retribution "FR" [8]. The "p" successive rewards are weighted by a function that increases with time ("t") to favor recent and positive rewards, without neglecting the past:

$$FR = \frac{\sum_{u=0}^{p-1} coef(u) \cdot R(t-u)}{\sum_{u=0}^{p-1} coef(u)}$$

With coef(u) = p-u   if R(t-u)>0

              1   else

Taking the past of a classifier into account allows to decrease the effects of parasites in the reward. Then, the system is more robust to unpredictable events and keeps high strengths to efficient classifiers.

2.2. Extension of αCS

Cooperation. In collaborative environment, it is necessary to define a way to favor cooperation. Then, a second level of fitness functions has been added. These functions are called global fitness functions (GFF). They are totally independent from the set of fitness function. Their role is to maintain a defined state or to maximize a parameter of the simulation. In the application, they will favor the auto-organization of the entities and make them more efficient in the accomplishment of their tasks.

When a GFF is triggered, it updates the strength of a rule with a classical "Bucket Brigade" algorithm [4]. These GFFs are activated by special events and contributes to the interactivity and the diversity of the behaviors by bringing punctual constraints to satisfy.

Communication. The communication between entities is used to exchange efficient rules [5]. Our classifier system is equipped with a module that supervises the reward. When bad rewards are detected, the entity starts a communication request by sending its actual state to other entities. This state corresponds to the environmental message of the entity. The other entities may search for a rule which condition part could be triggered by the message, and eventually send it back to the entity.

This very simple mechanism enables to speed up the search of efficient rules in the basis. With the rule-sharing, the entity gets a rule with the condition part corresponding to the environmental message and an effector. The question is "will this effector be efficient for this entity ?". the experience shows that it only depends on the simulation.

When entities do not have the same sensors and effectors, the communication needs a translation stage to convert a message from an entity to another. Thus, we use an intermediary binary language known by each entity to make each message understandable.

3. Applications

We evaluate αCS through two different applications. The first application uses the abilities of classical classifier systems. It is composed of two entities: Mouse which behavior is pre-programmed and Cat which behavior is managed by αCS. The role of Cat is to move towards Mouse and to follow it. The second application consists of two concurrent teams of 11 entities playing soccer. In this example, each entity will be able to use the cooperation ability to favor auto-organization and the communication ability to be more efficient.

3.1. Mouse and Cat

This application is composed of two entities. The first one is Mouse, which behavior is pre-programmed. Mouse indefinitely follows the same path represented by a circle. Cat is totally autonomous as it is equipped with ☐CS. Cat has 8 sensors to perceive the relative position of the Mouse {N, NW, W, SW, S, SE, E, NE}. It owns 8 effectors to move in eight different directions {moveN, moveNW, ...} and a unique fitness function "F" that represents the progression of Cat towards Mouse:

$$F = D(t)-D(t-1)$$
$$\text{with } D = \text{Distance(Mouse, Cat)}$$

The speed of the two entities are identical to enable Cat to reach and follow Mouse. The main difficulty of this problem comes from the perpetual movement of Mouse. Even if Cat moves towards Mouse, the fitness may not be positive and penalize the action, for example if the directions of Mouse and Cat are the same.

Learning. We test αCS with different configurations to optimize some parameters like the number of classifiers and α.
We start with 100 classifiers and α=5. The simulation immediately shows that the best adapted moves to the circular path are diagonal moves (NE, NW, SE, SW). After a short time (500 iterations), Cat can follow Mouse by using 4 rules, each one representing a different direction.
The use of the diagonal moves enables us to optimize the number of classifiers by reducing α and rearranging the effectors. By setting the four diagonal moves at the beginning of the list {NW, NE, SW, SE, E, W, S, N}, the system will implicitly give a higher probability of presence to these first 4 effectors. Taking into account this new parameter, the learning speed is reduced about 20% and the system quickly converges towards a solution (figure 4).

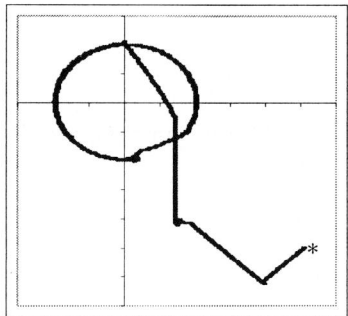

Fig. 4. One of the best trajectories obtained by Cat. The parameter α is set to 2. The initial position of Cat is down-right (*). The trajectory of Mouse is perfectly followed by Cat after a few iterations with optima parameters. The speed of Cat and Mouse are identical

Whatever the number of classifiers is, the system finally uses four rules. In the figure 5, we test the system with a decreasing number of classifiers. This figure shows that the minimum value we can use is 6 classifiers. Even if the simulation is longer, we do not reach the theoretical value 4. The same test with a classical LCS gives 16 classifiers for 10000 iterations and 12 classifiers for 15000 iterations. These conditions are extreme and they demonstrate that we can strongly optimize our system if we have an idea of the result, without deleting any effector.

Nevertheless, the field of animation requires a fast learning stage to produce a coherent behavior and, with this simulation, we must keep a number of classifiers close to 100.

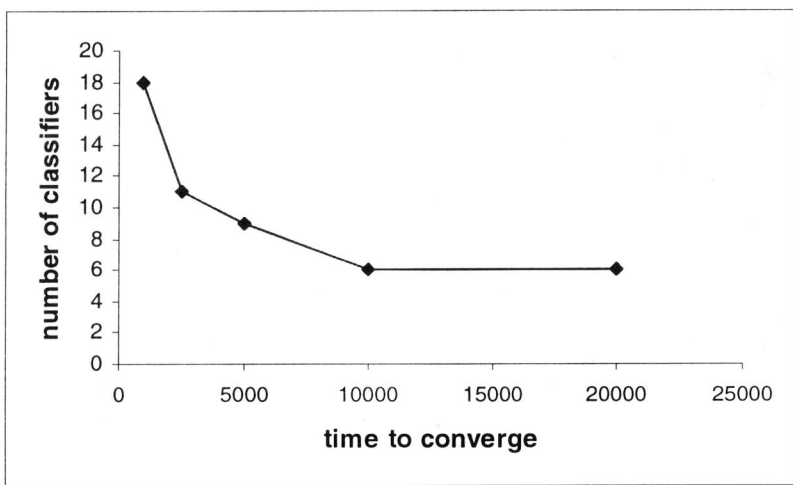

Fig. 5. Y-axis represents the minimum number of classifiers obtained on several simulations for a given number of iterations (X-axis)

190

In this part, we have shown the influence of selected parameters on the learning ability of αCS. Compared to procedural approaches, the main difference comes from the way to reach a goal. With our system, we do not describe the behavior of Cat with a static algorithm but we give the tools to reach this goal and we let the solutions appear by emergence. At this level, the performances could be the same for the two methods. But if the environment changes, the algorithm defined for the procedural approach needs to be rewritten. With a classifier system, the rules can immediately evolve to cope with new parameters of the environment as shown in the next part, and surpass classical approaches.

Adaptation. We evaluate αCS through the same problem but, during the simulation, we invert the 8 effectors of Cat (figure 6). For example, the effector moveN becomes moveS...

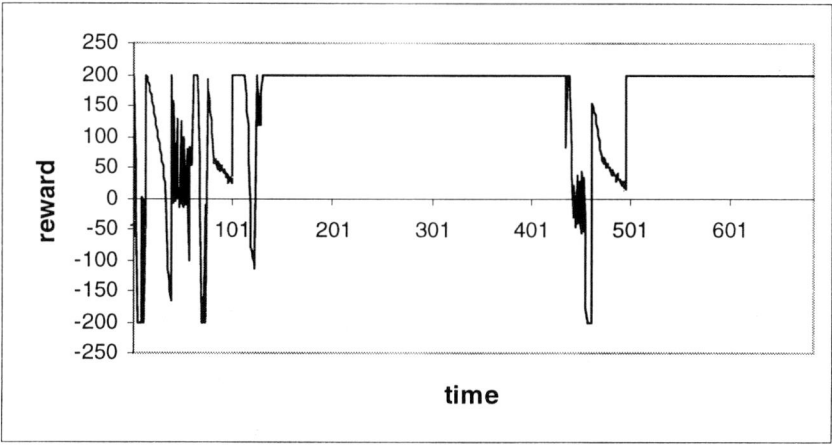

Fig. 6. X-axis is the reward of Cat during the test. The inversion appears after the convergence of the system to ensure a complete new learning stage. In this simulation we use 100 classifiers

The curve is composed of 4 parts. In the first part (from 0 to 129), the system gets immediate bad rewards and tries to find new rules. In the second part, Cat has found 3 new classifiers and uses them with success. The third part corresponds to the last rule discovered by Cat. After the time 500, there is no longer evolution.

This test shows that the adaptation of αCS to the new effectors is very fast (500 iterations). This performance is largely due to the genetic algorithm that maintains the diversity in the set of rules. By using the mutation operator, the genetic algorithms lightly modifies selected rules and then enables the system to be more efficient. By using the crossing-over operator, the genetic algorithm creates new rules that will be used when the system is confronted to a new situation.

3.2. NeVis

The second application is called NeVis (Networked Virtual Soccer [9]). NeViS is a distributed 3D environment where avatars and autonomous entities interact in real-time in a virtual soccer game. The world is composed of the scene, 22 players and the ball (figure 7).

The distribution of the application is assured by the World2World client-server software [12] and it runs both on Unix and Windows platforms. The principle of World2World is to define sharing properties (rotation and translation) on the objects of the simulation and to update these properties on the different machines when an object moves.

The environment and the characters are designed by WorldToolKit [12]. WorldToolKit is powerful tools that enables to create real-time virtual worlds and to manage many devices.

Each player is represented by a 3D animated character. The movements of the arms and legs are played by motion capture. The global movement is triggered by αCS that uses high-level behaviors.

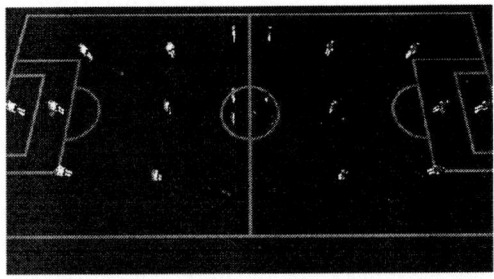

Fig. 7. NeViS enables several users to interact in a Virtual Soccer game. Several users can take the control of players with a SpaceMouse and use the graphical interface to communicate. Each player perceives a global vision of the game

In this simulation, we test all extra-abilities of αCS. The list of sensors and effectors are below:

Sensors:

#1: with-ball
#2: without-ball
#3: no-collision
#4: in-front-of-initial-position
#5: behind-initial-position
#6: far-from-initial-position
#7: near-from-initial-position

Effectors:

#1: go-to-ball
#2: go-to-initial-position
#3: shoot-strong-to-goal
#4: shoot-weak-to-goal
#5: pass-to-player
#6: move-forward
#7: roam

As for Cat, the fitness functions are computed from distances. For each player, we use three fitness functions built thanks to the same formula $D_i(t)-D_i(t-1)$ with

- D1= distance between the player and the ball
- D2= distance between the player and its initial position
- D3= distance between the ball and the goal

We use two GFFs. The first GFF is activated when a team scores, by rewarding this team and penalizing the other. The second GFF penalizes close players to favor the dispersion of the entities on the field.

Results. In the simulation, all the players have the same sensors, effectors, FF, GFF and parameters (100 classifiers randomly initialized, $\alpha=3$). By setting identical parameters to the 22 entities, there is no specialization before the game starts.
Each simulation runs in real-time, with approximately 30 frames per second and starts by setting the players to their initial position. The most common characteristic we have noted on the different simulations are presented in the next paragraph.

After the first iterations, the first behaviors emerge. Some players learn to move towards their initial position and others learn to move towards the ball. Then, the entities start to kick or pass the ball and this kind of interaction generates new rules.
Each entity creates approximately five efficient rules. In this sub-set, we find three kind of rules: allowing to move towards the initial position, to move towards the ball and to kick the ball. Even if the action part may be common to all the players, they have different condition parts. It demonstrates that the entities become specialized in different tasks. Some of them become more defensive and some become more offensive.
These five classifiers do not last for a long time. There is a constant evolution of the rules that emerge and die periodically, according to the adaptation of the other team. All along the simulation we remark that the most generalized rules (with few "0" and many "1" in the condition part) are the first to disappear. As the interaction generates a lot of different situations, a rule will be solicited by many environmental messages and the risk to be inefficient increases. Then, the most robust rules are the most specialized (with many "0" and few "1" in the condition part) with an average of three conditions per rule.

Cooperation. The cooperation system is responsible for the evolution of the rules. The role of the two GFF is double. It enables to reward a rule that could not have enough strength with the FFs alone. It penalizes classifiers that would not be without the GFFs. In the first case, a GFF can be useful for rules which are few used. In the second case, the effect of a GFF can be the destruction of a rule and the necessity to find a new behavior.

Communication. The evaluation of the rule-sharing is realized though two simulations by the analyze of the average reward. The first simulation works without any kind of communication and the second enables one team to communicate. Then, we run twice the same scenario by using the same number seed (making the same initial ruleset for the two simulations). An example of average reward of the two teams is presented on the figure 8.

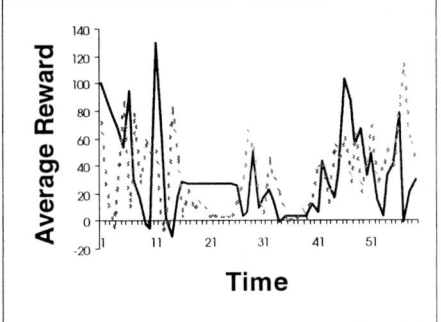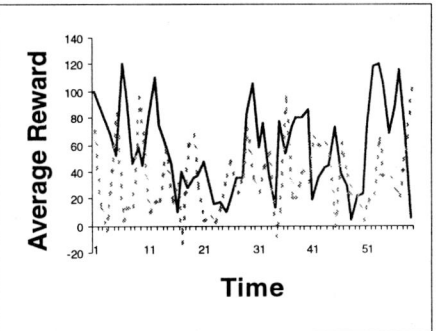

Fig. 8. At the left, the figure corresponds to a simulation without communication. At the right, we enable communication for the team whose average reward is represented by a full line (noted team 1). X-axis is the time (1 unit = 5 seconds) and Y-axis is the average reward of a team during 100 time steps

During the second run, the average reward of team 1 remains positive and higher than the one obtained in the first simulation. Moreover, the average reward of team 2 is directly influenced by the communication. Logically, the benefit for a team becomes a penalization for the other.

The communication happens during various events, for example when many players collide, or when they mutually fight for the possession of the ball.

The main advantage of the communication is to reduce the time to find a rule. The entity does not need to test several rules before to find the one that will be correct. This feature is particularly interesting at the beginning of the simulation to speed up the learning stage. Communication is less efficient for long simulations. Soccer requires various specializations in the game and sharing the same rule could involve a standardization of the behaviors.

4. Conclusion and Further Work

In this paper, we have described a system inspired from LCS devoted to the behavioral simulation of virtual entities. The features of our system are the ability to generate autonomous behaviors thanks to rewards and the ability to automatically adapt to the evolution of the environment. The most interesting contribution of this work is the adaptation. Indeed, virtual worlds become more and more interactive. Then, αCS enables the behaviors of the entities to evolve all along the simulation to provide high performances.

The first application shows that the main characteristics of classifier systems like robustness and adaptation are preserved with αCS. The second application presents new mechanisms for cooperation in multi-tasks environments. The high level of interaction that appears in the soccer simulation implies various behaviors for αCS. The simulation generates a specialization of the players and the performances of the system can be improved by the rule-sharing during the learning stage.

The next stage is the evaluation of αCS with several users immersed in the same game. The first results with a single user [9] have shown that classifier systems are efficient enough to ensure a coherent interaction between real and autonomous players. Indeed, compared to procedural or declarative approaches, the emergent approach produces unpredictable results and enables to simulate the adaptation of the entities to their environment in a realistic way.

References

1. Blumberg B., Galyean T., "Multi-Level Direction of Autonomous Creatures for Real-Time Virtual Environment". Proceedings of Siggraph 95. Computer Graphics Proceedings. Aug 1995.
2. Butz M., Stolzmann W. "Action-Planning in Anticipatory Classifier", IWLCS'99, Second International Workshop on Learning Classifier Systems, Orlando USA, 13 Juillet 1999.
3. Holland J. H., "Adaptation in Natural and Artificial Systems", Ann Arbor, University of Michigan Press, 1975.
4. Holland J. H., "Adaptive Algorithms for Discovering and Using General Patterns in Growing Knowledge Bases", International Journal for Policy Analysis and Informations Systems, Vol 4, No 3, pp 245-268, 1980.
5. Lattaud C., "Non-Homogeneous Classifier Systems in a Macro-Evolution Process", IWLCS'99, Second International Workshop on Learning Classifier Systems, Orlando USA, 13 July 1999.
6. Mataric M.J., "Reward Functions for Accelerated Learning" in Machine Learning: Proceedings of the Eleventh International Conference, William W. Cohen and Haym Hirsh, eds., Morgan Kaufmann Publishers, San Francisco, CA, 1994.
7. Musse S.R., Kallmann M., Thalmann D., "Level of Autonomy for Virtual Human Agents". Proceedings ECAL'99, 5th European Conference on Artificial Life. Lausanne, Switzerland. Sep 1999.
8. Panatier C., Luga H., Duthen Y., "Collective Learning for Spatial Collaboration", SAB'98, From Animals to Animats 5, Zurich, Switzerland, August 1998.
9. Sanza C., Panatier C., Duthen Y., "Communication and Interaction with Learning Agents in Virtual Soccer", VW'2000, 2nd International Conference on Virtual Worlds, Paris, France, Juillet 2000.
10. Stolzmann W., "Anticipatory Classifier Systems", Genetic Programming'98, Proceedings of the Third Annual Conference, Morgan Kaufmann p. 658-664, San Francisco, USA, 22-25 July 1998.
11. Wilson S.W., "Classifier Fitness Based on Accuracy", Evolutionary Computation, Vol 3 (2), MIT Press, 1995.
12. http://www.sense8.com

Appendix:

Colour Illustrations

Bechmann and Elkouhen (pp. 29–35)

(a) bent cube

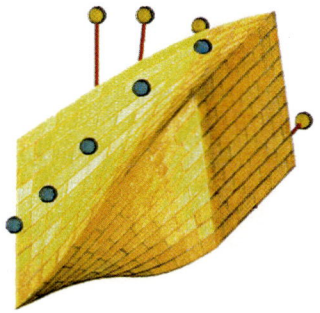

(b) twisted cube

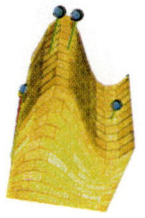

(c) tapered cube

(d) twisted and bent cube

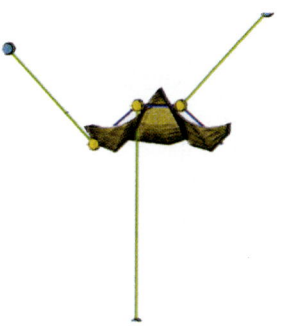

(e) bad placement of the handles

(f) correct placement

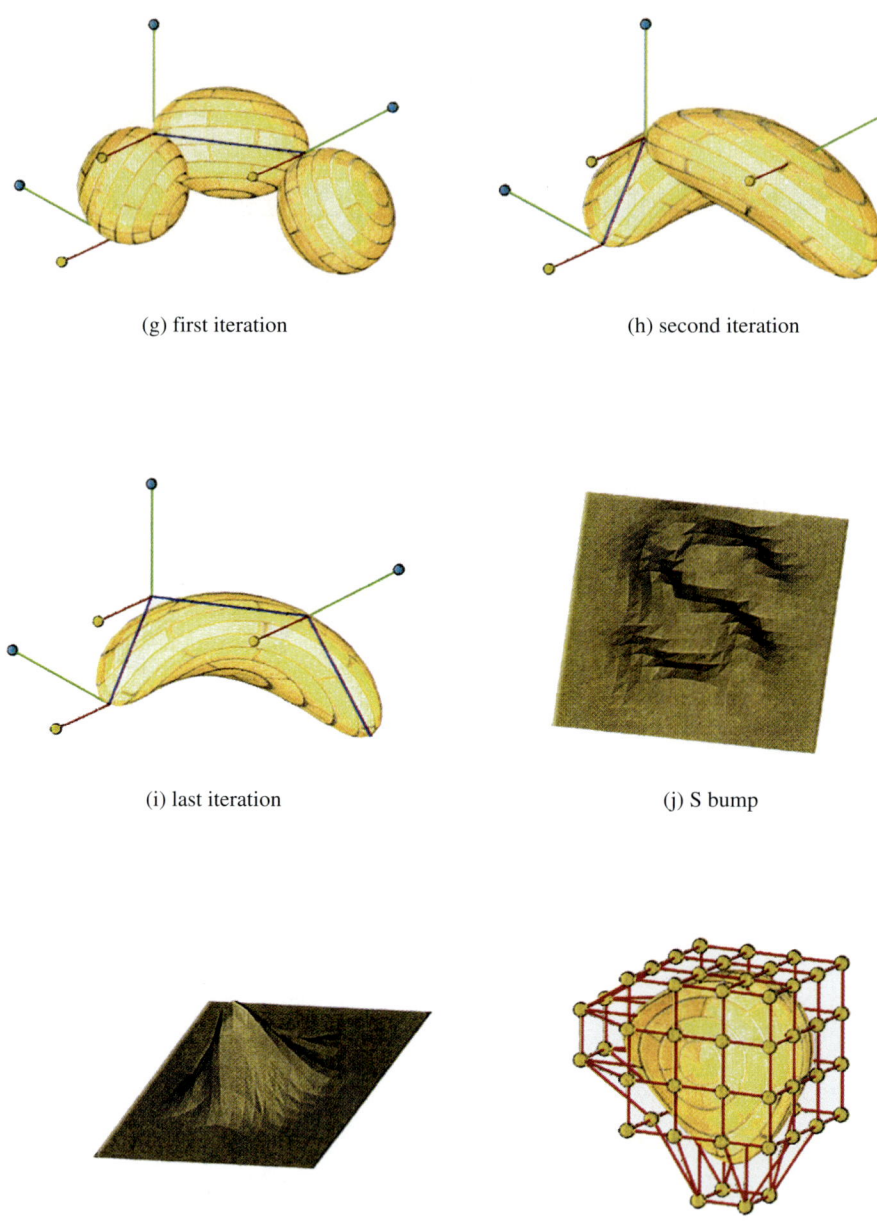

(g) first iteration

(h) second iteration

(i) last iteration

(j) S bump

(k) bump

(l) Generalized hyperpatch deformation

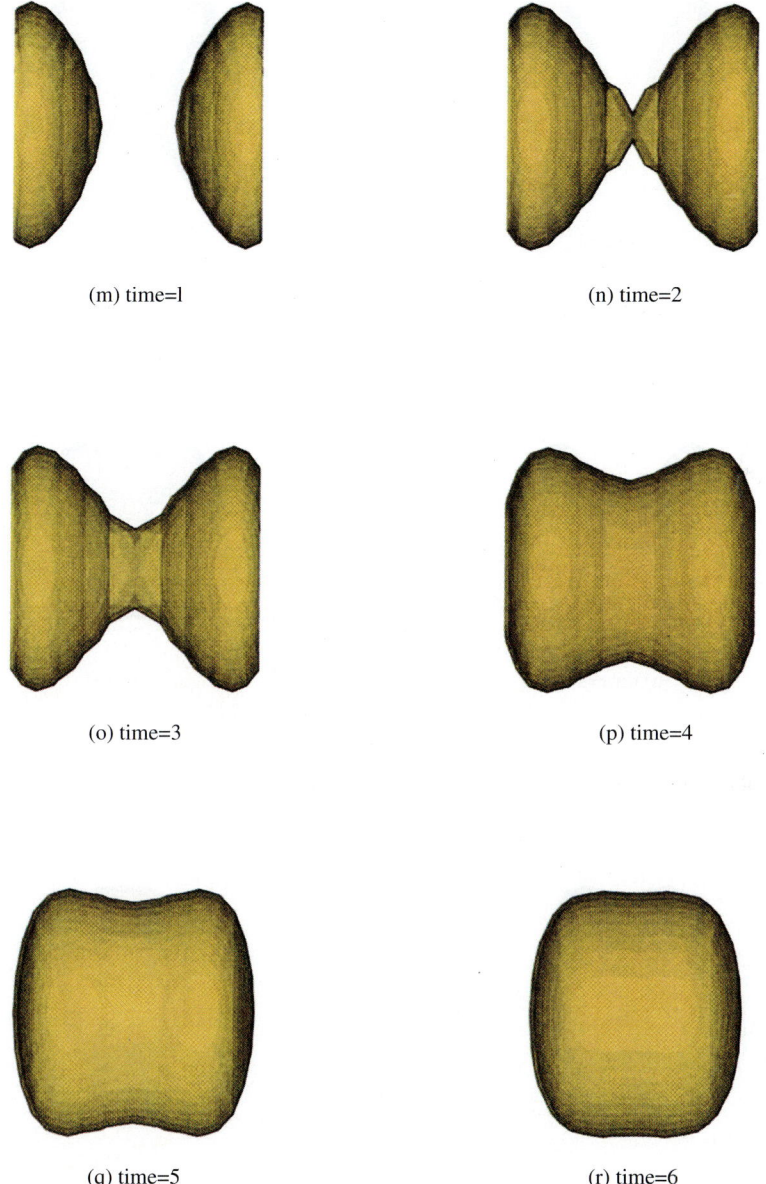

(m) time=1

(n) time=2

(o) time=3

(p) time=4

(q) time=5

(r) time=6

(s) time= I

(t) time=2

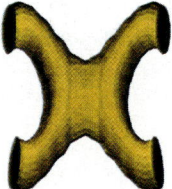

(u) time=3

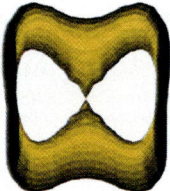

(v) time=4

(w) time=5

(x) time=6

Neyret and Praizelin (pp. 53–64)

Fig. 9. Source and vortex perturbations make the brook quasi-stationary, showing evolving wave features (images are part of animations, which are available on our web site).

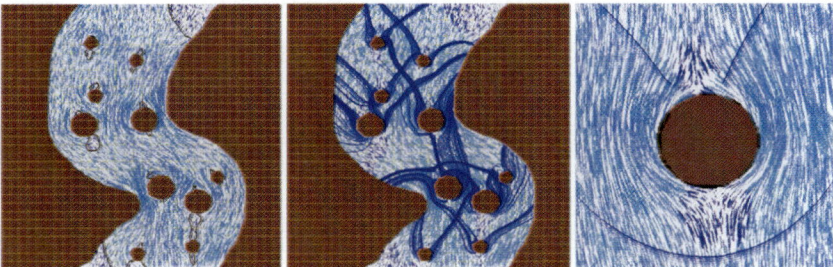

Fig. 10. *Left:* iso$_{Fr=1}$ curves built from the velocity field (the flow comes from the bottom of the image). *Middle:* ripples on obstacles sides (without any stop criterion). *Right:* close view of ripples upstream shockwaves.

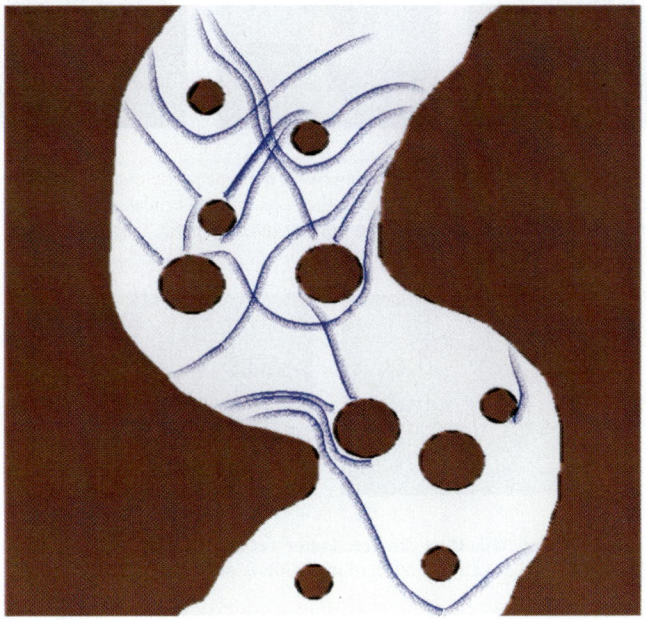

Fig. 11. Shockwaves built upstream and downstream obstacles.

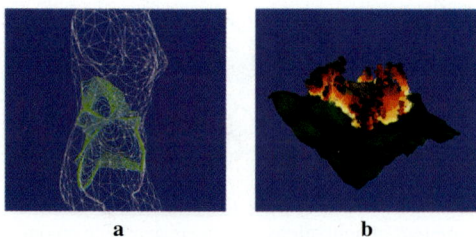

a b

Fig 5. a The flame front (in green) propagates on the surface according to the wind field and geodesic flow. **b** As the front progresses, flame particles [10] are dropped to visualize the fire.

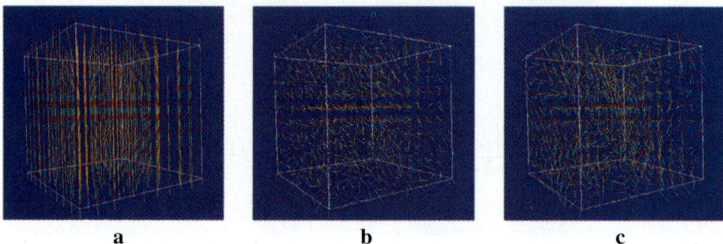

a b c

Fig. 6. Wind field: **a** large scale (upward direction), **b** small scale, **c** sum of the two scales.

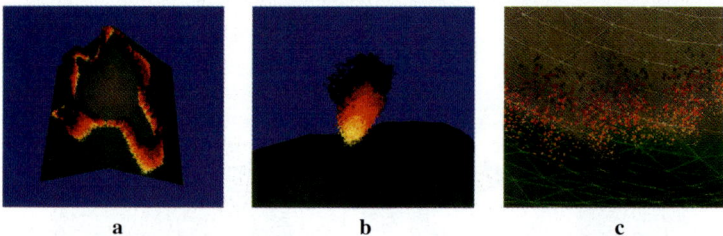

a b c

Fig. 7. a Flame emitters are deposited by the moving front. **b** Flame particles are emitted to give shape to the fire out of the surface. **c** Changing the luminance or the color of the vertices depending on their distance to the front allows for a smooth transition. Note that we only used a sparse field of emitters to clearly see the mesh surface.

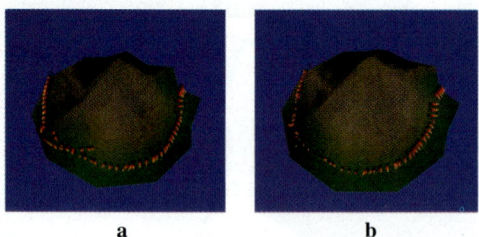

a b

Fig. 8. Swallow tail: **a** Swallow tail effect generated after a conjugate point. **b** The swallow tail is removed by simple particle deletions where an inversion of direction is detected (see Section 2).

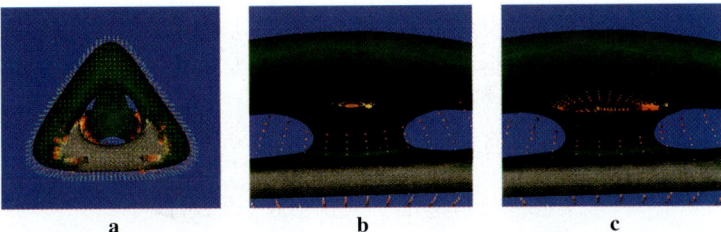

a   b   c

Fig. 9. Multiple Fronts: **a** The closest point transform generates the distance from each grid point to the closest surface as implicit representation. The color of the grid nodes indicates the proximity of the surface. **b** New fire starts at the intersection between a flame and a surface. **c** New flames start spreading from new origin. Note that each flame is represented by very few particles in order to illustrate the new ignition more clearly.

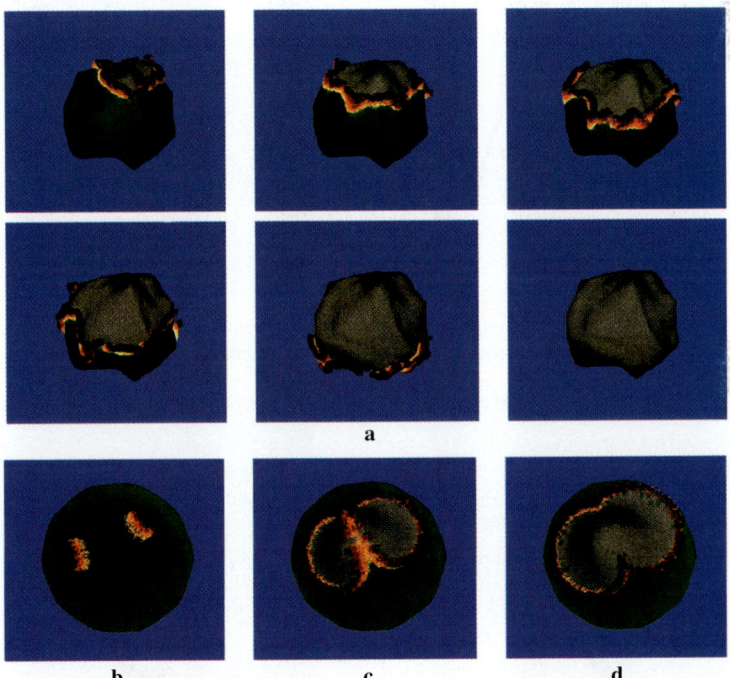

a

b   c   d

Fig. 10. Grass fires: **a** Animation with wind and slope effects of a fire propagation on a mesh. **b** to **d**: Fire fronts merging – when a front reaches a burnt region, it merges with the other fire front(s) appropriately. On all these snapshots taken during an interactive session, we can see the blackening of the mesh around the fire fronts.

Nocent and Remion (pp. 87–97)

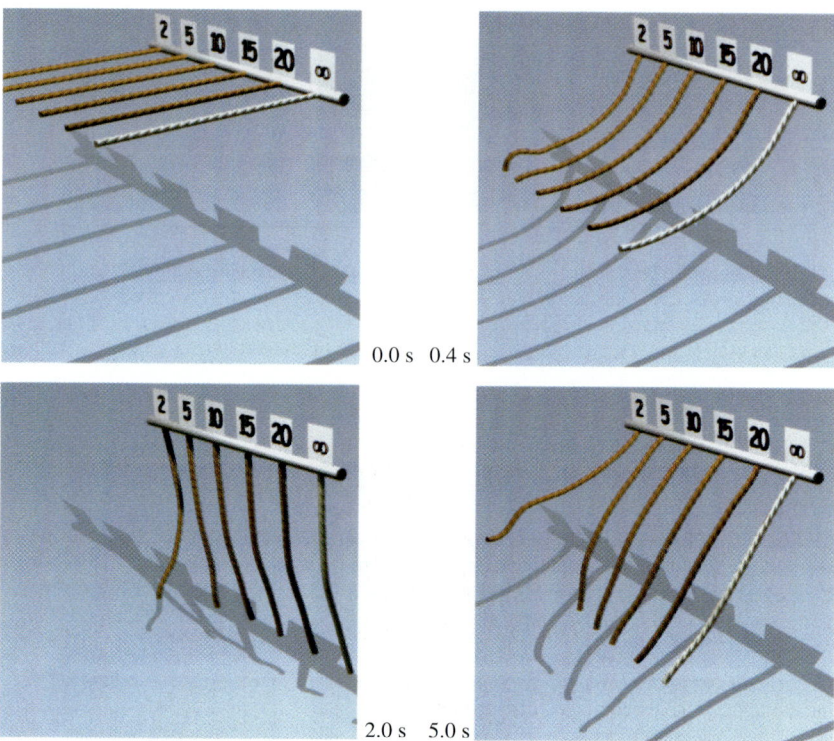

Appendix A. Frames drawn from simulations of ropes hanging from one end (labels give the number of springs for each of the 4 spline segments of the rope below; ∞ stands for continuous elastic modelling)

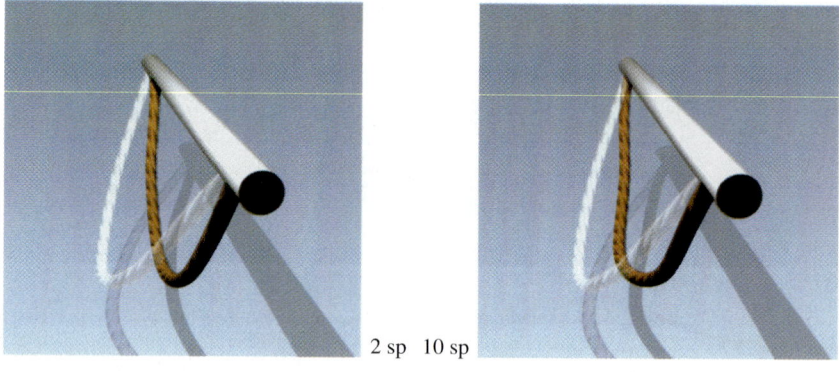

Appendix B. Frames drawn from simulations of a rope hanging from both of its ends. The white transparent ropes use continuous internal energy, while brown ropes use the indicated (# sp) number of springs per segment.

Fisher and Lin (pp. 99–111)

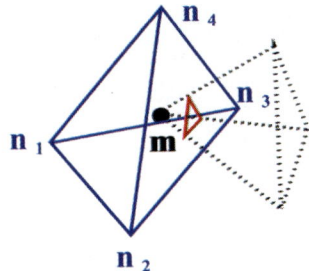

Fig. 2. A node **m** penetrates into another tetrahedral element. The distance between **m** and the red triangle is the penetration depth.

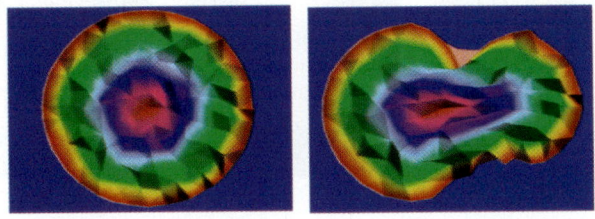

Fig. 3. *Left:* The distance field of a sphere. *Right:* The distance field of a deformed sphere computed using linear interpolation of the precomputed distance field.

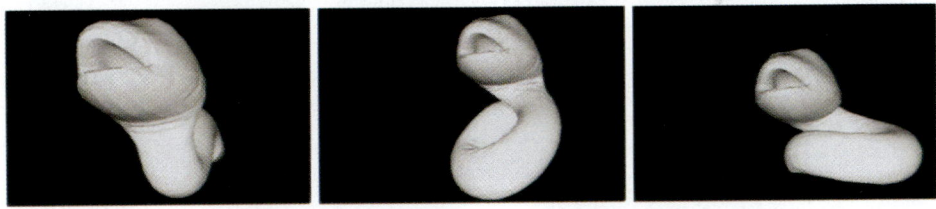

Fig. 4. Large Deformation: A snake coiling up

Fig. 5. A snake swallowing an apple from a bowl of fruits

Müller et al. (pp. 113–124)

Fig. 3. Drop of a vase demonstrates brittle fracture

a   b   c

Fig. 4. Clay teddy bear after dropping (**a**), front view before (**b**) and after deformation (**c**)

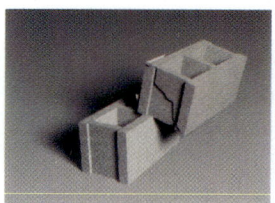  

Fig. 5. Collision detection demonstrated with two cinder blocks

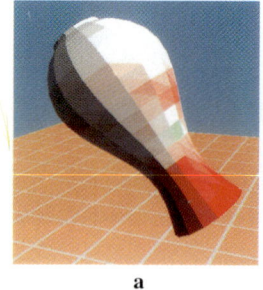  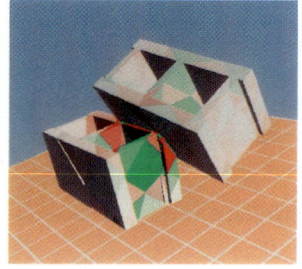

a   b   c

Fig. 6. Visualization of tensile stress within objects

SpringerNews

S. J. Gortler, K. Myszkowski (eds.)

Rendering Techniques 2001

Proceedings of the Eurographics Workshop
in London, United Kingdom, June 25-27, 2001

2001. VIII, 350 pages. 198 figures, partly in colour.
Softcover DM 118,–, öS 826,–, as of Jan. 2002 EUR 60,–*)
(Recommended retail prices)
*) All prices are net-prices subject to local VAT.
ISBN 3-211-83709-4
Eurographics

This book presents state-of-the-art methods in computer graphics rendering. The 29 papers in this volume were selected after careful review by an international committee of experts.

Included are a wide variety topics related to the generation of synthetic images: methods for local and global illumination, techniques for acquisition and modeling from images, image-based rendering, new image representations, hardware assisted methods, perception, shadow algorithms, visibility, texturing, and filtering.

SpringerComputerScience

SpringerWienNewYork

A-1201 Wien, Sachsenplatz 4–6, P.O.Box 89, Fax +43.1.330 24 26, e-mail: books@springer.at, Internet: www.springer.at
D-69126 Heidelberg, Haberstraße 7, Fax +49.6221.345-229, e-mail: orders@springer.de
USA, Secaucus, NJ 07096-2485, P.O. Box 2485, Fax +1.201.348-4505, e-mail: orders@springer-ny.com
Eastern Book Service, Japan, Tokyo 113, 3–13, Hongo 3-chome, Bunkyo-ku, Fax +81.3.38 18 08 64, e-mail: orders@svt-ebs.co.jp

SpringerNews

David Ebert,
Jean M. Favre, Ronald Peikert (eds.)

Data Visualization 2001

Proceedings of the Joint Eurographics - IEEE TCVG
Symposium on Visualization in Ascona, Switzerland, May 28-30, 2001

2001. XI, 364 pages. 212 figures, partly in colour.
Softcover DM 118,–, öS 830,–, as of Jan. 2002 EUR 59,90*)
(Recommended retail prices)
*) All prices are net-prices subject to local VAT.
ISBN 3-211-83674-8
Eurographics

This book contains 33 papers presented at the Third Joint Visualization Symposium of the Eurographics Association and the Technical Committee on Visualization and Graphics of the IEEE Computer Society. The main topics treated are: visualization of geoscience data; multi-resolution and adaptive techniques; unstructured data, multi-scale and visibility; flow visualization; biomedical applications; information visualization; object representation; volume rendering; information visualization applications; and automotive applications.

SpringerComputerScience

SpringerWienNewYork

A-1201 Wien, Sachsenplatz 4–6, P.O.Box 89, Fax +43.1.330 24 26, e-mail: books@springer.at, Internet: www.springer.at
D-69126 Heidelberg, Haberstraße 7, Fax +49.6221.345-229, e-mail: orders@springer.de
USA, Secaucus, NJ 07096-2485, P.O. Box 2485, Fax +1.201.348-4505, e-mail: orders@springer-ny.com
Eastern Book Service, Japan, Tokyo 113, 3–13, Hongo 3-chome, Bunkyo-ku, Fax +81.3.38 18 08 64, e-mail: orders@svt-ebs.co.jp

SpringerNews

Bernd Fröhlich, Joachim Deisinger,
Hans-Jörg Bullinger (eds.)

Immersive Projection Technology and Virtual Environments 2001

Proceedings of the Eurographics Workshop
in Stuttgart, Germany, May 16-18, 2001

2001. XI, 284 pages. 150 figures, partly in colour.
Softcover DM 110,–, öS 770,–, as of Jan. 2002 EUR 55,90*⁾
(Recommended retail prices)
*⁾ All prices are net-prices subject to local VAT.
ISBN 3-211-83671-3
Eurographics

17 papers report on the latest scientific advances in the fields of immersive projection technology and virtual environments. The main topics included here are human computer interaction (user interfaces, interaction techniques), software developments (virtual environment applications, rendering techniques), and input/output devices.

SpringerComputerScience

Springer Wien New York

A-1201 Wien, Sachsenplatz 4–6, P.O.Box 89, Fax +43.1.330 24 26, e-mail: books@springer.at, Internet: www.springer.at
D-69126 Heidelberg, Haberstraße 7, Fax +49.6221.345-229, e-mail: orders@springer.de
USA, Secaucus, NJ 07096-2485, P.O. Box 2485, Fax +1.201.348-4505, e-mail: orders@springer-ny.com
Eastern Book Service, Japan, Tokyo 113, 3–13, Hongo 3-chome, Bunkyo-ku, Fax +81.3.38 18 08 64, e-mail: orders@svt-ebs.co.jp

SpringerNewsComputerScience

G. Alefeld, Xiaojun Chen (eds.)

Topics in Numerical Analysis

With Special Emphasis on Nonlinear Problems

2001. XII, 249 pages. 12 figures.

Softcover DM 168,–, öS 1180,–, as of Jan. 2002 EUR 85,–*)

Reduced price for subscribers to "Computing":

DM 151,20, öS 1062,–, as of Jan. 2002 EUR 76,50*)

(Recommended retail prices)

*) All prices are net-prices subject to local VAT.

ISBN 3-211-83673-X

Computing, Supplementum 15

This collection of papers on numerical analysis with special emphasis on nonlinear problems covers a broad spectrum of fields. Several papers are involved in applying numerical methods for proving the existence of solutions of nonlinear problems, e.g. of boundary problems or of obstacle problems.

Naturally the solution of linear and nonlinear problems by iterative methods is the subject of a couple of papers. Here topics like the fast verification of solutions of monotone matrix equations, the convergence of linear asynchronous iteration with spectral radius of modulus one or aggregation and disaggregation methods for p-cyclic Markov chains are treated. On the other hand papers involved in optimization problems can be found. Nearly all fields of modern numerical analysis are touched by at least one paper.

SpringerWienNewYork

A-1201 Wien, Sachsenplatz 4–6, P.O.Box 89, Fax +43.1.330 24 26, e-mail: books@springer.at, Internet: www.springer.at
D-69126 Heidelberg, Haberstraße 7, Fax +49.6221.345-229, e-mail: orders@springer.de
USA, Secaucus, NJ 07096-2485, P.O. Box 2485, Fax +1.201.348-4505, e-mail: orders@springer-ny.com
Eastern Book Service, Japan, Tokyo 113, 3–13, Hongo 3-chome, Bunkyo-ku, Fax +81.3.38 18 08 64, e-mail: orders@svt-ebs.co.jp